Eagles on the Crescent

The Eastern Mediterranean, 1913

Scale in miles

0   100   200   300

AUSTRIA-HUNGARY

RUSSIA

RUMANIA

SERBIA

BULGARIA

MONTENEGRO

ALBANIA

Durazzo

Valona

Salonika

GREECE

Adrianople

Constantinople

BLACK SEA

Poti

Batum

Ardahan

Kars

Sarkamish

Trebizond

Erzerum

Erzincan

Musho

Bitlis

Van

Diarbekr

Ras-el-Ain

Baghdad

Zonguldak

Adabazar

Mudanya

Gallipoli

T U R K E Y

Konya

TAURUS

Adana

Alexandretta

Aleppo

Damascus

Joppa

Jerusalem

Beersheba

El Kantara

Ismailia

Cairo

Alexandria

Smyrna

Aidin

MEDITERRANEAN SEA

Eagles on the Crescent

GERMANY, AUSTRIA, AND THE DIPLOMACY
OF THE TURKISH ALLIANCE

1914-1918

FRANK G. WEBER

Cornell University Press

ITHACA AND LONDON

First published 1970

International Standard Book Number 0-8014-0566-1
Library of Congress Catalog Card Number 70-109339

7-11-77

PRINTED IN THE UNITED STATES OF AMERICA
BY VAIL-BALLOU PRESS, INC.

For Marie Weber

Acknowledgments

In the course of my research I have contracted several outstanding debts that must be acknowledged. Mr. Robert Wolfe of the National Archives and Records Service gave me valuable direction for the use of the microfilmed German Foreign Ministry files and often suggested avenues of approach that I might have overlooked. Drs. Mommsen and Bruchmann of the Bundesarchiv, Koblenz, furnished me with additional papers or informed me where I could find them. Dr. Richard Blaas, Haus-, Hof- u. Staatsarchiv, Wien, patiently assisted me in the task of collecting and microfilming the Austrian diplomatic documents, and I am grateful to Dr. Weis, Oberregierungsarchivrat, Geheimes Staatsarchiv, München, for similar and no less important service. The Public Record Office, London, made available a number of important documents, and Mrs. Judy Egerton was of invaluable assistance in helping me to microfilm some of these and in abstracting others. I was denied permission to use the Ottoman Foreign Ministry Archives, but Merih Erhan translated the Turkish printed histories. Hannelore Wissner deciphered the more gnarled portions of Hans von Seeckt's script. And Mrs. Mary Matteson typed the manuscript indefatigably and expertly through its various stages. A generous grant from the Department of History, Boston University, helped me to defray many of my expenses, so that the costs of this book never seriously detracted from my joy in writing it.

F. G. W.

Philadelphia
April, 1970

Contents

Eagles on the Crescent

Introduction

German diplomats during the First World War failed to persuade more than a few of the powers to support Germany's cause. There was much talk in the Wilhelmstrasse of bringing in Italy and the Balkan states as allies, but in the end Germany had to depend on only Austria-Hungary, Bulgaria, and the Ottoman Empire through most of the fighting. The Ottoman Empire was no inconsequential factor. Opinion about the fighting capacities of the Sultan's troops varied widely, but by its geographical position alone, the Ottoman Empire blocked Russia from communication with her allies, denied her badly needed materials, and finally brought her war effort to grief as the Germans alone could probably not have done. Moreover, Turkish troops on several fronts tied down not only Russian but also British forces, while her espionage and guerrilla activities harassed the governments of Italy and France.

All in all, then, the Turkish alliance appears a real achievement of German diplomacy, and at first glance it would seem the fruition of several decades of German maneuvering in the Near East. The story, so viewed, would begin with the first visit of the German Emperor William II to Constantinople in 1889, continue with the building of the famous Baghdad Railway, and culminate in the signing of the Turco-German Pact on August 2, 1914.

This book suggests that the standard interpretation is not entirely adequate. The Germans were not unaware of the value of a Turkish alliance, and many in the Wilhelmstrasse rejoiced when the Sultan's help was assured by a formal treaty. Yet a parallel conviction seems to have existed in Berlin that it would be futile to uphold the Ottoman Empire at the cost of alienating Russia. There is evidence that German policy toward the Ottoman Empire was undergoing a modification in 1913 and early 1914, only to be turned back in the old direction by the outbreak of the European war. Expediency rather than well-reasoned conviction persuaded the Germans to sue for the help of the Turks, but as soon as the initial anxiety had passed, there were regrets in Berlin and actions that belied a genuine brotherhood in arms.

It can be argued that the Turks, though their government was wracked with scandal and beyond the regenerative efforts of a whole series of foreign military and technical missions, were more impetuous and eager for the alliance and the fighting than were their supposed German mentors. Furthermore, the evidence suggests that urging on both Turks and Germans were the efforts of the Austrian Foreign Ministry. Like the Sultan, the Habsburger of Vienna often seemed one of the sick men of Europe. But like the Turks too, the Austrians were often able to lead German diplomacy down paths it might better have avoided. This was no less true in the Near East than the events of July, 1914, proved it to be in Central Europe.

This book attempts to analyze the conditions under which the alliance between Turkey and Germany was born. It shows that the alliance was the rather haphazard solution to one of a number of important Balkan problems confronting Germany and Austria in 1914. For several reasons, Austria had come to feel that the Ottoman Empire had too much scope for diplomatic maneuver by 1914 and that, if this latitude were not quickly circumscribed, it might prove dangerous to the Austro-Hungarian frontiers. The Germans did not share these Austrian fears but were unable or unwilling to forge a policy free of their influence. As a result, both German and Austrian policy in the Ottoman Empire betrayed signs of dissatisfaction and misdirection.

The Austrians advocated a Turkish attack on Russia from the Black Sea. It was to be linked eventually with their own thrust against the Tsar's troops from the west. The Turks, however, refused to deploy their men in this manner and, despite Austrian objections, decided to send their forces into Russian Armenia where they would not relieve any of the pressure on the Austrian lines. The Turks and the Germans then decided to attack the Suez Canal, but Vienna objected this operation could not succeed and feared that in any case it would provoke the Italian administration in neighboring Tripolitania. Austria was desperately concerned to keep Italy neutral; the Turco-German maneuver, she insisted, would drive the fence-sitting Italians into the Entente camp. Moreover, the Austrians suspected that the conquest of Egypt would turn the country into a German rather than a Turkish sphere of influence. Austria was determined not to be deprived of the Egyptian spoils and, unknown to Berlin, attempted to groom a rival to Khedive Abbas Hilmi, with whom the Germans intrigued.

The Austrians claimed the challenge given the British in Egypt would provoke them to a counterattack on the Dardanelles. While this contention was an oversimplification of the strategical questions involved, the Austrians became very bitter when their ideas were ignored in Berlin and Constantinople. During the critical Dardanelles campaign, they did nothing to deliver badly needed matériel to the Turkish front and, in some instances, used the tenuous lines of supply to export nonessential civilian commodities to Eastern Europe. The Germans discovered evidence that Austrian agencies allowed sales of war supplies to Serbia and Russia, though both were enemies of the Central Powers.

The Germans managed to curtail these activities, though not in the brusque and emphatic manner customary for the leaders of the Wilhelmstrasse and the General Staff. However, they could not curb Austria's pessimism and desire for a negotiated peace at the expense of the Ottoman Empire or her intrigues to achieve some kind of ascendancy, with or without the Germans, in what was left of the Sultan's domains after the war. At various times, the Austrians sought to undersell their German ally in consumer goods for Turkey or to supplant the Germans in various educational, technical, and medical projects that Berlin had

initiated. Toward the end of the war, the Austrian Foreign Ministry fancied that it might assume a religious protectorate over
Ottoman Catholics, using that position to limit the sovereignty of
the Turks in their own country.

Though the Germans promised to preserve and even augment
the Sultan's empire, they too attempted to exploit the Turks for
diplomatic purposes. Before the war, the Wilhelmstrasse apparently favored some cession of Turkish Armenia to the Tsar as the
price of a general reconciliation between Berlin and St. Petersburg. After the war began, some persons in the German Foreign
Ministry urged that the Tsar be given a corridor of Turkish land
to the Persian Gulf to relieve the traditional Russian pressure on
the Straits. These schemes of course clashed with the expansionist designs of the Young Turk party. To thwart such designs, the
Germans even limited the amount of Turkish manpower used in
the European theater of the war, fearing that the Sublime Porte
would demand a greater share in making the peace. Toward all
these German and Austrian tendencies the Turks were not blind
and for the four years of war had to guard against their allies
even while they fought against their declared enemies.

I

Germany, Austria, and the Young Turks

On October 29, 1914, Turkey entered the Great War on the side of the Central Powers. Outsiders assumed the decision was the inevitable outcome of nearly three decades of German diplomatic maneuvering in the Ottoman Empire, reinforced by the menace of German guns. The pointed stationing of the warships *Goeben* and *Breslau* off Constantinople seemed a crude maneuver for the German Foreign Ministry, rougher certainly than the foundation of the Baghdad Railway Company twenty-five years before; but the world thought ships and railroad were both tactics in the relentless pursuit of the same aim: the political and economic thralldom of Turkey.

Diplomatic documents, however, show that had war not broken out, Germany would probably have relinquished her interests in the Ottoman Empire and abandoned her close ties with Turkey. The war in fact imprisoned Germany in a diplomatic net not of her weaving and committed her to a policy in which she put little faith. The heyday of Germany's Near Eastern ambition had passed when the fighting began. By then, every German hope about the Turkish alliance carried in it a germ of disillusionment, and every pledge of material and military assistance had a grim afterthought of partition. In the recent Balkan Wars the Turk had proved a plucky and resilient, but not a persevering and decisive, combatant. Even the Germans had now been forced to admit all this, though many of their diplomatists had tried to dismiss such notions as groundless European prejudice.

Until 1908, German relations with Turkey were relatively un-troubled. The German Ambassador, Adolf Marschall von Bieber-stein, enjoyed great esteem at the Ottoman court and was called the Giant of the Bosphorus. But that summer the Young Turk revolution compelled Germany's old friend Sultan Abdul Hamid to rule according to a constitution, and the leadership of the lib-eral movement, calling itself the Committee of Union and Prog-ress, promised the abolition of all distinctions of class, religion, and descent in the Ottoman Empire. The Young Turks never had a chance to implement their program because, beginning in October, 1908, the European powers used the disturbances in Constantinople as a pretext for occupying and annexing portions of the Sultan's realm. Austria annexed Bosnia-Herzegovina on October 7; Italy fought for and won Tripolitania by 1912; and in 1913, a coalition of Bulgarians, Serbs, Montenegrins, Greeks, and Rumanians succeeded in annexing various parts of Turkish Mac-edonia, Thrace, Dobrudja, and the island of Crete.

The Austrian annexation of Bosnia-Herzegovina seriously em-barrassed Marschall von Bieberstein. Most Turks assumed that it had been done with the approval of the German government; in fact, the German Emperor was furious because Austria had sought neither his counsel nor concurrence. With some difficulty Marschall persuaded the Sublime Porte that Berlin was as aston-ished as Constantinople by the annexation, yet he felt that the Turks believed him only because they had no other choice. Be-fore the Bosnian crisis, a Turkish diplomat in St. Petersburg re-marked that his government was convinced that Britain was no longer willing to risk war to defend the integrity of the Ottoman Empire, while Russia was a declared and ancient enemy. The Turks therefore had no choice but to sue for German support, whatever their doubts and reservations about German policy.[1] Thus, after the crisis *Tanin,* a prominent Constantinople newspa-per affiliated with the Young Turk party, declared that the Com-

[1] Pourtalès to Bülow, Aug. 22, 1908, Auswärtiges Amt, Bonn (herein-after abbreviated A.A.), Türkei #158, Bd. 9, #A13882.

mittee of Union and Progress did not believe that Germany had approved the Austrian annexation.[2]

Turkey might not be so forbearing next time. Marschall had to be especially careful that the Porte's feelings should not be hurt soon again, and the strain of apprehension and forethought wore down even this man, whose optimism and egotism the society of Constantinople had many times remarked. In his memoir of Marschall, Hans von Miquel, First Secretary of the Constantinople embassy, described the Ambassador as sick of the Turkish capital and eager for recall. He wanted to match wits with Grey, Nicolson, and Delcassé and now scorned his Turkish associates as merely petty and garrulous. Miquel must have relished this, because he and the other junior members of the embassy resented their cavalier and overbearing chief. In an earlier time when he thought German potentialities in Turkey unlimited, Marschall had been ready to ignore, hurt, humiliate, and override his staff and his countrymen resident in the Ottoman Empire. He not only blinded himself to the faults of the Turks and exaggerated their merits to whoever would listen; Miquel states that a favorite and habitual tactic of Marschall was the surrender of German citizens to Turkish justice when the capitulations would have made them secure under their own law. Whenever he wanted a concession, the Ambassador would waive the trial in a German consular court and send the German accused to a Turkish judge. He even suggested to the Grand Vizier that his concession might be regarded as a precedent for the other members of the Constantinople diplomatic corps.[3] It is no wonder that during the war Germany was unjustly accused of having instigated the abrogation of the capitulations, which gave the European powers a variety of commercial and economic privileges in the Ottoman Empire.

Marschall felt he had good reason to do what he did, and his motives were at once a mixture of hope and frustration. The Ambassador had sought gradually to introduce German colonists

[2] Marschall to Bülow, Oct. 12, 1908, *ibid.*, Bd. 10, #A17014.
[3] Marschall by Hans von Miquel, no date, A.A. Nachlass von Miquel.

into Turkey, tradesmen along the Syrian coast and farmers in the
middle of Asia Minor. These people, he believed, would be the
only lasting and pervasive basis of German influence in Turkey.
While the pace of immigration had not nearly been up to Marschall's hopes, the Turks had turned suspicious and balked at
further settlement.[4] No amount of tampering with the capitulations would change their mood, and the Vizier Mahmud Shevket
Pasha informed the embassy that future German settlers would
have to do service in the Turkish army or in the Turkish bureaucracy at a Turkish rate of pay. They would be liable to Turkish
taxes and laws. The German government must screen out and
forbid passage to Jewish settlers and, above all, not publicize its
plans in the German press before consultation with the Turkish
government. According to Miquel, Shevket in all his conversations with German officials wildly overestimated the number of
German immigrants. He referred to forty thousand Germans in
Turkey and refused to be disabused.[5]

The German press of which the Vizier complained troubled
Marschall too. In the Ambassador's opinion, however, it was not
as sympathetic to German imperialism as Shevket believed. In
fact Marschall accused the German correspondents in Constantinople not only of lack of support but of downright sabotage. He
complained to the Chancellor, Bernhard von Bülow, that German
reporting about Turkey was ill informed and unnecessarily negative. Journalists, Marschall claimed, had discouraged interest and
investment throughout his entire term of service and, when they
could not secure a hearing in German journals, thought nothing
of planting articles in British and Austrian newspapers. The
Daily Mail, which picked at him constantly, got much of its material from German reporters close to his own circle, and the Viennese papers were full of articles that had been rejected by the
German editors.

[4] Oppenheim to Bülow, Sep. 25, 1905, A.A. Türkei #189, Bd. 2,
#A17173.
[5] Mahmud Shevket by Hans von Miquel, July 1912, A.A. Nachlass von
Miquel.

It was the Austrians, in fact, who cultivated the notion that the Young Turk party would eventually prove anti-German and resume Turkey's older ties with Britain.[6] When Chancellor Bülow asked his opinion about subsidizing the native Egyptian press and sending more German reporters to Egypt, Marschall rejected the scheme resoundingly.[7] At the same time, the Ambassador feared that without press cooperation, German opinion about the Near East and Turkish ideas about Germans would be formed by Armenian café gossips and hack writers. These he knew were incorrigibly hostile to Germany, whose Emperor they believed condoned the Hamidian massacres of the Armenians.[8] Nevertheless, Marschall was angry enough to take that risk.

What Marschall complained of was not really the result of malevolence or treachery. Rather, it was a sensible and realistic assessment of German undertakings in Turkey. Though he hated to hear that work on the Baghdad Railway progressed only slowly and was frequently halted altogether, the German people deserved to know. They also needed to be told that even when the line was complete, prospects for trade would be modest. Before he left Turkey, Marschall apparently came to share many of the views of his critics, but he would not admit they were right.

In the meantime one of them supplied the Berlin Foreign Ministry with sobering, penetrating information intended to compensate for Marschall's distortions and suppressions. This was Paul Weitz, Constantinople correspondent of the *Frankfurter Zeitung* for many years. He was Marschall's frequent collaborator in the execution of Germany's Turkish policy and continued to serve his successors. A bachelor, he divided his time between dinner parties and the selfless pursuit of intrigue. But while loyal, he would not be uncritical, and the evidence shows his candor served Germany's best interests. After the war began, Richard

[6] Marschall to Bülow, Mar. 27, 1907, A.A. Türkei #158, Bd. 9, #A52521.

[7] Marschall to Bülow, May 15, 1909, A.A. Orientalia Generalia #9, No. 2, Bd. 2, #8787.

[8] Belart to Helfferich, Oct. 10, 1908, A.A. Türkei #158, Bd. 10, #A17903.

von Kühlmann, who worked for Germany's disengagement from
Turkey, wrote that Weitz had given him a "true insight into the
diplomacy of Marschall." [9] Marschall apparently never suspected
that Weitz played a double game and that the man regarded as
his alter ego was in reality his nemesis.

Weitz believed that the Young Turk revolution was a wa-
tershed in Ottoman history and that it had set a term to the German penetration of Turkey. It was no longer true, as Marschall
liked to insist, that "men make history and especially in Turkey."
The removal of Abdul Hamid from effective rule had replaced
one omnipotent man with an inexperienced and self-conscious
parliament and a rudimentary and impetuous public opinion. Behind both was the nebulous Committee of Union and Progress,
which embodied Young Turk political ideology and other interests that even now cannot be defined. Marschall could influence
these men only until they found their bearings and established
contacts with the outside. When this happened, they would
throw out lines to Britain, whose politics they admired in principle, and to France, whose hospitality many of them had known
at first hand as exiles before the revolution of 1908. Marschall
was furious when he learned that a parliamentary deputation
was leaving for Paris, London, and a reception by King Edward
VII. The Turks were going to propose the foundation of an international parliament for peace in Constantinople or even the removal of the Hague Court to the city on the Bosphorus. One of
the members of the mission was Talaat Bey, later Grand
Vizier.[10]

Thus, Germany watched the onset of the First Balkan War in
1912 with mixed feelings. The Turks were overwhelmed by a coalition of Serbs, Greeks, Montenegrins, and Bulgarians, but there
was no genuine regret in the German attitude, only a little
cool concern at the damage to Germany's military prestige. The
Prussian General Colmar von der Goltz, chief of the German military mission in Turkey, had supervised the training of many of

[9] Kühlmann to Weitz, Sep. 7, 1915, A.A. Nachlass Paul Weitz, Bd. 6.
[10] Miquel to Bülow, July 2, 1909, A.A. Türkei #158, Bd. 11, #A11382.

the defeated forces, and he now bore the burden of ridicule and blame. General Helmuth von Moltke, head of the General Staff, went so far as to state that Germany's whole mistaken Near Eastern policy was based on Goltz's overly optimistic reports. For his alleged failures Goltz was denied an active field command at the beginning of the World War. Nevertheless, Goltz was not really to blame, and his charge that the Turkish army leadership suffered from a "Napoleon complex" and declined to pay much attention to his advice was probably true.[11] In any case, the odds against the Turks were too great, and the German Foreign and War Ministries were seeking ways to excuse a policy that they already had decided to abandon.

The correspondence of Emperor William during the First Balkan War reflected the shift in policy. Despite his long and well-publicized friendship for Turkey and his two trips to Constantinople, he declared that the Turks must now show their capability and, like the other Balkan peoples, prove their right to exist. The war of 1912 he described as a "free-fight and no favor" conflict, in which he would not interfere. He even believed that the Bulgarians might take Constantinople and was prepared to greet the accession of King Ferdinand as "Tsar of Byzantium" with equanimity. These observations must have bewildered his ministers and quite certainly frightened his Austrian ally. The Balkan *status quo* was a first principle of Austrian foreign policy, and the Foreign Ministry in Vienna nervously awaited the outcome of the Balkan War, fearing that one of the Balkan states would emerge with overwhelming power. To this Austria was opposed whether the chief victor was Bulgaria or Serbia. Nevertheless, the German Emperor had his Foreign Ministry declare that he would not support Austria in the Balkans, whatever boundary changes occurred there.[12] The Austrian Foreign Minister, Leopold von Berchtold, complained that the German atti-

---

[11] Colmar von der Goltz, *Denkwürdigkeiten* (Berlin, 1929), p. 321.

[12] R. W. Seton-Watson, "William II's Balkan Policy," *The Slavonic Review*, VII (No. 19), 6 (citing *Die Grosse Politik*, XXVI, #12339—hereinafter abbreviated G.P.).

tude amounted to the betrayal of an ally, but Emperor William merely replied by suggesting that Berchtold consider his resignation.[13]

Subsequently the German Emperor changed his mind. In October, 1913, barely a year later, he visited Vienna and told Berchtold that the Habsburg hegemony over the Balkan states must continue. Specifically, he recommended that the Balkan armies be brought under Austrian supervision and control. If, as the Emperor suggested, the Serbian King would not agree, then he might be bribed or his capital, Belgrade, threatened with bombardment. This control would prevent the eruption of another Balkan war and the further reduction of Turkish territory in Europe. As both Emperor William and Berchtold agreed, this could only serve the perilous cause of Balkan irredentism and ultimately endanger the Habsburg monarchy. According to Berchtold's memorandum, William made these remarks on October 28, 1913.[14] They mark the end of his enthusiasm for Slavdom triumphant, which may never have been more than a rhetorical gambit. But the documents suggest that the Austrians did not forget the incident. The memory remained to agitate and shape their Turkish policy and to convince them that they must shift for themselves in Near Eastern affairs.

The Emperor was not long gone from Vienna when the Austrians began to take an independent tack. The occasion was a disagreement between the Austrian and German Foreign Ministries over the management of the Balkan railroads and whether the Austrian government, chronically short of funds, might apply to the money markets of western Europe.[15] Most of the Balkan railroads had been built by European construction firms working under a series of Turkish concessions, because the Sultan was still master of most of southeastern Europe when the first tracks were laid in 1870. By the end of the century most of these construction companies had transferred their rights to the Oriental Railways Company, a holding company with headquarters first

---

[13] *Ibid.*, p. 16 (#13781).
[14] *Ibid.*, p. 19, 26, citing unpublished memorandum.   [15] *Ibid.*, p. 26.

in Vienna and then in Constantinople, but with financial control always residing in the Deutsche Bank of Berlin.

The arrangement presented no difficulties until the various Balkan states achieved their independence from the Turks. Serbia and Bulgaria, independent respectively in 1878 and 1908, spoke of purchasing Oriental Railways track that had been transferred from the Sultan's empire to within their own frontiers. They accused the Oriental Railways Company of making no effort to develop Serbian and Bulgarian local resources and industry. However, the Deutsche Bank, representing not only German but also Austrian investors, gave neither Serbia nor Bulgaria any satisfaction. Berlin realized that behind the Serbian and Bulgarian bids stood French money. Therefore, the Deutsche Bank's policy was to exclude foreign control from the Oriental Railways Company until both the German and Austrian Foreign Ministries decided to invite it.[16]

But this arrangement was put to a severe test during the Balkan Wars of 1912–1913. The victorious Balkan coalition advanced into Turkish Macedonia and occupied more of the Oriental Railways network. The Serbs and the Bulgarians renewed the old demands for a change in ownership, and the Greeks joined them with a bid to buy out all Austrian holdings in the Oriental Railways. Greece admitted that she would make her purchases with a French loan.[17]

In December, 1913, less than two months after William's visit, Austria indicated that she regarded this offer favorably. The Deutsche Bank, on the other hand, objected, although it had transferred much of its Oriental Railways stock to an Austrian consortium a short time earlier and thereby weakened its position.[18] Moreover, the Austrians pointed out to Berlin that the German government had favored international capitalization

---

[16] Notice of Austrian Embassy, Berlin, Sep. 15, 1915, A.A. Türkei #144, Bd. 26, #A27011. Additional information on the foundation and earlier history of the Oriental Railways Company may be found in Herbert Feis, *Europe The World's Banker, 1870–1914* (New York, 1961), pp. 296–298; 306–310.

[17] G.P., XXXVII (II), #15128.   [18] *Ibid.,* #15119.

for the Baghdad Railway in 1903 and should not oppose a parallel arrangement now.[19] Using this argument, Count Berchtold gave his provisional agreement to the Serbs and the Greeks, stressing that his decision was purely a business matter.[20]

However, M. Paul Doumer, a former French Minister of Finance, declared publicly that Berchtold's decision marked the beginning of a Franco-Austrian rapprochement and the end of German economic tutelage in the Balkans. According to Doumer, the German banks had been outsmarted and the Austrian government would be reconciled with Russia through the mediation of France.[21] The German Ambassador in Vienna, Heinrich von Tschirschky, reported that the Austrians were definitely interested in this prospect, as well as in placing their future loans in the Paris money market. The Foreign Minister in Berlin, Gottlieb von Jagow, was so disturbed by the news that he urged the Deutsche Bank to buy back its Oriental Railways shares as quickly as possible.[22]

In the end, the whole affair came to nothing because the Serbs and Greeks would not pay the price demanded by the Austrian stockholders.[23] Had not the World War broken out, however, the Germans suspected that the Austrians and French would have gone further with their plans, perhaps substituting a Swiss holding company for the Deutsche Bank organization.[24] This Swiss company would sell its shares to Serbian, Greek, French, and Russian investors, as well as to any Austrian and German participants. Furthermore, the Austrians were suspected of planning to push this scheme as a pattern for the management of the Baghdad Railway, an exclusively German concern. The Deutsche Bank indicated its fierce disapproval.[25]

[19] Friedrich Rosen, *Aus einem diplomatischen Wanderleben* (Berlin, 1931), I, 67–68; M. S. Anderson, *The Eastern Question, 1774–1923* (London, 1966), pp. 264–265.

[20] G.P., XXXVII (II), #15129.   [21] *Ibid.,* #15131.

[22] *Ibid.,* #15133.   [23] *Ibid.,* #15148, #15149.

[24] Notice of Austrian Embassy, Berlin, Sep. 15, 1915, A.A. Türkei #144, Bd. 26, #A27011.

[25] Gwinner to Foreign Ministry, Nov. 8, 1915, *ibid.,* no number.

There is no evidence that Austria was aiming at a political understanding with Russia via France, as Doumer asserted, but the Oriental Railways affair showed that Vienna was no longer willing to march in financial step with the German government, and nothing happened between the end of the Balkan Wars and the Sarajevo assassination to suggest that the Habsburgs would do so again in the future.

The railways problem was hardly settled when the Balkan victors raised indemnity claims against the defeated Ottoman Empire. Here again the great powers took a predictable line, with France espousing the claims of the Balkan confederates. France suggested that indemnity monies should be paid out of Ottoman customs revenues.[26] These revenues, however, were derived primarily from an import duty of only 11 per cent *ad valorem,* and the total sum collected was hardly adequate to service Turkey's foreign loans, let alone to bear the additional drain of war indemnities.[27] The British government pointed this out to its French ally and declined to support any more charges against the Ottoman customs. The Germans also objected to the French scheme and offered to work with the English Foreign Secretary, Edward Grey, to make the French back down.[28] The German government hoped that any Ottoman customs surplus would be used to give better financial coverage to the Baghdad Railway, in which it held the controlling interest, rather than given to the Balkan League.

But to both Grey's and the Germans' surprise, Austria would not make common cause with them.[29] The Austrians supported not only the French plan but also a simultaneous demand from Russia that she be given a seat on the Ottoman Public Debt Administration, an international council that represented the Euro-

[26] Notice of German Foreign Ministry, Jan. 25, 1913, A.A. Türkei #110, No. 2, Bd. 3, #A1563.
[27] Donald C. Blaisdell, *European Financial Control in the Ottoman Empire* (New York, 1966), pp. 159–170.
[28] Lichnowsky to Jagow, Jan. 27, 1913, A.A. Türkei #110, No. 2, Bd. 3, #A1847.
[29] French Foreign Ministry to Schoen, Jan. 27, 1913, *ibid.,* #A2106.

pean bondholders to the Sultan.[30] Grey, seconded by the Germans, insisted that Russian investment in the Ottoman Empire was not large enough to justify meddling in Turkish financial counsels.[31] The Austrian Foreign Ministry, however, declared such considerations to be irrelevant. What really mattered was that Russia not be exasperated to a point where she would retaliate. Vienna made it clear to Berlin that it was not ready to meet a military challenge.[32]

When the Great War opened, the powers still had not acted on either the French or Russian proposals, but these and similar experiences appear to have suggested to the Central Powers that concessions to Russia were not only opportune but perhaps inevitable. At any rate, Austria would support no other course, even if the Turks had to be sacrificed to their traditional foe in St. Petersburg. Germany's tide at the Bosphorus was ebbing, yet the Wilhelmstrasse strove to channel rather than reverse its flow. Apparently at his own request, Marschall von Bieferstein was transferred to the London embassy in the summer of 1912.[33] His successor as leader of the Pera embassy was less magisterial but fortunately more compromising. The policies of Austria and Russia now allowed of no other attitude.

[30] Wangenheim to Bethmann, Oct. 20, 1913, *ibid.*, Bd. 6, #A21247.

[31] Wangenheim to Bethmann, Oct. 27, 1913, *ibid.*, #A21646.

[32] Notice of Austrian Embassy, Berlin, November 21, 1913, *ibid.*, Bd. 7, #A23299.

[33] Erich Lindow, *Freiherr Marschall von Bieberstein als Botschafter in Konstantinopel, 1897–1912* (Danzig, 1934), pp. 193–194.

2

Germany's Choice: Tsar or Sultan

German policy toward the Ottoman Empire before the war was never officially changed, but it was certainly modified. Marschall's successor, Hans von Wangenheim, did not insist on the inviolability of the Turkish frontiers or on the ascendancy and exclusiveness of German economic imperialism within them. Instead he was encouraged to seek agreement with the Russians about Turkish affairs. These negotiations did not exclude the cession of Constantinople to the Tsar nor a more forthright control rather than mere economic influence for Germany in Armenia. The Germans were not prepared to write off the Turks completely, but they could not ignore the fact that, in any final reckoning, their friendship was worth less than Russia's.

Turkish reactions to this new policy were muddled and divided. Mahmud Shevket Pasha, Grand Vizier until his assassination in June, 1913, was reconciled to some contraction of the Ottoman frontier under pressure from the European powers. Enver Pasha, who became the most important figure in Turkish politics after Shevket's death, strove to thwart or at least defer the agreement of the powers. Austria was also bound to be concerned by the prospect of a Russo-German accord in the Near East, unless it made allowance for Austrian aims in the area and carried no threat to the stability of the Balkan frontiers. However, the Germans gave no assurance on these points, tending to write off as insignificant matters the Austrians considered vital.

Germany and Russia in Armenia

Hans Freiherr von Wangenheim seemed at least physically able to take up the work of the Giant of the Bosphorus. A big, burly Thuringian, he had served in the cavalry as a young man and had already seen diplomatic service in St. Petersburg, Copenhagen, Madrid, Athens, and Mexico City. Brimming with energy, he could become so overwrought during a policy debate that he would have to pace, even run, around a room to relieve his agitation. The singularity of his behavior increased markedly during his time in Constantinople, ending in a nervous breakdown and heart failure in 1915. His death, however, came as a surprise to everyone, particularly Henry Morgenthau, the American Ambassador, who had found him a healthy, full-blooded, though somewhat overpowering animal.[1] Morgenthau set him down as the perfect embodiment of Prussian militarism. The Turks, on the other hand, liked him for his gamey and unpredictable ways: they thought him bohemian. During the suspenseful summer of 1914, Wangenheim could be seen, knees crossed and smoking a cigar, on a bench outside his Therapia summer embassy reading dispatches as if they were trivial trade advertisements. His eye for the ladies was well known; it had cost him his first wife and prompted Morgenthau to forbid his daughters to sit next to him at diplomatic dinners.[2] In short, Wangenheim was too much a veteran to let the Turks get the better of him but too much a man to look down upon them. When he died on the Golden Horn four years later, the Sultan himself reviewed his funeral cortege.[3]

Though Wangenheim became a friend of the Turks and was mistaken by some as the sinister progenitor of the wartime alliance with them,[4] his first encounter with the Sublime Porte had

[1] Henry Morgenthau, *Ambassador Morgenthau's Story* (New York, 1918), p. 5.

[2] Henry Morgenthau, *All in a Life-Time* (New York, 1922), pp. 190-191.

[3] Joseph Pomiankowski, *Der. Zusammenbruch des Ottomanischen Reiches* (Vienna, 1928), p. 175.

[4] Alan Moorehead, *Gallipoli* (New York, 1956), pp. 21-22, 332.

been unsatisfactory and bitter. In 1901, as a special emissary, he tried to negotiate the sale or long-term lease to Germany of the Farasan Islands in the Red Sea. The German navy had used these as coaling stations during the Chinese Boxer Rebellion and, though the insurrection was over, did not want to relinquish the islands completely. Wangenheim informed a secretary of the Grand Vizier that Chinese affairs were too "unpredictable" to allow Germany to return the islands and offered to put German bases at Turkey's disposal should the Ottoman Empire ever find itself involved in a similar war.[5] But the Turks foresaw no such necessity and demanded evacuation. Wangenheim called for a German warship to cruise the Farasans twenty-four hours a day. The navy, however, withdrew its request.[6]

In 1908, Wangenheim served as chargé in Tangier during the absence of the German Minister, Friedrich Rosen. He used that occasion to encourage desertions from the French Foreign Legion. Morocco was ordinarily full of deserters, but upon Wangenheim's directive, they were sought out by the German consuls and given money and passage back to Europe. France brought the affair into the Hague Court, where the judges rejected the German argument that the deserters were Germans, Austrians, or Serbs and therefore entitled to the special consideration of their kinsmen.[7] Rosen himself discountenanced Wangenheim's actions as bad policy and bad judgment; but he still held that Wangenheim was a brilliant and learned man.[8] He noted, incidentally, that Wangenheim did not believe that Germany should extend her Turkish program beyond the completion of the Baghdad Railway or attach any territorial claims to the railroad line.[9]

When his embassy opened, his ideas had changed somewhat, but from the very beginning he did not believe in Germany's exclusive dominion over the Ottoman Empire and asserted that a Russian annexation of Constantinople must be reckoned with. It

[5] Wangenheim to Rosen, July 17, 1901, A.A. Deutschland #167, No. 5, Bd. 5, #A996.

[6] Schroder to Richthofen, July 20, 1901, *ibid.*, #A1014.

[7] Rosen, *Diplomatischen Wanderleben*, pp. 322–323.

[8] *Ibid.*, p. 320.   [9] *Ibid.*, p. 70.

was historically inevitable, strategically irresistible, but not necessarily politically dangerous for Germany. Wangenheim believed that if Germany could get a secure foothold in Anatolia, she had nothing to lose by a cession of the Turkish capital to the Tsar.[10] The forfeited glory would be more than made up for by the abundance of Anatolian grain and minerals. Germany's goal must be a sphere of influence divided with Russia, and to achieve it, he would have had his countrymen approach not the Ottomans, but rather their much reviled Armenian subjects.

Recent Russian policy, contended the Ambassador, showed that the St. Petersburg government knew how to appraise the Armenians at their worth, while the Germans had ignored and dismissed the race as "the Jews of the Orient." Wangenheim estimated that Russia had spent two and a half million rubles during 1912 on propaganda enterprises in eastern Anatolia, and the success gained would have been greater had not the Armenians had bitter memories of Pobiedonostsev and his program of harsh russification in the 1880's.

Here, then, was a point that Germans should exploit to their advantage, for the Armenians were not genuinely pro-Russian. One of Wangenheim's Armenian associates compared the situation of his people to that of a drowning man who will grasp at anything to save himself. They were therefore ripe and ready for a German protectorate because, though Europe and the German newspapers habitually forgot it, the Armenians were hardy, persevering farmers, not just the low tradesmen whom no power could long trust.[11]

Wangenheim advised the Foreign Minister to have the press depict the Armenians more sympathetically and also to increase the number of German consuls in their districts. He wanted an imperial representative sent to Erzerum immediately and thought funds should be found to set up a German school at Adana to educate Armenian children.[12] With proper training this race could supply the best executive and manual labor for the Baghdad Railway, while the Turks, on the other hand, were

intellectually obdurate and incorrigible.[13] He was himself prepared to contact the Armenian church hierarchy; with the requisite inducements, it would cease to be the customary channel
of Russian infiltration. The whole program might be capped by a
German squadron cruising in Anatolian waters. Significantly,
Wangenheim warned that the ships should be kept away from
Syria lest France take umbrage.[14] As ambitious as his Armenian
program was, the interests of France and Russia must be respected.

The German Foreign Minister agreed with this program in
principle but was reluctant to take the initiative in Armenia or to
implement Wangenheim's suggestions in every detail. He did not
call his ambassador up short, however, and only cautioned him
to do nothing that the Russians might misunderstand or seem to
the Turks at variance with Berlin's long-standing professions of
friendship.[15] In other words, he left his man in Constantinople
considerable latitude. But the Foreign Minister's apprehensions
were soon justified: the Grand Vizier quickly sought to frustrate
German intervention in Armenia by injecting a third competitor,
Britain. Wangenheim had apparently been too free with his
blandishments for the Armenian bishops, who warmly supported
the dispatch of the German navy. The Vizier, Mahmud Shevket
Pasha, therefore invited the British government to send inspectors for the western vilayets of Anatolia. When Wangenheim objected that Germans should have been called upon, the Grand
Vizier answered that his decision was taken solely to win British
support for the return of the Dodecanese, which Italy had seized
in the Tripolitanian war and the Porte wanted back.[16]

But Shevket cannot have been unaware that summoning the
Englishmen would make Russia furious, because she had just
commissioned the first dragoman of her Constantinople embassy
to develop her own program for an increase of Armenian freedom and for the prevention of murderous rioting between the
Armenian and Turkish peoples. This plan would have accorded

[13] *Ibid.*   [14] *Ibid.*, #15293.   [15] *Ibid.*, #15299.
[16] *Ibid.*, #15303.

autonomy to the six Armenian vilayets under a commissioner appointed by the Sultan.[17] Through Shevket's maneuver, this scheme now stood to fail through the untimely appearance of Britain and Germany in the area under discussion, and Russia would blame the Wilhelmstrasse and its man at the Pera embassy. The possibility of a Russo-German rapprochement in the Near East, adumbrated by Wangenheim in his reports, would become an impossibility, and St. Petersburg would cherish its shadow hegemony in Armenia more than ever. Yet Russia might have been willing to depart quietly from Armenia if she could have been assured safe arrival and permanent lodging in Constantinople. Wangenheim's mistake was telling his ultimate intentions to the Armenian prelacy [18] first rather than to the Russian Foreign Minister.

Wangenheim tried to dissuade Shevket from an address to Britain but stopped short when the Grand Vizier reminded him that Germany already had effective control of the Turkish army through the supervisory mission being organized under General Otto Liman von Sanders.[19] The exact date on which the organization of this group was decided upon cannot be determined, but the middle of March, 1913, is most likely. Almost at once, then, the mission proved a diplomatic handicap of the first water for Germany, because she could not object to a few Britons trailing the peripheries of the Ottoman Empire when forty-two of her own soldiers were quartered in its very heart. So the threat of British involvement in Armenia remained to harry the Russians; and for the moment a bilateral compact with St. Petersburg was impossible. At the end of the year Serge Sazonov, the Russian Foreign Minister, was complaining that Liman's mission was empowered to lock the entire diplomatic corps in the city of Constantinople.[20] He might not have felt so bad had he realized that the Germans had locked themselves out of the entire province of Armenia.

[17] Serge Sazonov, *Fateful Years* (New York, 1918), p. 143.
[18] G.P., XXXVIII, #15302.   [19] *Ibid.*, #15303.
[20] Sazonov, *Fateful Years*, p. 119.

Meanwhile, Grey had agreed to send the British inspectors, and Wangenheim could do nothing but feebly spar with the Grand Vizier. Shevket was told that Britain could not be trusted and that if the Dodecanese were not left to the Italians, London would see them awarded to the Greeks.[21] Shevket was ready to admit these charges, but claimed that his own hands were bound by the dictates of the members of his cabinet.[22] Then the German embassy learned that the British Ambassador to the Porte had secretly sent his dragoman to assure his Russian colleague that he would support the scheme of an autonomous Armenia.[23]

Worst of all, news from St. Petersburg showed that the Russian government was completely misinterpreting the character of Wangenheim and his mission. Sazonov had called in Friedrich Pourtalès, the German Ambassador, denounced Wangenheim as a consistent Russophobe, and speculated aloud as to whether he could secure his recall from Constantinople.[24] Pourtalès disclaimed any intrigue against Russia in the Ottoman Empire but privately advised Jagow that he would never be believed until Wangenheim was cashiered. The man was temperamental and without caution or foresight.[25] Yet Jagow covered Wangenheim against criticisms from within and without and confidentially told him that it was in the highest German interest that Sazonov be indulged. Jagow even compared Sazonov's situation with his own. He judged him sincere in the wish to maintain Turkey intact or else share the spoils equally. But, concluded Jagow, the

---

[21] G.P., XXXVIII, #15304.

[22] *Ibid.*, #15305. The distinguished Turkish historian Bayur suggests that the decision to call the British into Armenia came from Djavid Bey, the Minister of Finance and a consistent friend of the Entente. Bayur continues that both Djavid Bey and Shevket were unaware of the pro-German sentiments of the Turkish army, which received the new Armenian policy poorly. See Yusuf Hikmet Bayur, *Türk Inkilabi Tarihi* (Ankara, 1951), II/III, 53–58. The information is derived from recollections of Djavid Bey.

[23] G.P., XXXVIII, #15361.

[24] Pourtalès to Jagow, July 11, 1913, A.A. Deutschland #135, No. 1, Bd. 1, #A861.

[25] Jagow to Pourtalès, July 14, 1913, *ibid.*

Russian Minister worked against forces in St. Petersburg beyond
his own will. It was the same in Berlin—*"tout comme chez
nous."* [26]

Wangenheim and Jagow did not give up the Armenian project, though they both came more and more to believe that implacable forces could sidetrack any pacific intentions of Sazonov
and the Tsar.[27] Even while Jagow received additional sour notices from St. Petersburg, he instructed Wangenheim to study
the leaders and institutions of Anatolia best fitted to manage a
German protectorate over the area. He had considered but dismissed the possibility of transferring Prussian bureaucrats to the
Anatolian vilayets and believed it wiser to use native talent
alone. Wangenheim was to find a man who could function as a
regent or governor-general. Eventually, Jagow argued, the resistance of the Grand Vizier would end, or rather work itself out in
other directions. He speculated that the railroad network of the
Balkan peninsula ought to be improved and extended, because
such developments would draw Turkey's attention increasingly
away from Asia Minor. The lines to Adrianople and beyond
would involve her in European commerce where, he observed,
her true interests did not lie, but where inevitably her energies
would be confined. In the meantime, his policy would be to keep
the Sultan's empire free of crisis and trouble, so that no power
would have occasion to interfere until the German government
was ready to respond briskly.[28]

For that reason, on Jagow's orders the German consul at
Aleppo began negotiations with the Kurds, those wild tribesmen
who held it good sport to kill the Armenians and burn their villages. The Russians used such incidents to justify their autonomy
proposals and were even suspected of urging on the Kurds themselves. The Constantinople embassy suggested that German
schools be organized among the tribes and a few Kurds brought
to Germany for higher education.[29] A little culture and Euro-

[26] Jagow to Wangenheim, July 14, 1913, *ibid.*

[27] Wangenheim to Jagow, July 22, 1913, *ibid.*, #A15416.

[28] Jagow to Wangenheim, July 28, 1913, *ibid.*

[29] Mutius to Foreign Ministry, July 7, 1914, A.A. Türkei #183, Bd. 35,
#A13579.

pean society, it was hoped, would restrain them as Turkish and
Russian threats had never sufficed to do.

None of these proposals ever came to fruition, though they
were raised constantly during the war years. Jagow, Wangenheim, and undoubtedly many of the men in the German Foreign
Ministry believed in them, but they were supported by practically none of the other departments of the German government.
Particularly hostile were the German army and navy; members of
both services opposed any modification of Germany's earlier Turkish policy of complete and unequivocal control. There was nothing imaginary about the negative influences of which Jagow
warned Wangenheim, and though they cannot all be identified,
they were clearly influential at Constantinople. One enemy was
Corvette Captain Hans Humann, the naval attaché of the German embassy. Another was Enver Pasha, later Ottoman Minister
of War.

Humann's father was a former director of the Oriental Mu-
seum in Berlin.[30] He himself had a good grasp of the Turkish
language, an intimate acquaintance with many of the country's
leaders, and a broad grounding in Near Eastern history and culture. He also enjoyed the personal confidence and support of
Grand Admiral Alfred von Tirpitz, who authorized him to have a
special and direct call on the services of the Mediterranean fleet
superseding that of Wangenheim.[31] For the Ambassador, Humann had little tolerance. He accused him of professional incompetence and secret contempt for the Turks.[32] The counsellors of
embassy, Gerhard Mutius and Konstantin von Neurath, he regarded as defiant and obstructionist and better transferred to
other posts.[33] For its part, the Pera embassy responded in kind.
Wangenheim claimed that he did not need a naval attaché. He
emphasized his full confidence in Major von Strempel, his military attaché, who had given him reliable advice for some years

[30] Ernst Jaeckh, *The Rising Crescent* (New York, 1944), p. 119.
[31] Humann to Jaeckh, no date, A.A. Deutschland #135, No. 1, Bd. 1,
#A379.
[32] Humann to Jaeckh, Dec. 22, 1913, Jaeckh Papers, Drawer 69, #2.
[33] Humann to Jaeckh, no date, A.A. Deutschland #135, No. 1, Bd. 1,
#A379.

and was innocent of intrigue or political ambition.[34] But under
pressure from Tirpitz, Humann's appointment was confirmed,
and the Captain's relations with the German Ambassador remained little better than a truce. Strempel was recalled to
Berlin.[35]

Enver Pasha was Humann's close friend. The German officer
had given the Turk considerable hospitality when Enver was
military attaché at the Sultan's embassy in Berlin. From his service abroad the small, fastidious, but daring Enver acquired a
fluent if ungrammatical German and an almost ludicrous fondness for Prussian military mannerisms. With his stiff, corseted
bearing, elegantly tailored uniform, and Wilhelmian waxed mus-
tache, he aroused no little amusement among the European col-
ony in Pera,[36] but even his critics acknowledged his limitless patriotism. He dreamed of restoring the Ottoman Empire to the
heyday of power it had known under Suleiman the Magnificent,
and in that cause he could on occasion marshal a reserve of
ruthlessness that surprised even his closest colleagues.[37] He acquired a reputation for being pro-German, but the evidence, as
will be seen, does not show that he was particularly deferential
to Wangenheim. From Humann, he knew something of the Ambassador's views; and of these, with their talk of regional autonomy, foreign spheres of influence, and projected partitions, he
could not approve. Nor could he approve of those of his associates who were ready to negotiate such matters with the foreigner, however deviously.

One of these persons was of course the Grand Vizier. On June
11, 1913, Mahmud Shevket was abruptly removed from the scene

[34] Tschirschky to Bethmann, June 13, 1911, *ibid.*, Bd. 4, #A9448.

[35] Wangenheim to Bethmann, Sep. 19, 1913, and Lyncker to Jagow, Sep.
30, 1913, *ibid.*, #A19162, #A19638. On Strempel's career, see also George
W. F. Hallgarten, *Imperialismus vor 1914* (Munich, 1951), II, 349.

[36] Mary Mills Patrick, *Under Five Sultans* (New York, 1929), p. 260.

[37] Humann to Jaeckh, Nov. 27, 1915, A.A. Deutschland #135, No. 1,
Bd. 4, #A35948. On Enver's integrity, see a different comment in Alexander Aaronsohn, *With the Turks in Palestine* (Boston, 1916), pp. 11–
12.

by three assassins on the streets of Constantinople.[38] Though there is no evidence to implicate him in the crime, Enver could only benefit by the removal of this powerful rival. In January of the following year, he took over control of the War Ministry, a department with which the deceased Mahmud Shevket had especially concerned himself. This sudden accession to office was meteoric; Enver was only thirty-two years old at the time.

For the German embassy, on the other hand, the Grand Vizier's death was a setback. The Armenian negotiations were still in progress, and no commitment from the Turk as to full autonomy in that region had yet been obtained. Though he had been an obstinate haggler in the past, the evidence suggests that the Grand Vizier was on the verge of making concessions to the Germans and the Russians along the lines discussed by Jagow and Wangenheim.

Some observers thought that Mahmud Shevket had been the victim of a sworn vendetta by the leaders of the Turkish Liberal Party, who held him responsible for the murder of one of their members. Others charged the Grand Vizier with slack leadership in the Balkan Wars and even of treasonable negotiations with the Serb and Bulgar enemy.[39] A bad grain harvest was also counted against him, as was the heavy rate of conscription. But the American Ambassador believed that none of these factors caused the assassination. He claimed instead that it was the culmination of a fierce struggle over basic policy within the Committee of Union and Progress. Mahmud Shevket had been unable to persuade or reconcile his Committee opponents. The quarrel ended with his death.[40]

According to American reports, Mahmud Shevket clashed with his colleagues over the problem of the non-Turkish nationalities

---

[38] Rockhill to Secretary of State, June 14, 1913, United States Department of State Archives (hereinafter abbreviated D.S.), #867.002/27.

[39] Rockhill to Secretary of State, Feb. 21, 1913, D.S., #867.00/490; Kehl to Secretary of State, Mar. 15, 1913, D.S., #867.00/511.

[40] Rockhill to Secretary of State, Mar. 15, 1913, D.S., #867.00/507; Sauer to Secretary of State, Mar. 17, 1913, D.S., #867.00/517; Rockhill to Secretary of State, June 11, 1913, D.S., #867.002/26.

in the Ottoman Empire. The majority of the Committee insisted on no concessions and strict centralism, but the Grand Vizier sponsored a resolution that would have satisfied the Germans and Russians in many of its particulars. He proposed that certain surtaxes and property imposts be reserved to the vilayets in which they were collected and used for local needs. It was pointed out to the Vizier that financial autonomy was bound to end in political separation. Mahmud Shevket glossed over such objections and suggested vaguely that Turkey might acquire new territories for any old ones lost through his policies. He was reported in several of these debates to have broached the renunciation of Armenia or Arabia, and possibly both. The Porte had been recently bombarded with the demands of Arab secret societies, particularly one called La Markazieh, which insisted on financial home rule and on the reversion of many of the same taxes that Shevket had discussed.

Shevket also argued that it would be entirely feasible for Turkey to reconquer some of her former provinces in Europe.[41] From what is known of the correspondence between the German Foreign Ministry and its Pera embassy, it is not impossible that the Berlin government might have favored such an exchange. Jagow had spoken of shifting Turkey's center of gravity from the eastern to the western frontiers of the Ottoman Empire. Russia could be expected not to object if she made sufficient capital out of the deal, perhaps in Armenia or at the Straits.

Nevertheless, the Grand Vizier's proposals were ripped apart by the Ottoman War Minister, General Izzet Pasha. Speaking for the army, he declared Mahmud Shevket's dreams of Balkan ex-

[41] Sauer to Secretary of State, Mar. 17, 1913, D.S., #867.00/517; Rockhill to Secretary of State, Mar. 22, 1913, D.S., #867.00/509. Though his work contains little on Albania, Bayur charges that Shevket always undervalued Anatolia as the source of Ottoman political and cultural life. He notes also that Shevket's family originally came from Georgia, though it was for some time settled in the Arab provinces of the Empire. Bayur thinks this made Shevket relatively indifferent to the loss of Anatolia in a diplomatic exchange, especially if some foreign power would help the Grand Vizier to rule without the legislature, which Bayur states was his secret ambition. See Bayur, II/III, 59–60.

pansion to be absolutely suicidal. The troops, in light of their heavy losses in the Balkan Wars, were simply not up to them. Yet despite Izzet's criticism, the Grand Vizier plunged ahead and just before his death had a Turkish cruiser sail up and down the Albanian coast. By this gesture, as the government press enthusiastically pointed out, Turkey was staking her claim to the western Balkans.[42]

This naval gesture made the European powers uneasy in proportion to their nearness to the Adriatic Sea. Several probably did not regret Mahmud Shevket's death, and Russian embassy personnel in Constantinople were suspected of plotting against the dead man.[43] But given the facts of geography, they had less motive than the Austrians. All of the powers hoped for some time that the opposition of the Turkish army would scuttle Shevket's Balkan adventurism, but before the assassination, it was rumored that the Grand Vizier was planning to tap Bulgarian military resources in addition to his own. He was reported trying to arrange an alliance with King Ferdinand of Bulgaria for a war against Greece.[44] The victorious Turks and the Bulgarians would have cut away about equal shares of Greek land.

Neither Mahmud Shevket nor King Ferdinand considered what compensations might have to be paid to the other Balkan kingdoms in return for their benevolent neutrality. Among the first to be satisfied would have been Serbia, which had territorial claims against several of the Balkan states. And it was this

[42] Rockhill to Secretary of State, June 21, 1913, D.S., #867.002/28; Izzet Pascha, *Denkwürdigkeiten* (Leipzig, 1927), pp. 231–232; G.P., XXXVI(1), #14096. There is another version of Mahmud Shevket's assassination in Djemal Pasha, *Memoirs of a Turkish Statesman* (New York, 1922), pp. 21–23.

[43] Wangenheim to Foreign Ministry, June 15, 1913, A.A. Türkei #159, No. 2, Bd. 12, #A11970; Wangenheim to Bethmann, June 13, 1913, *ibid.*, #A12057.

[44] Rockhill to Secretary of State, Feb. 21, 1913, D.S., #867.00/490; Rockhill to Secretary of State, Apr. 26, 1913, D.S., #867.00/525. Turkey was of course at war with Bulgaria and had been since October, 1912, but such shifts of allegiance during combat were not unusual by Balkan standards.

Serbian reaction, entailing as it might a general redrawing of the
map of the Balkan peninsula, which concerned the Austrians.
This concern, it will be seen, deepened when they got no support from their German ally. Berlin was indifferent; and it was
reported that General Izzet, once the best hope for the Balkan
status quo, had been bribed heavily by Shevket's faction and
promised nothing less than his own kingdom in a restored Turkish Albania.[45]

When dealing with Turkey, Jagow and Wangenheim, like gen-
erations of their kind before them, always tried to apprehend the
reaction of Russia or Britain. To Austria-Hungary in such questions, the Germans paid scant attention or none at all. Their
concern, after all, was to shore up Austria, not spread her out
over the map. The time had almost come when the gentlemen in
Berlin would say openly what they privately held, namely that
the Dual Monarchy was only a little less sick than the proverbial
sick man of Europe.

But if the Turks were capable of vigorous rallies, the Austrians
proved themselves not less so. They would not lamely suffer
transgressions or diminution of their Balkan position. Wangenheim was astonished to learn that his elderly and amiable colleague from Vienna, Marquis Johann von Pallavicini, deliberately refused to help protect the embattled Grand Vizier against
his enemies. Nevertheless, the Grand Vizier had confided to Pallavicini that his life was in peril and had begged him for the use
of some Austrian property as a place of asylum and for Austrian
sailors to put some of his enemies under restraint. Pallavicini declared that he could not compromise his government and said little more about the affair, even to the police when they later tried
to question him about Shevket's murder.[46]

Pallavicini did not like the Turks, and all the artifice of the
venerable statesman could not conceal the fact. The longer he
remained in Constantinople—and as dean of the diplomatic

[45] Izzet Pascha, *Denkwürdigkeiten,* pp. 231–232.
[46] Wangenheim to Bethmann, June 27, 1913, A.A. Türkei #159, No.
2, Bd. 13, #A13160.

corps he had remained very long indeed—the more disgusted he became at the insuperable lethargy and dauntless corruption of the race. The conviviality and effusiveness that the Emperor William managed during his two trips to the city would have been unthinkable for him, and whatever the protean course of German policy, whether it waxed hot or cold on Turkey, Pallavicini remained steadfast in his cynical realism and well earned his name of the Cassandra of Pera. Indeed, he was more like a rotund Knight Templar, at his best but not at home in the Near East. In the Ambassador there remained something of the old Habsburg crusading spirit against the Ottoman Empire, a spirit that German, Magyar, and Slav troubles had put in abeyance at Vienna throughout the nineteenth century, but still not extinguished utterly. From time to time, he would in fact call up his Catholic conscience to rationalize an unfriendly decision against the Turks or to dignify some policy that became him as a diplomat but not as a gentleman.

Thus the Ambassador had no reason to save Mahmud Shevket, in whom he saw the specter of Turkish irredentism, and apparently made no effort to do so. The *status quo* of the Balkans was too precarious a thing under the best of conditions to survive the ambitions of this brilliant Turkish demagogue. Throughout the Balkan Peninsula there were many places where the Grand Vizier might have intrigued and intervened. Had he lived, he would probably have done so; at any rate, his successors took up the expansionist part of his policy, to which the assassination had only given pause. In time, Pallavicini found Enver as blameworthy as the murdered Shevket.[47]

The area that gave the Austrian government most concern was that part of the western Balkans called Albania. For most of Pallavicini's service it had never been a problem [48]—it did not even

---

[47] Pallavicini to Berchtold #4, January 7, 1914, Haus, Hof, und Staatsarchiv, Vienna (hereafter abbreviated H.H.S.A.) Türkei Karton 207.

[48] Stavro Skendi, *The Albanian National Awakening, 1878–1912* (Princeton, 1967), pp. 438–439. As early as 1910, Pallavicini was expressing the sympathetic, but also noncommital, view of his government toward Albanian nationalists in Constantinople.

exist as an independent state until 1913. But the Albanian question was brought to the fore by the outbreak of the First Balkan War in October, 1912. A league of Bulgaria, Greece, Serbia, and Montenegro made a concerted attack upon Turkey in Europe, each of them dispatching their troops over land they hoped to annex at the peacemaking. The Serbs advanced west and southwest, sweeping the Turks before them as they approached the Adriatic, and occupied northern Albania. Austria-Hungary and Italy, resolved to prevent the appearance of a new rival on the Adriatic, immediately objected. Serbia was landlocked, and Austrian policy required that she remain so. Russia, France, and Britain were inclined to support Serbia's ambitions on the Adriatic, but none of these powers was ready to go to war with Austria-Hungary over the question. A conference of interested powers awarded Serbia a railroad connection through Albania to the Adriatic, but the Serbs were denied any territorial access and required to evacuate their troops from northern Albania.[49]

The First Balkan War ended in May, 1913. By the end of June the Second Balkan War had begun with Bulgaria contesting the spoils with her former allies, the Serbs, Greeks, and Montenegrins, to which the Rumanians now joined. Serbia made good advances into Macedonia and the Sanjak of Novibazar, but the pressure of the powers again excluded her from Albania. Before the fighting ended, an ambassadors' conference agreed that Albania should become an autonomous principality with an hereditary prince. The powers were to guarantee its neutrality and regulate its finances and civil administration. All political ties with Turkey, Albania's suzerain until the Balkan Wars, were expressly declared dissolved forever. Instead of an Albanian magnate or even a Balkan prince, the powers named a German, Prince William of Wied, as the new sovereign.

The Serbs immediately denounced this settlement as a transparent ruse to block them from the Adriatic; the Austrians, though they sponsored the arrangement, despaired of its future; and the Germans without any enthusiasm mediated the settle-

[49] Anderson, *The Eastern Question*, p. 297.

ment. Though he was William of Wied's relative, the German Emperor advised the Prince to refuse the Albanian crown. He insisted that only a Moslem—perhaps a Turk, better an Egyptian —could rule a country where most of the regional chiefs were Moslem and maintained private armies of as many as nine thousand men. Austria was fully aware of Wied's difficulties, but she profited from this interim settlement by securing control of the National Albanian Bank and a concession to build a railroad through the country.

In the meantime, Serbian guerrilla bands slipped over the eastern frontier, while Greek irregulars moved in from the south. The Athens government alleged that the people of southern Albania were actually Greek and took to calling the area by the classical name of Epirus. Their troops pillaged and massacred, provoking Albanian peasant companies, led by semifeudal chieftains, to retaliate in kind. The Turks sent agents to intensify the chaos, while in Constantinople the Sublime Porte blandly observed that only an Ottoman prince could restore peace to Albania.[50] Against all the insurgents, the army of William of Wied made little headway. It was officered by Swedes and Dutch and without professional training. The Austro-Hungarian government, not insignificantly, refused to allow any of its officers on the spot to teach drill and marksmanship to the Albanians.[51]

In Constantinople, meanwhile, Pallavicini distributed liberal subsidies to persuade the papers to point out the weaknesses of the international settlement while at the same time denouncing any attempts at imperialistic intervention on the part of the Turks.[52] The policy of the Ballplatz, it would seem, was to reserve Albania for itself. But the Germans, it will be seen, became increasingly convinced that the country had to be given back to the Turks.

[50] J. Swire, *Albania, The Rise of a Kingdom* (New York, 1930), pp. 173–174, 179, 182–183, 190, 197.
[51] Swire, *Albania*, p. 213.
[52] Rockhill to Secretary of State, May 3, 1913, D.S., #867.00/532.

The Rise of Enver Pasha

The new Grand Vizier was Prince Said Halim, a relative of the Egyptian Khedive and a descendant of the celebrated Mohammed Ali. In manner, speech, and dress he was superbly and impeccably europeanized. He owned the most beautiful palace in the city and furnished it in a style whose symmetry and taste none of the other Ottoman grandees, including the Sultan, could match. With his English-cut ties and shoes, he made an overpowering contrast to his associates of the Committee of Union and Progress.[53] With the members of the diplomatic corps, whose languages and capitals he relished, he set a standard of cordiality and rapport that, after the end of the war, was not to be known in the city again. He told Wangenheim privately that he had destroyed much of the incriminating evidence concerning Shevket's death that the police had turned up against Russian and British diplomatic personnel. The German Ambassador took the gesture as proof that the Turk, or at any rate Said Halim, was the first gentleman of the East.[54]

Yet no one believed that the highest authority reposed in his well-manicured hands. The death of Shevket in fact cleared the stage for Enver Pasha, who had long worked behind the scenes and who, according to some observers, had regarded his way as blocked by the murdered man.[55] Though he was unquestionably pro-German, Enver remained above all a Turk and a good bargainer to boot. In the affair of the Liman von Sanders mission and its aftermath, he quickly showed that he could be a skilful negotiator. He put the Germans on the defensive and did not hesitate to play off the Russians against them.

It was Mahmud Shevket who had arranged for the calling of a German military training mission, subsequently under the command of Liman von Sanders.[56] As is well known, Russia pro-

[53] Wangenheim to Bethmann, June 20, 1913, A.A. Türkei #159, No. 2, Bd. 12, #A12585.
[54] Wangenheim to Foreign Ministry, June 28, 1913, *ibid.*, #A12948.
[55] Humann to Jaeckh, January –, 1914, Jaeckh Papers, Drawer 69, #3.
[56] Djemal Pasha, *Memoirs,* pp. 66–67.

tested the dispatch of this training group into a first-rate diplomatic crisis. Serge Sazonov charged that the Ottoman cabinet had become virtually German dupes, that the security of the foreign embassies was jeopardized, and that the Turkish army was being put on a war footing for action against Russia.[57] None of these charges was true, and almost any interpretation put upon the formation of the Liman group by the powers exceeded Germany's original intentions. These were of a purely technical nature, in no sense innovative or precedent-making. The German Foreign Ministry made constant reference to the presence of a British naval training mission in Constantinople, upon which it wanted to pattern its own undertaking.[58] The British themselves felt that the Germans were quite right in pointing out the analogy and could not understand why the Russians were so disturbed.[59] Most important, the Turks were not satisfied with either the depth or scope of the German commitment and suspected that the value of the mission had already been undermined by too much quibbling and qualification.

The first Russian response to the idea of Liman's mission had been positive. When the Emperor William mentioned it to him at a royal wedding in May, 1913, Tsar Nicholas did not regard the arrival of Liman's officers as strengthening the Turkish army to Russia's detriment but rather as contributing to force an armistice in the Balkan War. Nicholas believed the Germans could so strengthen the Chataldja lines in front of the capital that King Ferdinand of Bulgaria would be obliged to relinquish his hopes of seizing Constantinople.[60] This prospect frightened the Russians as much as the Turks, and Sazonov wondered whether he might have to send a Russian squadron into the Bosphorus.[61] The Russian attitude cannot have reassured the Turks; to whatever extent the Liman affair admitted of compromise with St. Petersburg, the Germans became suspect.

---

[57] G.P., XXXVIII, #15448.   [58] *Ibid.*, #15468, #15469, #15472.
[59] Harold Nicolson, *Sir Arthur Nicolson, First Lord Carnock* (London, 1930), p. 404.
[60] G.P., XXXVIII, #15462.   [61] Anderson, *The Eastern Question*, p. 296.

Furthermore, Russia did not at first work for the recall of the Liman group from Constantinople, but instead for its transfer to either Adrianople or Smyrna.[62] The latter was near the area in which the Germans were especially interested. This compromise accorded with the opinions of the Emperor William, who told the Russian Minister of Finance, Vladimir Kokovtsev, that Liman's position was still open to negotiation and that the General might be removed outside of Constantinople.[63] Jagow declared that the matter had already gone too far for such revisions to be made without Germany losing prestige.[64] But in the final instance, it was the surprise publication of the Sultan's proclamation of December 4, 1913, appointing Liman von Sanders commander of the First Army Corps in Constantinople, that deprived the Germans of any more room for maneuver.[65] The very day before Wangenheim had reported that he was trying to have the Bosphorus specifically excluded from Liman's command.[66]

All of these exchanges would seem to show that Wangenheim had not departed from his latently pro-Russian attitude. The Turks, however, at first rejected these compromises [67] and then wanted them postponed several months or indefinitely.[68] They yielded in the end, but not with any good grace. Only Sazonov was angrier at the outcome of the negotiations, and that probably because the Tsar had not troubled to inform him of his prior approval at the wedding festivities.[69] Because of his pique as much as anything else, Sazonov ignored all proofs of Germany's willingness to negotiate.

When on December 13, Russia, France, and Britain presented an identical note of protest to inquire whether the Turks regarded the Liman mission as infringing the security of the Straits, the Grand Vizier replied that the matter was Turkey's

[62] Robert J. Kerner, "The Mission of Liman von Sanders," *Slavonic and East European Review*, VI (1927), 352–354.

[63] *Ibid.*, p. 351.   [64] G.P., XXXVIII, #15452.
[65] Kerner, *op. cit.*, p. 359.   [66] G.P., XXXVIII, #15461.
[67] *Ibid.*, #15493.   [68] *Ibid.*, #15499.
[69] Sazonov, *Fateful Years*, p. 118.

business alone and not subject to foreign meddling. The reply had been agreed upon with the other members of his cabinet. Yet by that time Enver Pasha no longer believed in the German military mission and thought seriously of discharging it. He told Humann that as much good might be accomplished by simply sending more Turkish officers to study in Berlin.[70] This greatly disturbed the Captain, and he indicated that he alone managed to talk Enver out of going through with his threat. Just two months before, Enver had survived a serious appendectomy skillfully performed by a German surgeon.[71] Humann now reminded him, and Enver, who counted a certain barracks loyalty among his redeeming traits, agreed to allow Liman's mission to remain.

Furthermore, Humann and Enver were working out a program to send capable young Turks to Germany to study civil and electrical engineering. Humann convinced Enver that in time such trained personnel could replace the Armenian workers who predominated in these departments of the Turkish government. One of the first to go was Enver's brother Kiamel Bey. At first the young man was scheduled to study in Lausanne, but Humann warned Enver about malign French influences and had Kiamel posted to Berlin instead. There the Captain got him an interview with the distinguished electrical magnate Walter Rathenau.[72]

This sort of diplomacy was beyond Wangenheim for the moment. For whatever reason—and several have already been suggested—the Ambassador found it hard to work with Enver, though he recognized that he was the moving spirit behind the Grand Vizier Said Halim. During his convalescence, Enver had refused to see several members of the German embassy when they came to make courtesy calls. To Humann he accused them of hypocrisy and said that Wangenheim was too mercenary and self-serving to be trusted.[73]

[70] Humann to Jaeckh, Dec. 22, 1913, Jaeckh Papers, Drawer 69, #2.

[71] Humann to Jaeckh, Oct. 15, 1913, *ibid.*

[72] Humann to Jaeckh, Oct. 29, 1913, *ibid.*

[73] Wangenheim to Zimmermann, Nov. 1, 1913, A.A. Türkei #159, No. 2, Bd. 13, no number.

For his part, Wangenheim at first could find little more to commend in Enver than his military bearing, personal bravery, and freedom from graft. He noted that there was a picture of Frederick the Great over his desk, but also observed with as much satisfaction that the other members of the Committee envied Enver so much that he found it necessary to station a guard of twenty men around his house.[74] It was soon obvious, however, that a persistently reserved attitude would only diminish Wangenheim's effectiveness, particularly since the Russian Ambassador, Michael N. Giers, made haste to ingratiate himself with the little Pasha.[75]

Enver succumbed to these Russian overtures with an ease and rapidity that are striking in light of his later agreements with Germany. Early in January, 1914, the Grand Vizier appointed him Ottoman Minister of War. The news met with the reluctant concurrence of his Committee colleagues and the total astonishment of the Sultan, Mohammed V. The aged sovereign learned the news over his breakfast coffee and objected at once that Enver was too young for the office.[76] Mohammed did not trouble to protest, however, as no one knew better than himself that such action would be unavailing.

Giers, on the other hand, was very satisfied with the news, and the German embassy soon learned that Enver conferred several times with the Russians about the middle of January. Agents of Wangenheim made contact with a certain Alexander Tschernogortschevitsch, whom they treated to lunch and a bout of heavy drinking. Generously plied with liquor, Tschernogortschevitsch revealed that he had been sent to Constantinople to bribe the city and interior police to support a dictatorship of the country by Enver. Unlimited money had been given him, and all his drafts on Russian banks were signed by Giers. Enver was said to have told Giers that he wanted to be dictator and urged that

[74] Mutius to Bethmann, Jan. 9, 1914, *ibid.*, #A703.
[75] Mutius to Bethmann, Jan. 20, 1914, *ibid.*, #A1520.
[76] Liman von Sanders, *Five Years in Turkey* (Annapolis, 1927), p. 7.

Russia assist him "in great and small ways" to depose the House of Osman and abolish the caliphate.[77]

There is no way of definitely checking the accuracy of this report since its origin is murky and subterranean. However, it was considered credible enough to send directly to the German Chancellor, and Wangenheim made no attempt to qualify or countermand it, as he often did with intelligence from his assistants and consuls. Furthermore, he himself reported that Enver had secured the appointment of Hairi Bey as Sheik ul Islam. Hairi was a member of the *ulema* but had recently severed his connections with the priestly caste and denounced the caliphate as a pillar of corruption and obscurantism. He could be counted upon not to veto the progressive legislation of the Young Turks on religious grounds and would even be prepared to approve the accession of Enver as Sultan. It was rumored that Hairi would preach the liquidation of Enver's opponents as a pious act.[78]

So experienced a judge as Pallavicini believed that Enver had some such ambitions in mind and that Wangenheim sought a separate accord with the Russians to frustrate them. To do this, the German Ambassador sketched a compromise whereby General Liman would be appointed inspector-general of Turkish forces rather than commander of troops in Constantinople, where the foreign embassies were resident. Jagow approved Wangenheim's plan, as did the Turks. Pallavicini interpreted this arrangement as an attempt to dissuade the Russian government from further unilateral support of Enver Pasha.[79]

The rise of Enver and the solution of the Liman affair both profoundly disturbed Pallavicini. He would have preferred that Germany and Austria together oppose the Young Turk regime and force the Grand Vizier to reshuffle his cabinet in a more con-

[77] Mutius to Bethmann, Jan. 20, 1914, Supplement, A.A. Türkei #159, No. 2, Bd. 13, #A1520.

[78] Wangenheim to Foreign Ministry, Mar. 16 and 17, 1914, *ibid.*, #A5328, #A5644.

[79] Pallavicini to Berchtold #27, Jan. 11, 1914, H.H.S.A. Türkei Karton 207.

servative direction.[80] By the end of January, 1914, as will be
seen, Berchtold in Vienna, acting on his ambassador's advice, demanded of the Porte the dismissal of Talaat Pasha, the Interior
Minister. But the Berlin Foreign Ministry and Wangenheim
usually put off any suggestions of common action. Particularly in
the matter of the change in Liman's orders, the evasive replies of
the German Ambassador deepened Pallavicini's suspicion that a
deal must have been struck between Berlin and St. Petersburg. It
was, he feared, that an advance of Enver's people in Albania
and Macedonia might encourage their complete withdrawal
from Anatolia, which was to be left to the convenience of the
German Emperor and the Tsar.[81]

Enver lost little time in formulating his plans. A private informant told Pallavicini that he intended first to trigger an insurrection against the Serbian administration in Novibazar. To
that end a number of experienced Balkan bandit chiefs were
being trained and subsidized in the interior of Asia Minor. The
insurrectionaries would demand autonomy, subject, of course, to
the suzerainty of Sultan Mohammed V.[82] Thereafter Turkey
would declare war on Greece for the recovery of all the Aegean
islands occupied by the Greeks during the Balkan Wars. This
campaign, furthermore, would test the leadership and loyalty of
the Turkish officer corps, some of whom had already protested
the plans of their chief.[83] Enver, in the meantime, pensioned off
many of the older officers, alleging reasons of age and economy,
though Pallavicini insisted that they were retired for criticizing
the foreign policy of the Committee leaders.

Among those dismissed was a certain Shukri Pasha, prominent
in the defense of Adrianople and thus particularly offensive to
the Bulgarians. His removal from active service was seen at the
Austrian embassy as yet another sop thrown to King Ferdinand,
with whom the Young Turks aimed to contract an alliance. For

[80] Pallavicini to Berchtold #4, Jan. 7, 1914, *ibid.*
[81] Pallavicini to Berchtold #7, Jan. 19, 1914, *ibid.*
[82] Pallavicini to Berchtold #13, Jan. 7, 1914, *ibid.*
[83] Pallavicini to Berchtold #4, Jan. 7, 1914, *ibid.*

the moment, however, Enver would not move because the Turkish navy continued to elude his grip. Pallavicini learned that certain naval officers had formed a Ligue Militaire and approached Russia for subsidies and aid to bring down Enver and his faction. They wanted to place an order for bombs in Odessa but, Pallavicini believed, would have no success in light of Russia's Anatolian designs. Under these circumstances, the Ambassador suggested, Austria might step into the breach.[84]

At the end of January occurred a sharp exchange between the Austrian Ambassador and the Grand Vizier. Pallavicini demanded to know whether the rumors he had heard were true. If so, he warned Said Halim that the course followed by his party was "foolish, outrageous, and dangerous." The latter was quick to deny all these allegations and to dissociate himself from the opinions of his War Minister. Whatever truculence the Turkish government had been guilty of was only a means of pressuring the French and securing a loan that was at the moment under negotiation in Paris. Said Halim described the Turkish army and navy as barely strong enough to keep order in the provinces. But he did not let pass the opportunity to observe that the fault lay with the German military mission and to comment further that the Central Powers had given Turkey inadequate support in the Tripolitanian and Balkan Wars. Berlin and Vienna, he insisted, too often followed the lead of Grey in London, and under the circumstances, the Committee hotheads must be pardoned occasional outbursts of resentment and spleen.[85]

A few days later Pallavicini was shocked to find an unflattering cartoon of the three Triple Alliance sovereigns and their Ambassadors in *Tasfir-i-Efkiar*, one of the Constantinople papers. He again vigorously remonstrated with Said Halim, and the Grand Vizier had the sheet suspended.[86] But there was little satisfaction in this, because the Austrian Ambassador learned in the

[84] Pallavicini to Berchtold #7/p, Jan. 19, 1914, *ibid.*
[85] Pallavicini to Berchtold #47 and #10/p, Jan. 26, 1914, and Feb. 9, 1914, *ibid.*
[86] Pallavicini to Berchtold #8/p, Jan. 28, 1914, *ibid.*

meantime that the Porte had secretly opened discussions with the Italian embassy with a view to replacing all German drill instructors in Turkey with Italian army and navy officers. Furthermore, Italy, in return for certain economic concessions, was to undertake to supply arms of all types from her own arsenals at favorable prices. Said Halim was reported to have promised, whenever possible in the future, to purchase all ships from either Italian or American builders.[87] From Count Berchtold in Vienna came further intelligence that talks were under way with the Japanese, who had seized on the suggestion that their officers increasingly staff the Turkish navy. Turkey did not encourage Japanese hopes of turning this combination against Russia, but Tokyo nevertheless remained willing to help.[88]

Whatever the denials of Said Halim, news persisted that the Turks were preparing some action to recover Macedonia at the expense of Greece and Serbia. The project was taken up at several sittings of the Committee of Union and Progress, and the decision reached that even if an offensive with Bulgaria were unavailing, bandit chiefs should be encouraged to keep the area in turmoil until the Great Powers had been brought to the point of exasperation. A conference would then be convened and the powers obliged to return at least part of Macedonia to Turkish jurisdiction. The Young Turks spoke boldly of getting a foothold on the Adriatic by means of a corridor through either Albanian or Montenegrin territory and were reported to have formulated a plan of operations with the Bulgarian General Staff.[89]

Under the circumstances, Pallavicini called on Liman von Sanders himself to authenticate what he had heard. Liman proved a surprisingly ready informant, probably because his relations with Wangenheim were not altogether harmonious and he frequently felt slighted by the embassy staff. Wangenheim had

[87] Pallavicini to Berchtold #4/p and #26, Jan. 7 and 10, 1914, *ibid.*

[88] Berchtold to Pallavicini #29/410, Jan. 24, 1914. H.H.S.A. Türkei Karton 208.

[89] Pallavicini to Berchtold #10/p, February 9, 1914, H.H.S.A. Türkei Karton 207.

not even bothered to welcome the General at the railroad station when he arrived in Constantinople and since that time had seen him infrequently and accorded him little or no confidence.[90] The notion that Liman was in any sense the coordinating head or policy-maker of German operations in Turkey was recognized as completely groundless at the time. From the beginning he was treated as the orphan child of the German establishment and, for the sake of Russia's feelings, was never permitted to be prominent or at ease in the social circles of the capital. Liman felt the restrictions of his position quite keenly and before and during the war requested his recall several times. He was therefore delighted to unburden himself to Pallavicini, to whom he spoke frankly and even compromisingly.

Liman apparently lacked both the taste and talent for political intrigue and, not fully initiated into the higher designs of his superiors in Pera and Berlin, was reduced to guessing. Nevertheless, he had formed a pretty clear picture of Young Turk foreign policy, and his judgment was emphatically negative. He told Pallavicini that he would train and revitalize the Turkish troops as best he could but would not sanction their use in reckless Balkan aggression. If his objections were ignored, he would remove himself and all the members of his command from Turkey. His job, in his opinion, was strictly technical and without any controversial overtones except for the placing of a few profitable contracts with German munitions makers. Such dealings were not without precedent, and all the powers engaged in the arms traffic. Pallavicini, for his part, commended Liman's sincerity to Vienna but observed that the General was not the man to set a term to his government's involvement in the Ottoman Empire. Whatever Liman might wish, he would be overridden at every critical juncture and was even at that time being unfavorably reported upon by one of his subordinates, Fritz Bronsart von Schellendorff. This officer had the especial confidence of Berlin and was being groomed to replace Liman should he prove unsuitable or refractory in his post. However, the Austrian Ambassador felt that he

[90] Liman von Sanders, *Five Years*, p. 3.

had made a valuable contact in the head of the German military mission.[91]

In Vienna, Count Berchtold had in the meantime concluded that the Turks could not be reasoned out of their ambitions nor the Germans relied upon to assist in such efforts. Any attempt to bring Germany into line by making trouble in her ranks looked equally futile; Liman was more discontented than disloyal in his post. Moreover, there was no prospect of localizing the Turkish problem, because it was exciting the dangerous interest of other powers—the Italians and the Japanese—and the Turks themselves were ready to hit hard on more than one front. Fully as dangerous as Macedonia was the Albanian question; and despite Wangenheim's snide comment that Albania was only a neurotic apprehension in Pallavicini's mind,[92] there was every evidence that it was about to boil into a first-rate crisis.

When the cabinet of Said Halim first evinced interest in Albania, the Germans were inclined to write it off more as a Turkish means than an end. Mutius, Wangenheim's counsellor, described this tack as merely one phase of a larger anti-Christian and anti-Greek policy. The Committee needed some kind of diplomatic success but would make trouble on the Adriatic littoral only until Greece had been forced to evacuate the Aegean islands taken by her during the Balkan Wars. These islands rather than Albania were the basis upon which Turkey wanted to settle.[93] All the talk about General Izzet Pasha as King of Albania in opposition to Prince William of Wied, the choice of the Powers, and the arrival of an Albanian delegation in Constantinople to offer Izzet homage were dismissed as mere stage trappings and diplomatic tinsel.[94] The Germans argued that the Aegean is-

[91] Pallavicini to Berchtold #10/p, Feb. 9, 1914, H.H.S.A. Türkei Karton 207.

[92] Wangenheim to Bethmann, Mar. 2, 1914, A.A. Bulgarien #17, Bd. 20, #A4539.

[93] Mutius to Bethmann, Jan. 9, 1914, *ibid.*, no number.

[94] Mutius to Foreign Ministry, Jan. 5, 1914, A.A. Albanien #1, Bd. 1, #A290.

lands, whatever state eventually possessed them, were too far away to threaten the security of the Habsburg frontiers.

But the Turks were more persevering than the German Foreign Ministry thought and, furthermore, knew how to divide the Central Powers on this issue. In late December, 1913, Moslem Albanians began to contact the German embassy in Bucharest. There they described the Albanians as "Indogermans" and, as such, deserving of as much help as Russia gave the Slavs. The German government was urged to deal with the Albanian people more sympathetically, to reject the leading strings of Austrian diplomacy in that area, and to consider seriously the accession of a Hohenzollern prince to the Albanian throne to replace William of Wied.[95]

The Turks also added economic to dynastic considerations, and beguiled the Pera embassy with hints of limitless profits in Albanian mines and industries secured for Germany by the Sultan's concessions.[96] In this case the way of credulity led to profit, and all Austria's warnings about Turkish aggression were best discounted or dismissed. The Germans, moreover, found a certain justification for their policy in recurrent reports that Austria was herself conniving at Wied's deposition and the achievement of a naval base on the Albanian coast.[97]

Meanwhile, Bekir Effendi, a Turkish officer and veteran of the Balkan Wars, roamed Albania distributing guns, ammunition, and dynamite for an insurrection in favor of Izzet Pasha. However, he was tracked down by Wied's gendarmerie, mostly soldiers on leave from the Dutch army, and arrested together with numerous Turkish officers who had followed in his wake. During interrogation, these men were found to have leaves of absence signed by Izzet and, in Bekir's case, several telegrams from the Grand Vizier. Bekir confessed that the insurrection was to be cited as proof that the government of William of Wied was un-

[95] Waldhausen to Bethmann, Dec. 21, 1913, *ibid.*, #A25504.
[96] Mutius to Bethmann, Jan. 7, 1914, *ibid.*, #A594.
[97] Winkel to Bethmann, Dec. 31, 1913, *ibid.*, #A202.

stable and unpopular and should make place for a Turkish prince.[98]

Throughout the rumpus the German government remained unconcerned, though it was, of course, a party to Wied's appointment. It was apparently inclined to take at face value the assertions of Said Halim that his government had nothing to do with the affair [99] and did not raise at Berlin anything like the storm Berchtold made in Vienna. There, at the end of January, 1914, Hilmi Pasha, the Turkish Ambassador, was called to the Ballplatz and told that Austria must have the resignation of the Young Turk demagogues. Talaat Pasha, Minister of the Interior, was cited by name. Hilmi still denied Turkish complicity, but Berchtold hammered in his objections. He did offer, however, to end the affair with as little further noise as possible, if the Turks would sack Izzet and one or two other prominent offenders.[100]

A month later Hilmi was still brazening it out with the Austrian Foreign Minister. He not only refused to yield but trumpeted his country's policy in Albania as Austria's only hope for her own security in the Balkan Peninsula. When Berchtold asserted that Turkey's aggressive posture would set off the formation of another Balkan League, Hilmi retorted that Austria had better look to the movements of Montenegro and Serbia, who were negotiating a union and intended forcibly to rectify their frontiers to Austria's disadvantage. This disclosure caught Berchtold off guard, and he could only thank the Turk and instruct Pallavicini to track down the source of the news.[101]

The performance of the Turks was extraordinary. With an army lamed in the Balkan Wars and an economy mortgaged to the European bankers, they still had the temerity to challenge one of the great powers and entertain a reasonable hope of getting away with it. They could posture outrageously because they

[98] Nadolny to Foreign Ministry, both Jan. 9, 1914, *ibid.*, #A508 and A592.
[99] Mutius to Foreign Ministry, Jan. 10, 1914, *ibid.*, #A628.
[100] G.P., XXXVI (1), #14101.
[101] Berchtold to Pallavicini #55/747, Feb. 14, 1914, H.H.S.A. Türkei Karton 208.

knew that whatever else Austria might be prepared to lose, she could not afford to lose them to the Triple Entente. At the end of January, Ambassador Pourtalès had reported from St. Petersburg that some such rapprochement was in the offing. Sazonov had begun to regret the solution of the Albanian problem and the accession of William of Wied. He now thought that it would be much better to put "an intelligent Turkish pasha" in his place.[102]

A few days later it was learned at Constantinople that a Russian agent, Dimitrieff, had already arrived in Albania to work for the enthronement of a Russian prince subject to the Sultan's suzerainty. The Committee membership was reported as satisfied with such a solution as long as all Turkey's economic and cultural interests were guaranteed.[103] From another source, it appears that the Germans were not opposed to the appearance of the Romanovs and felt they would profit more certainly by their coming. According to a political observer attached to the Mediterranean Fleet, Germany would emerge from all this meddling of the powers as Albania's only disinterested friend and should lose no opportunity to exploit that position quickly. As many consulates as possible should be opened up at once, instead of allowing Austria, as hitherto, to represent German interests.[104]

By early spring of 1914, Turkey's relations with Russia, Bulgaria, and Rumania were warming almost as quickly as the weather. Talaat received an invitation to visit the Rumanian capital, which Pallavicini claimed both Constantinople and Bucharest tried to keep secret from him.[105] Then a Russo-Turkish Friendship Committee was formed in St. Petersburg, a move warmly hailed by the Young Turks and bitterly excoriated by the Austrian Ambassador. One of the founding members was a

[102] Pourtalès to Bethmann, Jan. 31, 1914, A.A. Albanien #1, Bd. 3, #A2170.

[103] Mutius to Bethmann, Feb. 8, 1914, *ibid.*, Bd. 4, #A2967.

[104] Schneider to Commander of Mediterranean Fleet, Feb. 16, 1914, *ibid.*, #A3966.

[105] Pallavicini to Berchtold #13/p, Feb. 18, 1914, H.H.S.A. Türkei Karton 207.

former editor of *Tanin* with many connections among Turkish journalists. Pallavicini believed this would make it all the harder to bribe the press in favor of the Dual Monarchy. He knew, moreover, that Giers and Wangenheim had lately exchanged a number of visits, and while the Russian criticized certain features of Germany's Balkan diplomacy, he declared that he believed his country and Germany could soon work out their problems in that area.[106] The Germans were reported to have approved recent Russian efforts to persuade Bulgaria to settle all her outstanding differences with the Ottoman Empire and to contract an alliance with the Porte. St. Petersburg had also influenced the Bulgarian clergy to suspend persecution of Moslem villagers in Bulgaria.[107]

The consequences of such an alignment Pallavicini accused the German Ambassador of underestimating or ignoring altogether. Germany had made her deal with Giers, whom all Constantinople regarded as Sazonov's imminent successor.[108] For Austria there was only isolation and speculation on the ruinous intentions of the many Bulgarian, Russian, and Rumanian emissaries who called on the Grand Vizier. The Rumanian General Coanda arrived at the end of March, but Said Halim and Talaat declined to answer any Austrian inquiries about him.[109]

The last restraint on Turkey seemed to have snapped when Liman von Sanders threatened to throw up his commission. The General ranted that his position had become impossible, since Enver countermanded his orders and neglected to provide the troops with shoes and sufficient changes of linen. Whenever Liman scheduled an inspection, new uniforms were issued and sturdy recruits substituted for feeble ones, but when he left the line, the clothes were returned to their boxes and the men to their original stations. He and Enver had also quarreled about

[106] Pallavicini to Berchtold #20/p Secret, Mar. 23, 1914, *ibid.*
[107] Pallavicini to Berchtold #20/p, Mar. 23, 1914, *ibid.* Cavalla and Salonika had only recently passed to Greece as a result of the Balkan Wars.
[108] Pallavicini to Berchtold #16/p Secret, Mar. 11, 1914, *ibid.*
[109] Pallavicini to Berchtold #127, Mar. 31, 1914, *ibid.*

the hundreds of officers who were being retired or dismissed.[110] Probably because he took up the cause of some of these, the General was subjected to a barrage of petty annoyances without finding any cover or assistance at the German embassy. Two of his daughters were molested by Turkish soldiers malingering near his office. A French newspaperman spread reports that they had been raped. This was not true, and Liman threatened the man with a revolver and forced him to quash the story, but his nerves were so frayed and his position so compromised and ridiculous that he wanted to go home. He was unable to see Wangenheim, who had gone to Berlin for conferences, and Counsellor Mutius distinctly gave the impression that the embassy would view his departure with unconcern.[111]

But Liman did not depart, though not only the Pera embassy but also the Berlin Foreign Ministry would probably have welcomed his passing. In both quarters it was recognized that Liman's mission was a sore point with the Russians, and Jagow and Wangenheim were anxious to set things right as quickly as possible, as has been seen. However, the German Emperor in early April, 1914, intervened and refused to consider Liman's departure. While it might improve relations with St. Petersburg, the removal of the general would give freer play to the expansionist schemes of Enver and his Committee supporters. Liman was known to be opposed to these, and so was the Emperor, or at least to certain aspects of these schemes. William could approve a Turkish advance into Albania, but this would be achieved only by a joint effort with Bulgaria, and the Bulgarians planned to take their compensations not in Albania but in Greece. The thought that in the next Balkan war the frontiers of Greece might be in any way reduced went against every grain of Hohenzollern family sentiment and loyalty, for the Queen of Greece was William's sister. For her sake the German Emperor was moved to frown on the foreign policy of the Committee,

[110] Liman von Sanders, *Five Years*, pp. 8–10.
[111] Pallavicini to Berchtold #20/p Secret, Mar. 23, 1914, H.H.S.A. Türkei Karton 207.

which, for other reasons, he had apparently supported. Indeed, William was in a quandary. He called Wangenheim to Berlin not for routine talks but rather for a thorough dressing-down.[112] The Ambassador had apparently given the Turks too much moral support at the expense of their Greek neighbors.

In the mélange of Albanian bandit fighting, Greece had taken as large a hand as Turkey. Though most of the insurrectionaries were native born, they would not have lasted long without the help of one or the other of these powers. For as many Turks as championed the cause of Izzet Pasha, there were probably an equal number of Greek troops, out of uniform and pretending to be Albanian, who aimed at an independent Epirus. Since the foundation of the Albanian state, fighting in this southern province had never stopped and would probably end only when the area was incorporated into the Greek kingdom. For some months King Constantine of Greece had sought to win the support of Emperor William, but Jagow, always looking to Russian initiative, had so far restrained his sovereign.[113] Then the Turks abruptly refused to honor a private agreement between the Emperor and the deposed Sultan, Abdul Hamid, whereby German archeologists could freely remove all their diggings from the Ottoman Empire to the museums of Berlin.[114] Politically the disagreement was inconsequential, but it offended William and roused in him a philhellenism that, with his keen artistic sensibilities and dilettante's love of everything classical, had never been far below the surface.

There can be little doubt that the German people would have preferred a philhellenic rather than a pro-Turkish foreign policy. Even though, as Wangenheim and Jagow conceived it, this policy was intended to shift Turkey's center of gravity from Anatolia to the Balkans, its rationale could not have been disclosed; and had it been, it would not have overcome the question of

---

[112] Pallavicini to Berchtold #144, Apr. 9, 1914, *ibid.*
[113] Jagow to Treutler, Apr. 2, 1914, A.A. Albanien #1, Bd. 6, #A6463.
[114] Pallavicini to Berchtold #25/p Secret, Apr. 13, 1914, H.H.S.A. Türkei Karton 207.

conscience for most Germans. The religious difference between Berlin and Constantinople remained. If the Germans often ignored it, they could not altogether erase it. The German Emperor knew this and even cited an article in the *Vossische Zeitung* urging him to mediate the dispute over Epirus.[115] During his spring vacation on Corfu, he had several talks with the Greek King. Thereafter he declared that Greece's aspirations in southern Albania were reasonable and pursued for the most part in a legal and orderly manner. Constantine, the German Emperor described as an utterly sincere man, innocent of any collusion with the Epirote terrorists and determined to court-martial and shoot any Greek officer found in their ranks.[116]

These declamations were made before the German Chancellor, the Foreign Minister, and the Ambassador to Turkey, who were all invited to Corfu. They were believed by none of them. William's argument did not gain in conviction when even he admitted that if there were Greeks in Epirus, they were deserters and not regular army personnel.[117] Though crestfallen and humiliated, Wangenheim warned the Emperor that his absence from Pera had already stirred alarms among the Turks and Russians and urged imperial intervention to win pardons for the accomplices of Bekir Bey and to clear away any misunderstanding. William would not discuss the point and it was in any case already too late.[118]

Throughout the Corfu meetings, the Committee of Union and Progress had been in almost daily session. Enver was kept under heavy fire and told that Germany was false to her commitments and craven toward Russia. Despite the presence of Liman von Sanders, the Bosphorus defenses were still deplorable, and the least advance by Russia would find Turkey alone and at the mercy of her foes. The opposition therefore demanded an immediate address to the Tsar inquiring his price for guaranteeing the

---

[115] Jagow to Treutler, Apr. 2, 1914, A.A. Albanien #1, Bd. 6, #A6463.
[116] Zimmermann to Nadolny, Apr. 9, 1914, *ibid.*, #A6737.
[117] Quadt to Foreign Ministry, Apr. 12, 1914, *ibid.*, Bd. 7, #A7219.
[118] Wangenheim to Foreign Ministry, Apr. 13, 1914, *ibid.*, #A7257.

integrity of the Ottoman Empire—or rather what he chose to leave of it. For the Turks were convinced that nothing coming from St. Petersburg would be disinterested, but certain at the same time that they would have to yield less to it alone than in the company of Berlin. Pallavicini's military attaché discovered that the Committee ordered a reduction in garrison strength all along the Armenian frontier, as the Austrians saw it, an undoubted gesture of reconciliation toward Russia.[119]

When Wangenheim returned to the city, Pallavicini remarked in him the nervous tension that was soon to prove fatal. The man had lost his old self-assurance and drive, his sense of humor and disarming forthrightness. He mumbled his answers, squirmed, and withal indicated how painful the Corfu encounter had been for him. His Austrian colleague believed that it would continue to cloud his future and bar his advancement in the service. Any further talk about Wangenheim becoming Foreign Minister, Pallavicini was inclined forthwith to dismiss.[120]

For Giers, on the other hand, the future was as bright as it had ever been and free from encumbrance for the first time. Germany had apparently jilted the Turks and by her traffic with King Constantine of Greece raised doubts about her good faith at the Porte. The Turks appeared to be at the mercy of Russia and her allies. The Russian Ambassador boasted of his friendship with Sir Louis Mallet, British representative at the Porte, whom he claimed had pruned his staff of all old-line foreign service men suspected of Russophobia.[121] And he delighted in blowing up Pallavicini's small worries into large fears. The Austrian was coldly told that the Rumanian people were basically hostile to Austria, held in check only by their king, whose poor health gave no guarantee for the future. Were King Carol gone from the scene, Russia could turn the country to her will.

[119] Pallavicini to Berchtold #24/p Secret, Apr. 4, 1914, H.H.S.A. Türkei Karton 207.

[120] Pallavicini to Berchtold #32/p Secret, May 4, 1914, *ibid.*

[121] Pallavicini to Berchtold #20/p, Mar. 23, 1914, *ibid.*

The army particularly, Giers held, would prove Russia's ready instrument.[122]

Ernst Jaeckh, Swabian publicist, dean of German Turcophils, and Hans Humann's frequent correspondent, was the first to contend that the Turco-German Alliance of August 2, 1914, was basically an Austrian inspiration.[123] His argument was based on a few bits of documentation and much informed hearsay, but the papers now available show him to have been absolutely right. Pallavicini was as much concerned about Turkey as Wangenheim, perhaps more so because he led from a position of weakness. At the beginning of April, he began to warn that the Turks had too much room for diplomatic maneuver and did not know how to use it. They aspired to so much because they were certain of so little; as long as they remained insecure, they would use demagogic journalism, religious fanaticism, and subversive insurrections to plaster over the cracks of their state system. Genuine reform was impossible for them, as much because of their human nature as their politics. The only solution therefore was to tie them in the knot of the Triple Alliance, to which Bulgaria could subsequently be added. Rumania would have no choice but to court this combination, because the threat of isolation would otherwise be too oppressive. However, if none of this could be achieved, Austria must "rethink" her Turkish policy.[124]

The dispatches summarized here provide an accurate forecast of Austrian policy at Constantinople during the World War, except that, while Vienna got its alignment, it still rethought its policy. At bottom the men at the Ballplatz were unwilling to treat Turkey as an equal, whatever engagements they made in writing. And Turkey went far enough with Russia before the war to inspire only scant trust among her allies after it began. It may be argued that the Turkish government had no choice. It

[122] Pallavicini to Berchtold, no number, Apr. 13, 1914, *ibid.*

[123] Jaeckh, *Rising Crescent*, p. 112.

[124] Pallavicini to Berchtold #24/p Secret, Apr. 4, 1914, H.H.S.A. Türkei Karton 207.

could not afford to ignore the German Emperor's philhellenism or not guard against it. William's intervention was particularly shocking because it was he who, in his much publicized Near Eastern odysseys, had opened the era of good feeling toward Turkey.

Said Halim warned Pallavicini that the Committee had all but decided on a reorientation of Turkish foreign policy toward the Triple Entente. He personally regretted that Germany had to be given offense. He still praised the rehabilitative work of the military mission, which even then his colleagues were prone to ignore. But it nevertheless remained impossible for him to comprehend or justify the Grecophile maneuvers of the Wilhelmstrasse, and he had bowed before the insistence of Talaat and Izzet, who would go to Livadia on the Black Sea and deal directly with the Russian Tsar. The imperial court was to stop there in May so that the invalid Tsarevitch might enjoy the warm air and the curative mud baths. A Turkish delegation always arrived in the Sultan's yacht to salute Nicholas on these occasions, but this time, so both ambassadors of the Central Powers feared, the Turks would bear plenary powers to negotiate instead of the customary empty compliments. Only Sazonov, present in the imperial retinue, doubted that Talaat was commissioned to talk seriously; he put off the Turk, perhaps unwisely and, as it proved, forever.[125]

However, Pallavicini urged Berchtold to anticipate the Turkish detente and to offer the surrender of Constantinople to the Tsar. There was no time to lose, he added, because Russia was prepared to partition Asia Minor, with or without Germany, and immobilize Austria by bringing against her a Balkan coalition. By such a coalition, Austria would be militarily overwhelmed and dissolved. To avoid such a catastrophe, Russia astride the Straits was not too great a price. In any case, the Straits, he concluded, had lost their former significance.[126]

[125] Sazonov, *Fateful Years,* pp. 137–138.
[126] Pallavicini to Berchtold #34/p Secret, May 13, 1914, H.H.S.A Türkei Karton 207.

The Balkans, however, had not; and it was precisely in that area that the dangers continued to mount for the Dual Monarchy. Pallavicini insisted that Talaat had been guaranteed a Turkish Albania at Livadia; [127] and he knew more reliably that Turkish agents were swarming into Bosnia. At the same time, many Bosnian farmers were pulling up stakes and migrating to the Ottoman Empire. Each had been given his traveling money by the Turks, and Pallavicini feared these people were being induced to charge that the Austrian government had oppressed them.[128] Wangenheim tried to be sympathetic, but knowing his sovereign's mind all too well, he dared not go beyond a few showy but impotent gestures to recover Germany's position of trust at the Porte. He arranged for the crew of the *Goeben*, which had put in at Constantinople, to be given a brilliant party at the Sultan's palace of Dolma Bagtché, but the event made little stir in the Turkish press, whose efforts were far more taken up by the return of Talaat from his interview with the Tsar.[129]

No change in fact could be expected of the Turks, since the German Foreign Ministry remained inflexible in the matter of Greece. Germany favored giving southern Albania to Greece, while Turkey demanded all Albania for her own. While Sazonov was said to have promised Talaat that he would not recognize the jurisdiction of the Patriarch of Constantinople outside the city itself,[130] the Germans seemed to be making every effort to aggrandize the dignity and importance of that prelate. At the end of May occurred the anniversary of the Turkish capture of Constantinople, an event normally signaled by loud blasts of Turkish chauvinism, but on the advice of Wangenheim, the authorities of Constantinople let the day pass in relative quiet. Furthermore, plans to publicize stories of Greek atrocities against Turks in Macedonia were foregone at the insistence of the Ger-

---

[127] Mittag to Berchtold #223, May 28, 1914, *ibid.*
[128] Pallavicini to Berchtold #28/p, Apr. 22, 1914; Mittag to Berchtold #43/p, June 15, 1914, *ibid.*
[129] Mittag to Berchtold #38/p, May 25, 1914, *ibid.*
[130] Pallavicini to Berchtold #46/p Secret, June 24, 1914, *ibid.*

man Ambassador. On the birthday of King Constantine in early
June, on the other hand, the Greeks of the capital permitted
themselves a noisy parade that included a salute to the German
embassy. This gesture undoubtedly compromised Wangenheim
further than he wished.[131]

In the diplomacy of effrontery and brass, the Greeks quickly
showed that they could match the Turks. They offered the
Grand Vizier a series of provocations that would have been suicidal without the assurance of the German government's good
will. For no apparent reason, the Ecumenical Patriarch closed
down every Greek school in Constantinople, as well as a number
of churches.[132] Giers himself set down the man for a muddle-
headed charlatan and declared that not the Greeks, but rather
the Turkish peasants of Macedonia were the victims of oppres-
sion at the moment.[133] The Grand Vizier and the Turkish Ambassador in Athens, Ghalib Bey, got wind of the remark, and the
latter demanded his passports. Though the gesture might have
dramatized Turkey's grievances effectively, the Grand Vizier
sternly charged Ghalib to remain at his post.

Said Halim in his turn had again yielded to pressure from the
German embassy.[134] Very likely following a suggestion of the
Russian Ambassador, the Grand Vizier called for an international conference to discuss Greek and Turkish claims in Albania
and in the Aegean Islands. Preparatory to its meeting, Said
Halim wanted to send a mixed commission into Macedonia and
Smyrna to investigate the atrocity stories and to fix responsibility.[135] Rumania and France immediately expressed their interest, together with their assurances that Turkey had behaved toward Greece in good faith.[136]

[131] Wangenheim to Foreign Ministry, June 8 and 13, 1914, A.A. Türkei
#168, Bd. 10, no number, #A11661.

[132] Wangenheim to Bethmann, June 10, 1914, ibid., #A11823.

[133] Wangenheim to Foreign Ministry, June 15, 1914, ibid., #A11830.

[134] Quadt to Foreign Ministry, June 14, 1914, ibid., #A11724.

[135] Wangenheim to Foreign Ministry, June 16, 1914, ibid., #A11879.

[136] Waldhausen to Foreign Ministry, June 17, 1914, ibid., #A11924,
Quadt to Foreign Ministry, June 17, 1914, ibid., #A11955.

The Porte appointed Talaat to lead the commission and requested that its membership be as international and distinguished as possible. But the Wilhelmstrasse objected that the whole affair could be adjusted by Germany and Russia with possibly a third power. The German Foreign Minister also declared that if war did break out, Germany would take every step in cooperation with the other powers to see that the action was localized.[137] In other words, the Wilhelmstrasse had decided in advance to withhold any aid from the Turks. This declaration really made Talaat's commission unnecessary. It would never enjoy the publicity originally intended for it, and one of its members had come to a conclusion regardless of the evidence. Talaat did leave for Smyrna, but he was tailed by a few dragomans and reporters, not by the ambassadorial lights whom he had expected. Pallavicini wanted to give Said Halim or Talaat a medal to assuage their hurt and mortification, but the Porte rejected the gesture.[138]

Thus, on the eve of the World War Germany did, as her enemies charged, exercise an inordinate and overweening influence at Constantinople, but almost all of it worked toward her disadvantage and defeat. The policy of the Wilhelmstrasse lacked premeditation, and the contradictions of opinion emanating from Berlin were so sharp as to cut down the very men charged with expressing them. Wangenheim was an instance of this. He had lost all influence and seemed without any fixed opinions, except perhaps the one that Britain had first reached in Salisbury's time: Constantinople belonged inevitably to the Russian Tsar.[139] Yet apparently the Germans lacked sufficient technical dexterity to profit from this obvious geographical fact; they were permitting themselves to be pushed out of Turkey when they might have been paid handsomely for going. Emperor William was responsible for much of this fumbling, but the problem was not

[137] Aide-Mémoire, Berlin, June 17, 1914, ibid., #A11958.
[138] Wangenheim to Foreign Ministry, June 17, 1914, ibid., #A11976.
[139] William L. Langer, The Diplomacy of Imperialism (New York, 1935), I, 251.

of any one man's making. Marschall had years before reduced it to its elements: the Germans were too far away; they were too sparsely settled in the Ottoman Empire; and they had not the means or experience to shape the culture of the area in their image.

Perhaps some or all of these handicaps could have been overcome in collaboration with a friendly and absolute ruler like Abdul Hamid. But that Sultan now languished in close confinement, and no advance could be made with the wilful Young Turks. These men, themselves living on dreams and feeding on hopes, would not permit as much to the Germans. The Austrians, with an alertness and penetration into Turkish ways that only close geographical proximity could bring, knew all this better than their German colleagues. But perhaps the very nature of the historical relationship between Vienna and Berlin decreed that the experience could not be used in common, but served instead only to divide the Central Powers.

3

The Crisis of Turkish
Intervention and the
Egyptian Problem

On August 2, 1914, the German Ambassador and a few Young Turk leaders signed a military alliance. The Austrians concurred. In so doing, the Turks strove to enlarge their empire and protect what they already had against partition. Without this alliance, they felt, Germany herself might play the role of partitioner as well as any of the Entente powers. For their part, the Germans hoped eventually to use the alliance to draw off British and Russian troops from the main European sphere of conflict. With the Austrians this consideration weighed to some extent, but the Vienna Foreign Ministry had also to guard immediately against Turkish irredentist intrigues. These might have been begun had not the Ottoman government, on August 2, undertaken an obligation of honor to the Central Powers.

With such a mixture of motives the alliance was unsound from the start. In planning the first Egyptian campaign, it became clear that neither Germany nor Austria, for different reasons, was prepared to treat Turkey as a full equal. Germany was not above speculating on Egypt's passing into her own sphere of influence rather than the Sultan's; and Austria could not afford an Ottoman restoration in Egypt for fear that Italy would use such a development to desert the Triple Alliance and make war on the Habsburg monarchy. In short, there was, and could be, no brotherhood of arms.

The Signing of the Turco-German Alliance

The news of the Sarajevo assassination reached Constantinople on June 28 during a dinner party given by the Grand Vizier to the commander of the British Mediterranean Fleet, Sir Berkeley Milne. These parties were commonplace at the Porte. According to custom, every commanding British officer was expected to pay his respects to the Sultan. But to Sir Berkeley, Said Halim had paid the extraordinary honor of allowing a British cruiser, H.M.S. *Inflexible,* to pass through the Dardanelles, although a yacht would have been sufficient to carry the Admiral and his aides to the gala at Dolma Bagtché. It was the first time such an exception had ever been made; the British raised their eyes and took note.[1]

Quite possibly the gesture was intended to express the Grand Vizier's satisfaction at the treatment lately accorded him by the British government. Though Grey had spoken of localizing any conflict with Greece, his countrymen on the spot had been conspicuously busy in repairing and servicing Turkish warships at the Bosphorus docks for imminent action. Djemal Pasha, recently promoted Minister of Marine, got along famously with Admiral Arthur H. Limpus, the British technical adviser. Both men had seen to it that contracts for new vessels were judiciously placed with Armstrong and Vickers as well as with similar firms in France. The payments, usually a problem, seemed to be well covered by a public subscription that was going briskly.[2]

Curiously, when told of Franz Ferdinand's death, the Grand Vizier broke into a smile. Some observers believed that his reaction was merely one of relief and that he was glad of an excuse to end a long day of official functions. But in several of the provincial governments, the Turkish flag was not lowered in mourn-

[1] Andrew Ryan, *The Last of the Dragomans* (London, 1951), pp. 89–90.

[2] Hoffman Philip to Secretary of State, May 1, 1914, D.S., #867.-00/621; Morgenthau to Secretary of State, June 19, 1914, D.S. #867.-00/630.

ing, and Berchtold had to protest what the Grand Vizier excused as an oversight.[3] Wangenheim paid his respects at the Austrian embassy with ceremonial punctiliousness, and of greater practical importance, his military staff hastened to make good in a few weeks all those omissions of which Pallavicini had been complaining for months. The military mission at once appreciated the strategical importance of the Ottoman Empire should a general war break out; or rather they allowed this consideration to override every other idea that they had recently weighed. Liman von Sanders immediately telegraphed for six more staff officers to be added to his mission, a request on which the Berlin authorities had for some months delayed action.[4] Even at this late date, however, the General did not get exactly the type of men he requested because Wangenheim was still inhibited by nagging doubts.

The Ambassador had been recalled to Berlin upon the news of Franz Ferdinand's death, and he there warned the chief of the military cabinet against the appointment of as many engineers as Liman wanted. Liman's urgency to strengthen the Bosphorus fortifications was technically correct; but it was decided that the provocation this might give the Russians was of even greater moment. No work on the fortifications was therefore undertaken.[5] The Secretary of the Navy suggested that if the Turks were concerned about their defenses, they could send some of their own officers to Germany, where they could quietly learn methods of coastal fortification without giving offense to the powers.[6] The loss of time involved was perfectly obvious and extremely frustrating to General Liman, but he was unable to make his objections tell against the diplomats. The Turks went wild with anger

[3] Berchtold to Pallavicini #3239, July 10, 1914, H.H.S.A. Türkei Karton 208.

[4] Lyncker to Bethmann, July 3, 1914, A.A. Türkei #139, Bd. 33, #A13207.

[5] Lyncker to Bethmann, July 9, 1914, *ibid.*, #A12056.

[6] Department of the Navy to Foreign Ministry, Secret, July 8, 1914, *ibid.*, #A13602.

and threatened to place more arms contracts with the French and British.[7]

As always, these maneuvers had an upsetting effect on Pallavicini and the Ballplatz. Since his government's relations with Serbia were rapidly deteriorating, Berchtold deemed the moment right to press Jagow with his Turkish proposals, since Wangenheim had always been so curiously phlegmatic toward whatever Pallavicini transmitted to him. The Austrian Ambassador in Berlin, Count Szögény, therefore inquired whether it would be possible to bring Turkey into the Triple Alliance. Jagow dismissed Turkey as at best a "passive factor." He remarked specifically that it was not in Germany's interest to give the Porte an absolute guarantee for Armenia against Russian attack.[8] Wangenheim maintained that Turkey was incapable of carrying out an alliance, would only place burdens on her allies, and should be encouraged to preserve cordial relations with all the powers. Three days later, he implied that the Austrian gesture was essentially a matter of prestige, that in initiating the alliance scheme Berchtold was attempting to recover a Balkan pre-eminence lost during the wars of 1912–13.[9] Apparently none of Pallavicini's jeremiads had made a dent upon him, or he was more convinced that Germany's interests were better served in accord with Russia.

Roughly the same suspicions of German bad faith played upon Enver Pasha. For him inclusion in the Triple Alliance would bind Germany's hands and submit her to the dictates of honor. It would end Germany's flirtations with Russia and secure for the Ottoman Empire all of Armenia and the approaches to Asia. Of all Turks, Enver, a fervent Pan-Turanian, was least willing to give up these areas. At the same time, Turkish aspirations in Albania would not be prejudiced, but rather could be pressed as a strategic necessity against the Serbian enemy. Enver warned

[7] Mutius to Foreign Ministry, July 10, 1914, *ibid.*, #A13594.

[8] Jagow to Wangenheim, July 14, 1914, given in Jaeckh, *Rising Crescent*, p. 10.

[9] Wangenheim to Jagow, July 18 and 21, 1914, both given in Jaeckh, *Rising Crescent*, pp. 11–12.

Wangenheim that if Turkey were rejected by the Triple Alliance, she would turn at once to the Triple Entente.[10] Enver undoubtedly knew that the Porte could expect none of the desired advantages from such an alliance. The threat of adhesion to the Triple Entente was probably to satisfy his Gallophile colleagues, Djemal and Djavid Bey, the Finance Minister. But the Germans did not call his bluff. The prospects of closing the Straits with Turkey's help and cutting off Russia from her allies was compelling, the more so as it agreed with the thinking of the Austrian ally, whose interests the Germans could not always ignore.

About July 24, William ordered that the Turkish approach be followed up.[11] He totally disregarded the advice of his Foreign Ministry, and there is no evidence that the army believed wholeheartedly in closer association with the Ottoman Empire. The conduct and opinions of Liman von Sanders prove just the contrary. If any department of the German government actively favored the Turkish alliance, on the basis of the available evidence, it would appear to have been the Naval Ministry. Humann worked zealously for it and, later in the war, persuaded Tirpitz to take up the cause in return for naval bases in Turkey.[12]

The Emperor's command, however, was dutifully if not enthusiastically seconded by his representatives abroad, though their private opinions did not always tally with their public conduct. Wangenheim now proclaimed that Turkey's army would be a potent factor in the outcome of the war as long as it was under the command of German officers,[13] but he cannot possibly have believed this. He was in the best position to know that Turkey's troubles struck too deep to be erased merely by a new leadership,

[10] Wangenheim to Foreign Ministry, July 22, 1914, given in Jaeckh, *Rising Crescent*, p. 12.

[11] Wedel to Foreign Ministry, July 24, 1914, given in Jaeckh, *Rising Crescent*, p. 14.

[12] Holtzendorff to Bethmann, Dec. 26, 1916. A.A. Nachlass von Hintze, no number.

[13] Wangenheim to Foreign Ministry, July, 27, 1914, given in Jaeckh, *Rising Crescent*, p. 15.

however enlightened. In the last analysis, all that anyone in Berlin could be sure of was that Turkey would add a certain strength of numbers to the resources of the Central Powers and tie down Entente units that could be more crucially used elsewhere.

The Grand Vizier's original offer stated that the alliance must become active if Russia attacked Turkey, Germany, or Austria, or if any of these attacked Russia. Said Halim wanted the treaty contracted in the strictest secrecy and would not have revealed it even to his own ambassador in Berlin, Mahmud Muktar. Chancellor Bethmann, on the other hand, wanted to exclude Pallavicini from the negotiations and insert a clause into the treaty abrogating the whole arrangement if war did not break out between Russia and the Austro-German coalition. If it ran beyond the latest Balkan crisis, it would be of use only to Austria, which wanted the Turkish association with or without a more general war. Wangenheim advised, however, that the exclusion of Pallavicini would create unnecessary resentment, contradict earlier treaty obligations, and quickly prove unrealistic in the Constantinopolitan hotbed of intrigue. The Turks could also not be expected to accept the suggested terminal date, because without extended military coverage, Turkey would be subject to later Russian reprisals for even having considered a treaty with the Central Powers.

The Austrian Ambassador was accordingly told of the discussions, and the treaty was made to run until December 31, 1918. In his instructions to Wangenheim to sign the treaty, Bethmann permitted the Ambassador to draw back if he still had any doubts of Turkey's military capacity.[14] At that late date, Wan-

[14] Wangenheim to Foreign Ministry, July 28, 29, 30, 1914; and Bethmann to Wangenheim, July 28 and 31, 1914, all given in Jaeckh, *Rising Crescent,* pp. 16–19. On January 11, 1915, the German and Turkish governments agreed to a revision of the alliance treaty of the previous August. According to this revision, the alliance was to continue until July, 1920, and was to provide for German military assistance in any defensive war against France; against Britain, supported by another power; or against a coalition of Balkan states, Rumania excepted. All this was in addition

genheim had not much of an option, but the Chancellor's tele-gram puts beyond doubt his conviction that the treaty signed at Therapia on August 2 was not to the advantage of the Reich.

During the discussions, the Turks had spoken of giving the German military mission supreme control of the Ottoman army in the event of war and actual field command of at least one-fourth of it. It is not clear from the documents if Liman von Sanders ever knew of this (he took no part in the treaty negotia-tions), and the Turks showed in short order that they had no in-tention of conceding so much authority to a foreigner. The ap-proach of war brought to a head all of Liman's grievances against the Turkish government, and even while the treaty was being discussed, he had all he could do to check the discontent and demoralization among his men which had been mounting since the beginning of the year. At that time it had been pointed out to the Turks that the officers posted to their service took a considerable cut in pay, and it was hoped that efforts would be made to match the salaries given in the German army. Two days after the alliance treaty was signed, Enver claimed he could not do this. Again pleading expense, he disclosed that his office would not push for any further fortifications of the Bosphorus.

Liman was beside himself and completely deaf to the Turks' other argument that they did not want to force Russia's hand through precipitate action or frighten the Bulgarians, with whom they had exchanged projects of alliance and territorial expansion for a long time. In the question of the Bosphorus forts, Liman had personally intervened against the dithering of Berlin, so he took Enver's decisions as a betrayal and a personal humiliation.[15]

---

to the original German commitment against Russia. Bethmann was at first quite unwilling to agree to these additional clauses, and Austria did not formally accept them until March 21, 1915. The original treaty and its revision are to be found in Carl Mühlmann, *Deutschland und die Türkei 1913–1914* (Berlin, 1929), pp. 94–98. For comment, see Bayur, III/I, 436, and Gerard E. Silberstein, "The Central Powers and the Second Turkish Alliance 1915," *Slavic Review,* XXIV (1965), 77–89.

[15] Wangenheim to Bethmann, Aug. 4, 1914, A.A. Türkei #139, Bd. 33, #A1788.

He threatened to resign, but the War Minister not only agreed but suggested that the General take out at least half of his mission with him.[16]

The German Emperor's reprimand sufficed to check the rage of his general. Liman was informed that William valued his services as highly on an oriental front as in the western sectors. The German government understood how chafing and discouraging was the inactivity of the Bosphorus when shooting had already begun in France, but it demanded unquestioning and uncritical obedience of all its officers, as appropriate to their calling as any rash bravery in the field.[17] Wangenheim agreed that any change in the character of the military mission would now be taken by the enemy as surrender.[18] Just as important, however, was the policy of Austria, which made any withdrawal of the Germans even more embarrassing if not completely impossible. For shortly before, Berchtold telegraphed to Berlin that he intended to send most of the Austrian fleet to Constantinople and expected the German government to match his offer. He specifically requested that the *Goeben* and *Breslau,* which had recently been cruising off Albania, be directed to the Straits at once.[19]

On the face of it, Berchtold's offer was an ordinary comradely gesture in time of war, but made at that precise moment, it solidified the alliance of August 2 as no stroke of the pen could ever have done. It served to bind Bethmann and Liman as well as Enver and the Young Turk cabinet. Why Enver went back on his word hardly more than forty-eight hours after having given it is not clear. He may have simply changed his mind; yielded to the objections of his colleagues, many of whom were not consulted on the treaty; or been attempting an eleventh-hour deal with Russia.[20] If the last was his aim, Berchtold's move tended

[16] Wangenheim to the Emperor, August 19, and Wangenheim to Foreign Ministry, Aug. 20, 1914, *ibid,* #A17905, #A18019.

[17] Bethmann to Foreign Ministry, Aug. 20, 1914, *ibid.,* #A18211.

[18] Wangenheim to Foreign Ministry, Aug. 19, 1914, *ibid.,* #A17937.

[19] Berchtold to Szógyény #343/4910, Aug. 4, 1914, H.H.S.A. Allgemeines Karton 941.

[20] See Harry Howard, *The Partition of Turkey, 1913–1923* (Norman, 1931), pp. 92ff.

to confound it and to sow disunity among the leaders at the Porte. Said Halim was perfectly delighted at the news Pallavicini brought to him and declared that any doubts of the alliance that he had were completely dispelled. He even offered to abandon neutrality as soon as the Austrian ships arrived before the city.[21] This last remark is particularly important, since the Germans are usually represented as having been extremely dissatisfied that Turkey did not intervene soon after the signing of the August pact and waited instead until the end of October.[22] The documents suggest, however, that many of the German party in Constantinople were not eager for a Turkish declaration of war and would have preferred more time to consider how far Germany could prudently involve herself with the Porte.

In the money question, the Turks yielded nothing to Liman's complaints. Their own arrogance and Austria's encouragement were proof against all of Wangenheim's attempts at mutual accommodation. The Ambassador was brought to suggest that a monthly subsidy be added to the salary of each member of the military mission. He suggested that sixty thousand marks a month would eliminate the disparity between the German and Turkish wage scales and also cover the rising cost of commodities in the city market. But as he wrote, he was fully aware of how disgraceful his position had become and did not want it to be publicly examined or discussed. The money, he believed, should not appear in any official appropriation or be referred to any Reichstag committee. It might best be taken from the Emperor's privy purse. If it had been, one might observe, justice if not economy would have been served, because the feelings of the Turks were dearer to William than to any other German official at the moment.

A month later, the Deutsche Bank agreed to put one hundred thousand marks at the disposal of the military mission every

[21] Pallavicini to Berchtold #405/4010 and #407/2134, Aug. 5 and 6, 1914, H.H.S.A. Allgemeines Karton 941. In the end, the Austrian ships did not arrive, for reasons suggested in Franz Conrad von Hötzendorf, *Aus meiner Dienstzeit 1906–18* (Vienna, 1921–25), IV, 186–187, 190–191.

[22] Carl Mühlmann, *Deutschland und die Türkei, 1913–1914*, pp. 52, 57–59.

month, the Treasury promising to make good this charge in full at
a later date.[23] Captain Humann was sent to inform Liman of the
arrangement and to caution him against any future outbursts.
The incident was closed with a letter from the chief of the Emperor's military cabinet to the irascible General. The latter was
bluntly told that if he returned to Berlin, he could not expect
reassignment under any condition.[24]

Albania and Turkish Intervention

The surrender he had extorted from the Germans worked an
enormous change in Enver's personality. All traces of modesty
and diffidence disappeared, to be replaced by a self-confidence
that at times approached lunacy. He spoke as if he did not need
foreign advice or foreign leaders. His armies, he told Pallavicini,
were fully mobilized and eager to attack; he would have committed them long ago had not Berlin withheld its approval. The
Austrian Ambassador was pleased to note that most of the units
were stationed in eastern Anatolia for an eventual strike into the
Caucasus, but he warned Vienna that unless some move soon occurred, their effectiveness would fall off from its highest pitch, or,
worse still, they might be used elsewhere.[25]

Exactly what he had in mind cannot be definitely established,
but a fair guess is that it related to the Albanian question. In the
Adriatic area, the German and Austrian Foreign Ministries were
completely at loggerheads when the Great War broke out. With

[23] Wangenheim to Bethmann, August 4, 1914, A.A. Türkei #139, Bd.
33, #A17880; and Helfferich to Rosenberg, Sep. 24, 1914, *ibid* #A23701.

[24] Jagow to Zimmermann, Sep. 27, 1914, *ibid.*, #A24476. This and later
accounts of Liman's discontents in Turkey are hard to reconcile with
Turkish assertions that the General took a leading part in encouraging
the Porte to declare war. Bayur claims that Liman promised Crimea to
certain Turkish generals in return for intervention. Moreover, he offered
to furnish the Turks with instructors of the Russian language. Finally,
he is supposed to have asserted that both Russia and Austria were falling
apart, and the Turks had only to help themselves. For all this, Bayur cites
the recollections of General Ali i Fuat Erden for the period September,
1914. See Bayur, III/I, 198–199.

[25] Pallavicini to Berchtold #515/3525 and #522/3622, Aug. 29 and Sep.
1, 1914, H.H.S.A. Allgemeines Karton 941.

every passing day it became more certain that Turkish army officers organized and led most of the peasant insurrections against the tenuous government of Prince William of Wied.[26] The Greeks bore some of the blame, and the Serbs and Italians were variously involved, but at the heart of the problem was the mad drive for a Turkish restoration. This was an article of faith with the Austrians, and they had decided to set a mark to Turkish ambitions at just about the time their relations with Serbia began to deteriorate. Though they were able militarily to undertake unilateral action in Albania, they shied away from such a step for diplomatic reasons. Italy had long-standing interests on the Dalmation coast and would insist that these be satisfied if there were any change in the *status quo*. Austria therefore favored the withdrawal of William of Wied, but would have put in his place a joint occupational force organized with the Italians. Some kind of partition was expected to follow on this intervention to forestall another division between Serbia and Greece, a scheme favored by the Russian government.[27] Above all, the Austrians did not want the Triple Alliance splintered by a quarrel over Albania between two of its members.[28] It was a concern the Germans ought reasonably to have shared.

But Berlin did not favor any part of this scheme except getting rid of Prince William of Wied. The Prince had looked consistently, but almost always vainly, to the Germans for support, stressing kinship of origin and race. But though Jagow did not meet him with outright rebuffs, he made all sorts of impossible proposals that were even worse. Wied was told that if he wanted to stay on his throne, he had better find ways of satisfying, one after the other, the claims of the Greeks, Serbs, and Turks.[29] This was hardly feasible for a man who could barely pay his household servants. Then the German government ordered the

[26] G.P., XXXVI (II), #14466.
[27] *Ibid.*, #14460; and Michahelles to Foreign Ministry, June 8, 1914, A.A. Albanien #1, Bd. 11, #A11257.
[28] Flotow to Bethmann, June 26, 1914, A.A. Albanien #1, Bd. 12, #A12815.
[29] G.P., XXXVI (II), #14394.

Breslau from Alexandretta to Durazzo, a step the Austrians at
first understood as demonstrating solidarity with the other members of the Triple Alliance. Emperor William himself immediately warned Berchtold that such was not the case and that his
government could not count on unqualified German backing in
Albania.[30]

Indeed, the mission of the *Breslau* was to obliterate the last
faint thread of hope sustaining the government of William of
Wied. The Prince was invited aboard and told that Berlin would
not guarantee his safety and strongly advised his departure. That
thought had, of course, crossed Wied's mind more than once in
the previous troubled months. In the event of his leaving, he already had arranged to travel aboard a British cruiser. But Hell-
muth Lucius, the Foreign Ministry's man on the *Breslau,* insisted
that it would be a dreadful discourtesy to the Reich if a German
nobleman preferred the services of a foreign government over
those of his kinsmen. Should the Prince insist on such a preference, Lucius recommended to his superiors that it be advertised
as widely as possible that the German government had put the
Breslau at Wied's disposal for his retreat.[31] The Germans
wanted not so much to insure Wied's comfort and security, as to
gain all the credit for having gotten him out of the way. Berlin
wanted to be as certain as possible that Constantinople knew
who had created the vacuum into which the Turks were almost
being invited to move. The outbreak of war only served to confirm this policy, which had the primary advantage of deflecting
the Turks from the Russian front, where the evidence shows the
Germans pressed the attack most reluctantly, as well as the sec-
ondary attraction of possibly bringing pressure on Serbia for a
negotiated peace.

The Austrians were not interested in this kind of negotiated
peace. They saw no advantage in bargaining with an old enemy
while standing in the shadow of one newly arrived. They tried

[30] Wedel to Foreign Ministry, June 21, 1914, A.A. Albanien #1, Bd. 12,
#A12232.

[31] Lucius to Foreign Ministry, July 24, 1914, *ibid.,* Bd. 15, #A14125.

to recruit volunteer battalions in Vienna to fight against the Turkish insurrectionaries, and since the appeal was to the honor of the German race, they had the temerity to attempt enlistments in Berlin itself. But the Prussian police closed down the offices, and German ships rigorously interdicted the delivery of munitions through Durazzo.[32] Wied miraculously held on until the beginning of September, but then fled with his retinue to Venice. His palace was seized by the insurgents and the Turkish flag at once run up.[33] The Porte then requested the Austrian government to declare that it would not oppose the enthronement of a Moslem ruler. On Pallavicini's advice, the declaration was withheld.[34]

The Austrian ships never arrived in Turkish waters. From Berlin, Undersecretary Arthur Zimmermann replied to Berchtold that the *Goeben* and *Breslau* were sufficient to engage the Russian Black Sea squadron if trouble arose, and no additional strength beyond the Turkish vessels joined to the German cruisers would be required.[35] Accordingly, *Goeben* and *Breslau* arrived at the Straits on August 10 and were passed through, as many argued, in violation of the Paris and London treaties of 1856 and 1871, respectively. Though Turkey was not yet at war, the Porte was well aware that the two German ships were in flight from the British Mediterranean Fleet. Gibraltar and the Suez Canal had been heavily guarded to prevent just such an escape as now occurred, and in permitting it at the Straits, the Porte had in effect committed an unfriendly act against the British government. According to Ambassador Morgenthau, Wangenheim had ordered Admiral Wilhelm Souchon, commander of the *Goeben,* to raise the Turkish flag on his ship as early as August 4 to meet this objection.[36] A *pro forma* sale of the *Goeben* and

[32] Tschirschky to Bethmann, June 28, 1914, and July 7, 1914, *ibid.,* Bd. 12, #A12837, and *ibid.,* Bd. 13, no number.

[33] Lucius to Foreign Ministry, Sep. 5, 1914, *ibid.,* Bd. 16, #A20663.

[34] Wangenheim to Foreign Ministry, Sep. 6, 1914, *ibid.,* #A21109.

[35] Hohenlohe to Berchtold #481/8841, Sep. 1, 1914, H.H.S.A. Allgemeines Karton 941.

[36] Morgenthau, *Morgenthau's Story,* p. 75.

Breslau to Turkey followed on August 11.[37] No one, of course,
believed that the Turks would have made the purchase without
German prompting, and Said Halim objected to the maneuver
most vigorously.

Henceforward, until Turkey intervened in the war, the Grand
Vizier opposed the activism of Enver and Talaat. His reasons
were not pure neutralism, but probably had much to do with the
failure of the Austrian ships to materialize. Almost certainly he
did not know of Zimmermann's decision and was therefore left
to speculate that Berchtold was urging Turkey on, only to leave
her in the lurch at the critical moment, compromised in the judgment of the other powers and vulnerable to their retribution.
Since the offer of the ships had been given, Pallavicini had been
indiscreet enough to reveal that Austria favored a territorial realignment in the Balkans that would give her Salonica and a corridor of access through its hinterland. This news was picked up
by an agent of the British embassy and then revealed to the
Porte. Berchtold was obliged to issue an official denial and a
sharp reprimand to his man in Constantinople.[38]

Pallavicini was also secretly negotiating with a group of Georgian clergy, to whose followers the Turks were issuing arms and
munitions for a rising in the Caucasus against Russia. The Georgians, however, were not altogether confident that they would fare
as well under Ottoman jurisdiction as under the Tsar's regime
and therefore discussed with the Ambassador an Austrian protectorate over the area.[39] It is not clear whether Said Halim knew of
the Georgian discussions, but on the basis of what he did know,
he might have suspected Austria's double game.

The arrival of the *Goeben,* now called the *Sultan Selim,* and
the *Breslau,* renamed the *Medilli,* of course drew the protests of
the Entente governments,[40] but Wangenheim behaved as if the

[37] Pallavicini to Berchtold #424/1621, Aug. 11, 1914, *ibid.*

[38] Berchtold to Pallavicini #314/5209, Aug. 12, 1914, *ibid.*

[39] Pallavicini to Berchtold #533/2989, Sep. 3, 1914; and Berchtold
to Pallavicini #444/5942, Sep. 6, 1914, *ibid.*

[40] Great Britain, *Correspondence Respecting Events Leading to the
Rupture of Relations with Turkey,* Parliamentary Papers, LXXXIV, #13
(London, 1914), Nos. 10, 13, 20, 30, 32, 94, 164.

attack on Russia was no nearer and the role of Turkey in the strategy of the Central Powers still undetermined. He declared that no action in the Black Sea could begin until the Dardanelles were thoroughly mined.[41] When Pallavicini inquired of the German military attaché when this work might be completed, he was told that no less than three weeks would be required, though the Germans seemed to be making no special efforts to meet even that timetable.[42] In Berlin, the Austrian Ambassador, Gottfried von Hohenlohe, was shown a telegram from Wangenheim asserting that the German officers in Constantinople did not regard a bombardment of the Russian forts as feasible and recommended at most that the Turkish fleet cruise the Black Sea coast so that Rumania and Bulgaria might be persuaded to declare for the Central Powers. Such a turn of events, it was believed, could force Russia to leave the war, but any attack on her nationals or property, the army believed, would prejudice negotiations. Hohenlohe was described as beside himself with anguish, pleading with Zimmermann that the German government show more clarity and resolve. However, the Undersecretary simply replied that, while he could appreciate the Austrian viewpoint, he could not presume to question the technical competence of the military.[43]

On September 13, Enver held a council of war to which he invited Admiral Souchon. He was superbly confident and prepared, he assured Pallavicini, to put 800,000 Turks at the service of the Central powers. But the offer proved a dud and made no mark on the Admiral's wooden pessimism. Souchon declined to take the responsibility for anything more than a demonstration.[44] When Pallavicini heard the outcome of the meeting, he apparently thought the last word on the matter had been spoken. He indicated to his chief that it was now unlikely that Turkey would enter the war but that her alliance with the Central Powers was

[41] Pallavicini to Berchtold #538/3772, Sep. 4, 1914. H.H.S.A. Allgemeines Karton 941.
[42] Pallavicini to Berchtold #545/5668, Sep. 5, 1914, *ibid.*
[43] Hohenlohe to Berchtold #511/9148, Sep. 9, 1914, *ibid.*
[44] Pallavicini to Berchtold #581/5652, Sep. 13, 1914, *ibid.*

still valuable from the Austrian standpoint. It had prevented the formation of a Balkan League against Austria, with Turkey as a member and under Russian aegis. It would also prevent any Balkan state from declaring openly against Germany and Austria, even if none of these aided them actively.[45]

Two days later, Enver, in collaboration with the Austrian military attaché, Joseph Pomiankowski, attempted another sally against the Germans. The two men decided that a parade of the fleet would be held before the Sultan on September 17. Thereafter the ships would go immediately into the Black Sea with orders to fire on any Russian vessels encountered. Enver swore that he would have war with the Russians, victory over whose empire could alone assure a prosperous future for the Turkish people. But when another council was convoked to review this decision, the Grand Vizier and Talaat, the Interior Minister, moved its rejection in the hope of winning Russia's peaceful agreement to the abolition of the capitulations.[46]

Pallavicini tried to talk Talaat out of his stand, which he considered transparent obstructionism, and told Wangenheim that the situation required a common front. The German Ambassador professed outrage at Turkey's dallying and shouted that he would have the German flag run up on every ship and the attack on Russia begun on his own responsibility.[47] He had, however, neither the means nor the will to do this, nor had anyone else in his entourage. He may have been trying to bluff the Austrian Ambassador. Even as he raved, the Austrian embassy in Berlin was told that the German Emperor and Zimmermann still regarded a cruise as sufficient and a bombardment of Odessa as not practicable. About even the former, the strictest secrecy was enjoined, so that, as Vienna feared, the whole business could later be denied by Berlin.[48]

On September 20, a final meeting was called at the Porte to

45 Pallavicini to Berchtold #56/p, Sep. 13, 1914, *ibid.*

46 Pallavicini to Berchtold #589/7708 and #602/11, Sep. 15 and 17, 1914, *ibid.*

47 Pallavicini to Berchtold #66/1034, Sep. 18, 1914, *ibid.*

48 Haymerle to Berchtold #533/2031, Sep. 19, 1914, *ibid.*

decide what action if any should be undertaken in the Black Sea. The ministers were negative except for Enver, who stood up and assured his colleagues in the name of the Austrian Ambassador that Souchon could blow the enemy to bits if he wanted to do so. This remark, in Enver's words, "stuck" with the Young Turks, and they agreed to permit the fleet to leave the Bosphorus. Said Halim gave his assent, probably because the reference to Pallavicini diminished some of his own suspicions about Austrian intentions. At the same time the ministers agreed that the British Admiral Limpus should be relieved of his command and his functions as naval adviser assumed by Souchon.[49] This was a very sizable bait for the Germans, and in taking it up they indicated not so much that they had decided to let Turkey enter the war by an attack on Russia as that they wanted the very profitable contracts that Limpus had heretofore awarded to British shipbuilders.

As soon as the news was out, the Russian and French Ambassadors waited on the Grand Vizier to protest the entry of the fleet into the Black Sea and to inquire after the Porte's further intentions. Said Halim disclaimed all personal responsibility and stated that Gemany, as a sovereign nation, could send her ships where she liked. This was the grossest of fumbles, for it completely obliterated the fiction that the *Goeben* and *Breslau* were really Turkish. Moreover, the Grand Vizier contended that the ships had got through the Dardanelles because the British had taken no effective steps to stop them. This observation hit home because Sir Louis Mallet, the British Ambassador, had not joined in the exertions of Giers and M. Bompard. It seems to have surprised even the German embassy to discover that Mallet had confided to a Swedish colleague that Britain let in the German ships because she had a "lively interest" in not allowing the Straits to fall into Russian hands. That consideration had not grown less since the outbreak of war.[50] It may also help explain

[49] Cabinet Minutes by Enver, Sep. 20, 1914, Jaeckh Papers, Drawer 69.

[50] Report (probably by Humann) of Sep. 21, 1914, Jaeckh Papers, Drawer 69.

why no British torpedo flotilla was sent through the Straits to destroy the German ships at Constantinople, though Winston
Churchill and Morgenthau believed this ought to have been
done.[51] Mallet threatened that the *Goeben* and *Breslau* would be
shelled if they tried to leave the Dardanelles. Privately, however,
he advised his government to draw off from those waters as much
of the British fleet as "practical efficiency" would allow. This
gesture would demonstrate that Britain had no wish to deal
rigorously with Turkey.[52]

The presence of Entente or neutral ships in Turkish waters
was of vital importance for the outcome of the crisis. If there
had been any unusual naval activity off the coast of Syria or a
significant concentration of ships at the entrance to the Dardanelles, the Porte would have thought twice and longer about an
attack on Russia. The hawks in Berlin would have been scattered and the doves possibly carried the day. All this was perfectly obvious to the German Ambassador, and yet there is reason to think that he regretted the departure of such ships and
would even have augmented their number.

Though obviously the *Goeben* and *Breslau* would have been
deprived of their ascendancy of the Bosphorus in this manner, it
was reported to Washington from the American embassy in Copenhagen, which had the news in turn from Berlin, that Wangenheim actually favored American warships drawing up to protect
the lives of neutrals.[53] Secretary William J. Bryan, however, refused to permit this,[54] even though, in addition to the apparent
acquiescence of the German Foreign Ministry, he had positive
approval from the French. Gaston Doumergue, the French Foreign Minister, declared on August 29 that he had no objections
to American ships taking up positions in Near Eastern waters.[55]

[51] Morgenthau, *Morgenthau's Story*, p. 79.
[52] Mallet to Grey, Sep. 30, 1914, Public Record Office, London
(hereinafter abbreviated P.R.O.), Foreign Office Papers, Turkey 371-
2140, #54620.
[53] Gerard to Secretary of State, Sep. 14, 1914, D.S., #867.00/662.
[54] Morgenthau to Secretary of State, Dec. 12, 1914, D.S., #867.00/723.
[55] Doumergue to Secretary of State, Aug. 29, 1914, D.S., #867.00/669.

However, the American Ambassador in Constantinople, Henry Morgenthau, always maintained that such ships might create rather than avert a crisis.[56] His argument carried the day with Bryan, though Morgenthau's views were opposed to advice given him by his own consuls in Smyrna and Beirut, George Horton and Stanley Hollis.[57] Wangenheim had for some time tried to cultivate Morgenthau, who was born in Germany; [58] but on this occasion the effort paid no political dividend.

In the end the Porte, aware that the powers had not coordinated their policies, indicated that it would not approve the approach of American warships to either Constantinople or the Syrian ports. This decision may have been the concomitant of another Turkish policy put into effect at the same time: on October 1 began the abolition of the capitulations, those ancient agreements between Turkey and the European powers whereby foreign property had been protected against arbitrary search and seizure.[59]

The Austrian government would not in any case have approved the intervention of neutrals. Pallavicini was dismayed that Wangenheim could not be made more alert to the danger of American interference and pestered Berchtold to find out what was in the minds of the Ambassador and his superiors in the Wilhelmstrasse. Hohenlohe, the Austrian Ambassador in Berlin, was then instructed to take an inquiry to Undersecretary Zimmermann. Zimmermann was one of the few men in his department determined to bring Turkey into the war. At this time, he took the lead in persuading the Imperial Treasury and the Deutsche Bank to advance generous loans to Turkey to bring her

[56] Morgenthau to Secretary of State, June 19 and Nov. 12, 1914, appended telegram from Morgenthau to Hollis, D.S., #867.00/630 and #867.00/717.

[57] See, for example, Hollis to Secretary of State, Aug. 3, 1914, D.S., #867.00/638. On American policy in general, see further Laurence Evans, *United States Policy and the Partition of Turkey* (Baltimore, 1965), pp. 26–27.

[58] Morgenthau, *All in a Life-Time*, pp. 174–181.

[59] Confidential Notice by Humann, Oct. 2, 1914, Jaeckh Papers, Drawer 69.

to declare for the Central Powers. Now, however, he used the discreetest words and the blandest manner with the American Ambassador, who was told that the situation was not serious enough to justify an American naval demonstration. When Zimmermann let it go at that, the Austrians were dissatisfied and felt that their cause was being somehow ill served or even imperilled.[60]

The evidence seems to suggest that though American intervention posed no real threat, the Germans were anxious to proceed as if it did. On the other hand, the Austrians were quick to point out that the situation was improving for the Central Powers. By the end of September the Austrians reported the support of the Minister of Marine, Djemal Pasha, who was thoroughly fed up with Entente attempts to sabotage his ships. He was said to be ready to settle accounts with a declaration of war. Only Djavid Bey, Minister of Finance, still hoped for an understanding with France and Britain, but the Austrians were glad to have the encouragement of the indefatigable Zimmermann to find ways "to make him disappear." [61] Yet the attitude of the United States gave Zimmermann's associates genuine pause, and with appropriate reference to Bryan and Morgenthau, they declared that now not even a Black Sea cruise to impress Rumania and Bulgaria was possible. Pallavicini was told that the German Ambassador in Bucharest had advised against it, although the Austrian did not believe Admiral Souchon would take the ships into the Black Sea whatever he was advised.[62]

The position of Admiral Wilhelm Souchon was perplexing, both for Pallavicini and the Entente ambassadors. He had come to Constantinople with the *Goeben* and *Breslau,* and it was assumed by many that his services had been sold to the Turks along with his ships. Such was not the case, however, and Souchon was not appointed a Turkish vice-admiral until September 24. Even after that date he did nothing to show that he considered himself

[60] Berchtold to Pallavicini #370/5556, Aug. 25, 1914, H.H.S.A. Allgemeines Karton 941.

[61] Hohenlohe to Berchtold #567/401, Sep. 27, 1914, *ibid.*

[62] Pallavicini to Berchtold #645/9604 and #660/1415, Sep. 26 and 28, 1914, *ibid.*

seriously subordinate to Turkish jurisdiction and was not notably quick to carry out the directives of Berlin either. Pallavicini was glad when Souchon was presented with a formal Turkish commission, because he evidently believed that the Ottoman Ministry of Marine could galvanize the otherwise sluggard German admiral. It might also curtail the sloppy discipline that Souchon permitted in the "Turco-German Navy," whose ships sailed out of the Dardanelles, as it seemed, not so much to stop as to rendezvous with the British.

On September 28, a Turkish torpedo boat under the command of German officers was halted near Tenedos. The ship's company was informed that in the future all such vessels would be treated as prizes of war, though the torpedo boat itself was released. But more disturbing to the Austrians was an offer, made to the crew, to deliver to Turkey two dreadnoughts being built in Britain on commission from the Ottoman Ministry of Marine. These ships had been confiscated for British service as soon as the war began. The fury of the Turks was stupendous because both ships had been popularly subscribed. Nothing served better to justify Turkey's association with Germany, as the British government quickly realized. Sir Louis Mallet was reported to have gone to the Sultan himself on September 27 to offer the return of the ships, and apparently the encounter off Tenedos was to confirm the offer.[63] If such a deal were concluded, Enver would have thus lost a major grievance to incite his people against the Entente, and characters like Djemal would quickly renounce their newly found truculence and go back to fence-sitting.

The Sultan, claiming that he was a constitutional sovereign and would have to consult his advisers, let Mallet's proposals drop. The Aga Khan, charged by the British government to make similar overtures to the Turkish Ambassador in London, is probably correct in stating that Turkey remained adamant because the Entente wanted only her neutrality and not her active alliance. The Young Turks, on the other hand, felt that only if

[63] Pallavicini to Berchtold #655/531 and #571/2453, Sep. 27 and 28, 1914, *ibid.*

they were definitely and forthrightly included in one of the belligerent coalitions would they be safe from schemes of partition on the part of the powers.[64] For their neutrality, they could expect and were offered only the two ships and the territorial *status quo*, whereas for intervention they could demand a redrawing of the map in the Balkans and in Eastern Anatolia. Sazonov was not averse to some increment of the Ottoman Empire, in areas of no intimate concern to Russia; but Grey could not bring around his cabinet, where Lord Kitchener proved the chief stumbling block.[65]

Kitchener, then, abetted the Turkish policy of the Dual Monarchy, as did Richard von Kühlmann, who came as special emissary from Berlin to Constantinople at the beginning of October. Kühlmann was born in the Turkish capital, where his father had served the railroad enterprises undertaken jointly by the Sultan and the syndicate of German banks. Before the war he had seen diplomatic service at the London embassy and played an important part in negotiating with the British government a series of agreements determining the further construction of the Baghdad Railway and the navigation of the Persian Gulf.[66] Later in the war, Kühlmann was himself to assume the Constantinople embassy and to be accused of pursuing too "English" a policy. In the autumn of 1914, however, his attitude was uncompromising, and almost everyone but Wangenheim knew that he had come to reprimand and in effect to supersede the German Ambassador to Turkey.

Wangenheim had not requested any assistance and had to listen to Pallavicini, with superb temerity, extol the great competence of the new member of his staff. The Ambassador strictly forbade any hospitality to be shown Kühlmann, who would not even have had a place to sleep if Captain Humann had not put a

[64] The Aga Khan, *The Memoirs of Aga Khan, World Enough and Time* (New York, 1954), p. 164.

[65] *Ibid.*, p. 165; Howard, *Partition of Turkey*, pp. 96–100.

[66] Maybelle Kennedy Chapman, *Great Britain and the Bagdad Railway, 1888–1914* (Northampton, 1948), p. 173.

small ship's cabin at his disposal.[67] But such petty annoyances could not impair Kühlmann's mandate, which came from Zimmermann or from a person in still higher authority. The Ambassador was brought to heel, and Souchon, as befitted his lesser eminence, was subjected to a proper dressing-down. Both men tried to make it clear that any alleged superiority of Turkey in the Black Sea depended on the *Goeben* alone; if the ship went under, so would the hope of the Turks.[68] But at a party held for the German emissary, the ubiquitous Enver Pasha routed all such doubts. Darting back and forth among the guests, he asked Kühlmann several times why Germany had not given the word to strike.[69]

Kühlmann was empowered to give that word. The month of October was taken up with negotiations about a large subsidy that would enable the Turks to move. Talaat and Enver suggested that the German government put two million Turkish pounds at their disposal and, to press this arrangement on Wangenheim, invited themselves to a breakfast at the German embassy. The Turkish leaders indicated that there were now no dissenters from a policy of war, except perhaps Said Halim and their ambassador in Berlin, Muktar Pasha.[70] Even Djavid Bey favored a forward policy and had probably set the amount of the subsidy.[71]

[67] Richard von Kühlmann, *Erinnerungen* (Heidelberg, 1948), pp. 446, 449.

[68] Pallavicini to Berchtold #679/6743, Oct. 7, 1914, H.H.S.A. Allgemeines Karton 941.

[69] Kühlmann, *Erinnerungen*, p. 447.

[70] "Discussion with Enver," Oct. 9 and 11, 1914, Jaeckh Papers, Drawer 69. Jaeckh describes even Muktar as deeply involved in a plot to force intervention by deposing both the Sultan and the Grand Vizier (Jaeckh, *Rising Crescent*, pp. 114–115).

[71] Though the Germans were quite concerned about Djavid's opposition and Entente sympathies, the Russian Ambassador to Bulgaria, who met Djavid some months before, represents him as obnoxiously pro-German (A. Savinsky, *Recollections of a Russian Diplomat* [London, no date], p. 231). Later, Djavid tried to give the impression that he went along with the German alliance only because Wangenheim threatened that otherwise Germany and Russia would partition Turkey (Bayur, III/I, 82).

Though there is no evidence that the Germans tried to rein in all this enthusiasm, there is also no clear indication that they tried to spur it on. The sum of two million pounds had barely been mentioned when Enver declared that he could bring off the attack for only one million. Enver proposed further that the money could be held "in storage until after the first battles." This behavior would seem to indicate that the Turks were not being bribed and wanted to make war at almost any price. However, Captain Humann was present at the conference and interjected a goad that the Turks did not need. He pointed out that since the pro-German King Carol of Rumania had just died, the neutrality of his country would henceforth be assured only if Turkey joined the Central Powers. This observation probably only caused the Turks to raise their price. Djemal opposed selling his services cut-rate. When the conference concluded, Germany made herself responsible for the payment of an additional million pounds, while the Turkish leadership promised to issue sailing orders to Souchon within a few days.[72]

The Russian embassy had a fairly clear idea of these arrangements made on October 11. Sazonov alerted the Black Sea squadron to be ready for imminent war, and Giers, informed of the arrival of the subsidy trains at Constantinople, made desperate attempts to contact Wangenheim. Paul Weitz was approached by a Russian journalist, Olguenine Berezovsky, whom he had known for many years and trusted. This man, in Giers's name, warned the Germans that they were becoming Austria's dupe. The Dual Monarchy was described as fanatically intent on the destruction of Russia. Germany should not allow herself to be inveigled into a course contrary to all the historical and economic ties between Berlin and St. Petersburg and should even now weigh the advantages of collaborating with Russia in an under-

[72] The breakfast conference was probably held on October 11, 1914. I have followed Humann's memorandum for that date in the Jaeckh Papers. The subsidy arrangement is also discussed by Ulrich Trumpener in "Turkey's Entry into World War I," *Journal of Modern History*, XXXIV (December, 1962), 375–376.

standing about the Habsburg monarchy. Berezovsky stated that "powerful circles" in the Russian capital had instructed Giers to offer Russia's withdrawal from the war if Germany forced Austria to relinquish Galicia to a newly created Kingdom of Poland and concurred in the cession of Bosnia-Herzegovina to Serbia. Russia would welcome the incorporation of Salzburg and Tyrol by the German Empire and would agree to any other reasonable territorial rectifications.[73]

The Berezovsky interview did not of course lead to its desired end but almost certainly postponed Turkey's attack until the end of October. "The few days" mentioned on October 11 passed, and Souchon's ships were still in port. The Russians knew Wangenheim and may have even struck home with men who set a higher value on Turkish intervention. A certain Janson, attached to the German staff at Therapia, wrote to Ernst Jaeckh that the Turkish operation in the Black Sea recently decided upon would be of no real strategical value and might easily become a political disaster. The really important thing, Janson continued, was for Germany to attack Britain in Egypt. That move would destroy Britain's "world position" and deprive her of the power to intimidate Spain and Italy, which would then join the Central Powers. Relieved of the British menace in the Mediterranean, all the nations abutting on that sea would recover a freedom of choice that they had not been able to exercise in almost a hundred years. The attack on Egypt, Janson concluded, thus became a "moral duty" for Germany.[74]

Meanwhile, Enver, unaware of Berezovsky and "morality," speedily prepared his plan of attack—and caused more difficulty and delay. The plan called for an advance into Transcaucasia and a thrust at the Suez Canal. The bulk of the Ottoman army, however, was to be held in readiness for eventual service against Russia's southern flank. This plan was approved by the German General Staff after Zimmermann had observed that to do any-

[73] "Confidential Report by Paul Weitz," Oct. 13, 1914, Jaeckh Papers, Drawer 69.

[74] Janson to Jaeckh, Oct. 13, 1914, *ibid.*

thing else was to gamble too dangerously with Enver's instability
and vainglory.

The order to Souchon was then formulated, but it was not
shown to Liman von Sanders, and significantly, Humann was responsible for any correction or editing.[75] The exact contents of
Enver's plan surprised Pallavicini. They did not accord with the
various hints he had thrown out to the Ottoman War Ministry
nor justify at all the energy he had expended on Ottoman intervention.

The plan in fact obliged the Austrian Ambassador at the end
of October to contradict all he had insisted upon since the eruption of the Serbian crisis. Like his German colleagues, the chief
of the Austrian General Staff, Baron Conrad von Hötzendorf, had
closely watched the Turkish situation. On his behalf, Berchtold
had ordered Pallavicini to persuade Enver to order a march by
Turkish troops along the railroad line from Odessa to Proskurow.
If an alliance with Bulgaria could be arranged in time, General
Conrad also wanted Turkey to attack Serbia.[76] But Enver informed Pallavicini that it had never been his intention to land
troops at Odessa since, in the judgment of his General Staff and
Ministry of Marine, the season of the year would not allow it.
Pallavicini did not accept this excuse and wired Berchtold that
it was certain that Wangenheim and Liman had put Enver up to
it.[77]

The day after this meeting, October 24, Enver sent for the
Austrian military attaché, Pomiankowski, and assured him that
the welfare of Austria was being given due consideration. He
was willing to have the mouth of the Danube River laid with
mines, which would prevent Russia from dispatching help to her
Serbian ally. But Pallavicini was not at all mollified and argued
that these indirect expedients were too feeble to diminish the
Russian pressure on Austria's lines. Enver retorted that he would

[75] Humann to Wangenheim, Oct. 22, 1914, *ibid.*

[76] Berchtold to Pallavicini #637, Oct. 21, 1914, H.H.S.A. Allgemeines
Karton 942.

[77] Pallavicini to Berchtold #720/1236, Oct. 23, 1914, *ibid.*

fight the war for the Sultan, not for Emperor Franz Joseph. The Proskurow operation that Pallavicini had in mind was dismissed as out of the question unless Rumania came into the war.[78]

On October 27 the Ottoman navy at last entered the Black Sea with orders to attack Russian ships and harbor facilities, and Pallavicini, the man who had had so much to do with bringing on this encounter, was no longer enthusiastic about its successful outcome. He realized that the Austrians and Germans had reached the fork in the road of their Turkish diplomacy and that if he did not want to tag after Wangenheim, he would have to travel a path separate from that of the German Ambassador. He knew that his German colleague had found out about Enver's offer to put mines in the Danube channel and was striving, by invoking the veto of the German General Staff, to sabotage this slight and utterly unacceptable Turkish accommodation. Before the fleet left, an Austrian agent learned that Wangenheim had had as much as 300,000 Turkish pounds distributed to the ships' companies, ostensibly as a present for the next Bairam festival. Pallavicini suspected the money might have been distributed to contain rather than to enlarge the scope of the Turkish attack. In this light, he reported that Giers knew of the fleet's departure at least twenty-four hours in advance, though Djavid Bey was named as the actual informant of the Russian embassy.[79]

The damage done to the Russians was, according to the Austrian Ambassador, not overwhelming. The *Goeben,* by hits on five oil tanks near the shore, was able to set afire the dock works of Odessa. She also damaged five steamers moored in the harbor. Subsequently, a mine layer, a torpedo boat destroyer, and a cruiser were sunk. But at Theodosia only the small railroad station and the Greek Orthodox Cathedral were set afire. At Novorossik, the Turkish cruiser *Hamidie* added an almost comic touch to the enterprise by drawing up and demanding the surrender

[78] Pallavicini to Berchtold #729/3423 and #731/4013, Oct. 24 and 25, 1914, *ibid.*

[79] Pallavicini to Berchtold #740/1290, #736/5389, #63/p, Oct. 27 and 29, 1914, *ibid.*

of the municipal treasury. The demand was refused, the Turks fired off a few shots, and the ships then sailed away.[80]

On November 1 the British, French, and Russian ambassadors left the Turkish capital. The Grand Vizier implored Mallet not to "abandon" him, and four members of the Turkish cabinet resigned in protest against their government's policy. The Entente diplomats do not seem to have been particularly incensed at the Germans, perhaps merely testifying to the chivalrous ways of the old diplomacy or aware at least vaguely of how the Turkish intervention came about. When Mallet travelled to Dedeagatch aboard a French ship, he protested when the sailors burned the German emperor in effigy.[81] Giers sent the Italian Ambassador, Marquis Camillo Garoni, to bid Wangenheim a special farewell. Garoni was anathema to Pallavicini because he had been several times used by the German Ambassador to press his doubts and pessimism about Turkey on the Austrian embassy. Now the Italian diplomat assured Wangenheim that Giers considered himself to be only his "official" enemy. As gentlemen, they would always remain friends. The Russian fondly recalled the negotiations they had undertaken together and urged the German to leave no means untried when he was ready to talk again.[82]

The Diplomacy of the First Canal Campaign

The mediation of Marquis Garoni was perhaps as close to a disinterested gesture as diplomacy permits. It might be argued that as an Italian, it was in his interest to embroil Turkey, Germany, and Russia as deeply as possible in the Black Sea basin. For if this did not happen, then, according to Enver's plan, the Turks would pursue their Egyptian expedition all the more vigorously, and since Egypt bordered on Tripoli, the Italians entrenched there would be made all the more apprehensive. Ga-

[80] Pallavicini to Berchtold #749/0048, #756/460, Oct. 30 and 31, 1914, *ibid.*

[81] Ryan, *Last of the Dragomans,* pp. 105–106; also "Confidential Information," Nov. 2, 1914, Jaeckh Papers, Drawer 69. One of the four was Djavid Bey.

[82] "Confidential Information," Nov. 1, 1914, Jaeckh Papers, Drawer 69.

roni did not know Enver's plan, but he knew enough of the drift of it to be seriously concerned.

In July, 1914, the Italian embassy began to report that Enver was actively planning the recovery of Tripoli. He was said to have distributed ten thousand pounds to the Senussi tribesmen and stationed agents all over Egypt for further training in sabotage and insurrection. The British counsul-general, Lord Kitchener, had called these machinations to the attention of the Turkish authorities in Constantinople, but so discreetly that the Young Turks could not have been expected to forego their plans. Enver not only stuck to his tactics but broadened them to include activities in India and Java. The Dutch Ambassador confirmed to the Italians that officials in the East Indies were becoming increasingly aware of the spread of Pan-Islamic propaganda. Unless the powers formed a common front, it would be impossible to stem the tide.[83] At that point neither the Central Powers nor the British were anxious to cross the Turks for fear of irrevocably driving them into the other's camp.

When the war began, the British no longer felt such inhibitions, and it was rumored that they would annex Egypt and run her economy and politics to suit themselves. Legally Egypt was still a province of the Ottoman Empire, a situation with which the British administrators had wrestled with increasing difficulty ever since they moved in in strength in 1882. But the war forced them to abandon all such fictions, lest the pro-German Turks occupy the country and cut them off from India. The British never did deny the Sultan's legal right; they simply rode roughshod over it, incurring an ineffaceable reputation for brutal highhandedness among Moslem peoples and compounding the difficulties of relations with them after the war. The British anticipated all this, were honestly concerned about blackening their reputation, and at least sought excuses for the measures they took. Their greatest justification, they were quick to point out, was the massing of Turkish troops and supplies against the Suez Canal.

[83] Richthofen to Bethmann, July 14, 1914, A.A. Aegypten #3, Bd. 83, #A14351.

Most European chanceries assumed that Britain had been pre-
meditating the complete annexation of Egypt for three decades.
But the Austrian government now professed to believe that the
war had not brought the conflict between the Sultan's titular sovereignty and Britain's actual control to an ineluctable breaking
point. Berchtold held that the problem could remain as far as
ever from a final solution if nothing was done to force Britain's
hand.[84] But the German Foreign Ministry was convinced that
Britain did not need to be forced down her chosen path and
should instead be headed off as quickly as possible. Even though
the recovery of Egypt was one of the most important of Turkish
war aims, the German government had clearly decided to reserve the area for itself against the claims of both friend and foe.
In his memoirs, Liman von Sanders scoffed at the Egyptian campaign as ridiculous and doomed to failure; and Ernst Jaeckh, a
straightforward and honest authority, insists that the phrase
"Turkey, a German Egypt" never meant that the Reich aspired
to so thoroughgoing a control as the British achieved along the
banks of the Nile.[85] Yet the documents indicate that at some
points Germany was inclined to prefer the old Egypt as "the
German Egypt" and to turn Turkey over to Russia and her associates.

These Egyptian designs seem preposterous in retrospect, but
perhaps not more so than Germany's conviction that she would
win the war. Against all the difficulties, her diplomats were inclined to set the overriding fact that Britain had done the spade
work, surmounted nearly all the obstacles, and left few rough
places unplaned. Many years would pass before the Germans
reached this point in Turkey; and the Turks' inexhaustible gift
for playing one European power against another would make
the job still more difficult. But Egypt, the Germans were convinced, was the Khedive and the British. The war might elimi-

[84] Tschirschky to Foreign Ministry, Aug. 19, 1914, *ibid.*, #A17841.
[85] Liman von Sanders, *Five Years,* pp. 25–26; Jaeckh, *Rising Crescent,*
pp. 138–140.

nate the latter, while the former had already shown himself
ready to follow wherever Germany might lead.

In the previous August, Khedive Abbas Hilmi had visited the
German embassy in Constantinople. It was his annual custom to
vacation in the city, but that summer was made memorable by
an attempt on his life. It had occurred a few weeks before he
conferred with the German Ambassador, and the Khedive, convinced that the Porte was behind the plot, was in a black mood
when he delivered himself to Wangenheim. He stormed against
the intimidations of the British, who made a mockery of Egypt's
neutrality, and detailed his lively hatred of Kitchener, a hatred
warmly returned. And then he declared himself ready to do anything with Germany to end British rule. He offered to put his
army entirely under German command and suggested an advance
against the Canal to be coordinated with an insurrection of
Egyptian army units and police. The British officers were to be
overpowered and murdered. It is likely that Abbas Hilmi conceived of this Egyptian campaign as an exclusively German operation; the Turkish expeditionary corps was not part of his original proposal because he distrusted Enver and hated Said Halim.
He wanted this and future conferences carefully concealed from
the Turks.[86]

Wangenheim's reaction was a most striking contrast to his opinions about Turkish intervention in the war. He recommended
that the Foreign Ministry take soundings from its informants in
Egypt and encourage the Khedive if these reports gave no reason to doubt his seriousness. All correspondence about the affair
should be sent in a secret cipher, as the Grand Vizier was especially interested in anything concerning Egypt and would not
hesitate to read the German embassy's mail. Evidently Wangenheim let the Khedive's name come up in a conversation with
Enver, who blasted Abbas Hilmi as completely untrustworthy
and ready to be bought at any time. Enver further disclosed that
the Khedive was suspected of plotting to make himself king-ca-

[86] Wangenheim to Foreign Ministry, Aug. 22, 1914, *ibid.*, #A1801.

liph of all Arabs. But this news failed to dismay the German Ambassador, who seems to have expected something like it and even considered what he heard reassuring for his plans.[87]

The Khedive's scheme was never put to a test because Enver quickly and cleverly merged it with his own program. On September 4 the War Minister called at the German embassy while Wangenheim and the Egyptian ruler were in conference. He shouted charges of treason at the flustered Abbas and challenged him to demonstrate his loyalty to the Sultan by leading the Turkish columns toward the Suez Canal. The Khedive could only agree, certainly without any enthusiasm; in a few moments, he had apparently exchanged the efficient rule of the British for the incompetent sway of the Turks. He was no soldier, and the fear of being done away with *en marche* must have crossed his mind.

It was a cruel jest of Enver's to impress him into active service, and he was soon to plead for more time to recuperate from the wounds inflicted on him by the assassin. Nevertheless, Enver demanded that he put himself at the Padishah's disposal and promised that the victory would make him greater than Mohammed Ali. This assurance was nothing compared with the further disclosure that forty high officers of the Egyptian army had sworn loyalty to the Committee of Union and Progress. With secret trainbands under their command, they were to sever all communications and confine the British to one or two cities.[88] Though Enver's bluster considerably exaggerated their chances of success, the Khedive could not doubt that this kind of conspiracy could be turned against him if he proved stubborn. It was much like the political freemasonry that had destroyed Abdul Hamid. Like the Khedive, he had had little prior intimation that it was even at work.

The British found out about the Khedive's plot almost as quickly as the Young Turks. Anticipating trouble, they sent more

[87] Jagow to Foreign Ministry, Aug. 22, 1914, *ibid.*, #A1805; and Wangenheim to Foreign Ministry, Aug. 29, 1914, *ibid.*, #A19587.

[88] Wangenheim to Foreign Ministry, Sep. 4, 1914, *ibid.*, #A20361.

than a hundred ships from the Canal and the Red Sea to the safety of Indian harbors. They closely interrogated and disarmed large numbers of Egyptian army officers and police, many of whom would probably have carried out the coup outlined to Wangenheim.[89] Consequently, the Germans could not thereafter hope for all the rewards that Abbas Hilmi had offered, but they could also not entirely renounce the attack because Enver urged it on them as a question of honor. Confronted by the War Minister's enthusiasm, Wangenheim found it difficult to be too captious or behindhand. The capture of the Canal, furthermore, might drive the British to the wall of negotiation, oblige their allies to follow suit, and leave the Russians relatively unscathed. The last consideration was never far from Wangenheim's view.

Yet when all is said and done, the Egyptian expedition was Enver's brainstorm and not essential to Germany in her prosecution of the war. The longer the German government entertained proposals for a march toward the Canal, the more tightly it became committed to the full restoration of Turkish authority in Egypt. That the Germans allowed themselves to be lured so far showed once again the weakness of their Near Eastern diplomacy and the strength of Enver's powers of persuasion.

It seems reasonable to conclude that the Wilhelmstrasse still thought it might acquire a profitable position in Egypt, somewhat like the offer of Abbas Hilmi, for otherwise it would have supported Talaat's plan to have the country declared neutral by the powers. If this were done, the Minister of Interior believed, the British would have no excuse for annexation and would give up the idea. Not all the membership of the Committee of Union and Progress shared Enver's belief in the success of the expedition. But Wangenheim simply relayed the proposal, without a recommendation that it be acted upon formally in Berlin.[90]

---

[89] Quadt to Foreign Ministry, Sep. 5, 1914, *ibid.*, #A20533.

[90] Wangenheim to Foreign Ministry, Sep. 9, 1914, *ibid.*, #A21273. Wangenheim did, however, personally assure the Grand Vizier that Germany would undertake no aggressive moves against Egyptian territory without his prior consent (Wangenheim to Bethmann, Sep. 11, 1914, *ibid.*, #A23140.)

However slight would be the rewards of German involvement in the area, the benefits of the *status quo* were slighter still.

But Pallavicini had no such dreams and delusions to occupy him and vetoed any help for Enver with all the means at his command. He sent his attaché, Pomiankowski, to the War Minister to make it clear that an invasion of Egypt would agitate Moslems in a manner impossible to contain. The wave of anti-Christian violence would lay waste not only Egypt, but spill over also into Cyrenaica to undermine Italian control there. Pomiankowski left no doubts that Vienna was desperately concerned about the attitude of Italy in the war and anxious to avoid any step that might cause her to leave the Triple Alliance.[91]

Enver was at least temporarily impressed by the Austrian objections and asked Wangenheim whether he should continue to prepare the Turkish forces. But the German Ambassador minimized the danger of Italian intervention and forwarded to the Foreign Ministry such professional opinions as tended to support the Turkish plan of attack. Though General Liman was later to represent his attitude toward the matter as aloof and indifferent, at the time he estimated the conquest of Egypt at a relatively modest 100,000 Turkish pounds, adding that it might be possible to bring off a victory for even less.[92]

When informed of it, Jagow took the General's opinion quite seriously, merely observing that the cost should absolutely be kept under 100,000 pounds. About two weeks later, he instructed the Turks to be told that the attacks of German submarines on British cruisers had already shown that Britain's control of the seas was very precarious. If the Porte would only rely on a fleet of German submarines, there was no question that Egypt could easily be rewon. Jagow urged the Turks to storm ahead.[93] Though he formerly held Talaat's diffident opinions on the sub-

[91] Wangenheim to Foreign Ministry, Sep. 9, 1914, *ibid.*, #A21288.

[92] Wangenheim to Foreign Ministry, Sep. 11 and 12, 1914, *ibid.*, #A21818 and #A21557.

[93] Jagow to Foreign Ministry, Sep. 13 and 29, 1914, *ibid.*, #A21889 and #A24495.

ject, Said Halim was so heartened by this trumpet blast from Berlin that he had a note prepared for Sir Louis Mallet, stating that Turkey could not logically be accused of making aggressive moves against Egypt, because that country belonged to her to begin with.[94]

Although this note emanated from the Porte, Mallet quite wrongly held Abbas Hilmi chiefly responsible for all the steps leading up to it. In any case the episode was a handy excuse to embarrass and expel the troublesome Khedive. The British Ambassador charged him with being the unqualified leader of the one hundred thousand troops massing along the Syrian frontier and demanded that he retire to Europe to keep himself from further mischief. Palermo, Naples, and Florence were all suggested as places of comfortable exile. They were well known to Abbas Hilmi, who had always liked to hobnob with members of the Italian court. However, the Khedive now refused to travel and appeared undaunted even when Mallet threatened him with annexation. After the departure of Mallet, Wangenheim urged him not to flinch or yield because, as he put it, the British had already decided on their course whether the Khedive stayed or went.[95]

But Pallavicini was less reassuring to the Egyptian ruler, and his eagerness to retire Abbas was critically reported to Vienna. Berchtold then lamely denied that his office opposed the Egyptian campaign. Pallavicini was accused of having sent Pomiankowski to Enver without official authorization.[96] Yet it was hardly credible that the Austrian Ambassador should have taken such a step independently, and no one in Berlin and Constantinople believed the professions of his chief.[97] The incident simply showed that the Austrians were abashed by their differ-

[94] Wangenheim to Foreign Ministry, Oct. 7, 1914, *ibid.*, Bd. 84, #A25732.

[95] Wangenheim to Foreign Ministry, Sep. 28 and 29, 1914, *ibid.*, Bd. 83, #A24370 and #A24535. Mallet's figure of 100,000 troops was grossly exaggerated.

[96] Tschirschky to Foreign Ministry, Sep. 14, 1914, *ibid.*, #A21978.

[97] Wangenheim to Foreign Ministry, Sep. 15, 1914, *ibid.*, #A22245.

ences with their German ally—abashed but no more. To some
extent, moreover, the Austrian position was more encouraging
once the hand of Abbas Hilmi had been exposed to all sides. For
if the outcome of the Egyptian campaign were successful, the
fame and advantage would accrue to Turkey, and not to the
Germans working behind the transparent sham of khedival authority. That being now the case, Berchtold could afford to support the enterprise with deliberately limited means, as in fact he
intimated to Berlin that he would do.

Relieved of Austria's strictures, the Germans prepared the
campaign in an atmosphere of fevered haste and anticipation.
On September 11 their consular agents had been expelled from
Egypt, and thereafter they had no accurate information about
British troop strength. Wangenheim and Jagow amused themselves with all sorts of widely divergent estimates, but the net
conclusions they drew from all of these were still confident and
optimistic.[98] The German embassy sent a mission throughout
Syria to test local attitudes toward an Egyptian campaign. A report was returned that the Arabs were not only pro-German but
even pro-Wilhelmian: the name of "Hadji Gallium" was everywhere spoken, and the young men sported mustaches like the
German Emperor's.[99] The British were thought to have about
forty thousand soldiers in Egypt, but concentrated chiefly along
the Canal, while the frontier defenses were given over to native
recruits. It was believed that these would desert when the Turks
approached and that the few men who stuck at their posts
would be overrun by swarms of Arabs eager to rally around the
Sultan's standard.

The Germans had no high opinion of the British infantry: it
was held to be too small to patrol the whole country adequately
and to consist, furthermore, of the worst elements of the British
population. Wangenheim described the recruits as raw and un-

[98] Wangenheim to Foreign Ministry, Oct. 20 and 28, 1914, *ibid.*, Bd. 84,
#A27502, #A28552; and Quadt to Foreign Ministry, Dec. 20, 1914,
ibid., #A35575. The estimates varied from 17,000 to 40,000, and as high
as 200,000 men.

[99] Held to Wangenheim, Oct. 15, 1914, *ibid.*, no number.

seasoned and made much of the ridicule heaped upon them by the crowds of Cairo and Alexandria. He also emphasized a report that the Indian government was reluctant to dispatch too many of its units for fear of encouraging Pan-Islamic disturbances in the subcontinent. He steadfastly maintained that the Australians and New Zealanders landed at Suez resented their service and would mutiny at the first opportunity against their callow British officers.[100] In short, the Germans accepted rumors and speculations as compelling truths.

Liman's attaché, Major Karl Laffert, who was assigned by the War Ministry in Berlin to go over all the Syrian vilayets, at this time put his finger on what was to be the final failing of the Egyptian and indeed of all the Turkish campaigns of the First World War: transportation. The Major believed that Egypt could be taken, but he had doubts whether the Turks could maintain themselves there. If a railroad were built immediately, the prospects would be substantially enhanced. Laffert estimated that the construction of a line from Turkish headquarters in Jerusalem to the Egyptian frontier could take as little as three months, if the finest engineers and the best German materials were set aside for the job.[101] But the cost would be a drain on the German treasury well beyond the limit set down by Secretary Jagow.

Wangenheim saw this paper but did not believe that the railroad was indispensable. He argued that the British would be beaten by an inferiority of numbers impossible for them to redress in wartime. Their control of Egypt was secure only as long as it was maintained by predominantly white troops. Neither Egyptian nor Indian troops could be substituted because, being Moslem, they were both liable to defect or revolt in a battle with the Turks. From his colleague in Athens, Count Albert Quadt, he

[100] Wangenheim to Foreign Ministry, Oct. 20, 1914, *ibid.*, #A27502.

[101] Laffert to War Ministry, Dec. 30, 1914, *ibid.*, Bd. 85, no number. This paper does not mention the fact that there was no complete rail connection from Constantinople to Aleppo. The tunnels through the Taurus and Amanus Mountains were not finished, and supplies had to be transported by pack trains at these points.

had evidence that the British were perilously short of manpower and were begging Prime Minister Venizelos to send them forty thousand Greek soldiers for Egyptian service. In effect, they were pleading for Venizelos to abandon his neutrality, which, despite large promises from London, he was not ready to do. Venizelos, according to Quadt's report, had declared that he would not move until he had Rumania firmly on his side or until Germany was clearly losing the war. For Wangenheim, disclosure of these British difficulties closed off further argument about Germany's chances in Egypt. And when he heard, on November 23, that the Turks had inflicted a loss of thirty-two men on a small British scouting party fifteen miles east of the Canal and induced the desertion of all the native camel drivers, he became ecstatic.[102]

A few days before this skirmish at El Kantara, Sultan Mohammed V proclaimed the Holy War. It thus became incumbent on all good Moslems to support the Sultan-Caliph against his enemies, specifically, for Moslems under Entente jurisdiction to turn against their governments. The desertion of the camel drivers was only a small indication of what the Holy War might yield, but the ensuing months showed that the maximum damage to the Allies from this source might already have been reached. The whole notion that a Holy War could arouse Moslems in the twentieth century was unsound from the start, and even the people of Constantinople greeted its proclamation with only idle curiosity instead of fervent support. The government declared a holiday and organized a parade led by the Sheik ul Islam for the occasion. But when the city prefect sought two women to impersonate the Prophet's wife and her servant, no better-class women would volunteer, and two pea-sellers from Galata Bridge had to be used for a small fee. The government was mortified, and as the procession wound through Stamboul, it evoked only a few shouts and some scattered clapping.[103]

[102] Quadt to Foreign Ministry, Nov. 14, 1914, *ibid.*, Bd. 84, #A30911; and Wangenheim to Foreign Ministry, Nov. 23, 1914, *ibid.*, #A31918.
[103] Patrick, *Under Five Sultans*, p. 289.

More serious was an argument that developed between the government and the allied and neutral powers about the wording of the Sultan's proclamation. His Majesty had set the number of his adherents at three hundred million, and the Central Powers were quick to observe that the number must include persons under their own as well as the Entente's jurisdiction.[104] Moreover, the appeal seemed to encompass subjects of neutral states like Bulgaria and Italy, and unless the apprehensions of the latter could be cleared away, Germany and Austria might have to pay for the largely verbal sympathy coming out of the Moslem capitals of the world with the very real hostility of Sofia and Rome.[105]

The Turks themselves wanted no trouble with Italy and proposed a curious alliance to Rome on November 3. It would have guaranteed all Italian possessions in North Africa and even obliged the Turks to help fight off any and all aggressors. The Italians, on the other hand, would not have to defend any part of the Ottoman Empire, and the possibility therefore remained that they might help themselves to another piece of it in the future. By implication this treaty would have recognized the sovereignty of Italy in Tripoli, which the Porte had withheld at the signing of the Treaty of Lausanne in 1912.

But the offer, however, was formulated by Halil Bey, President of the Ottoman Chamber of Deputies, and not by the official who should have taken the responsibility, the Grand Vizier Said Halim. Marquis Garoni found him "temporarily invisible" when he attempted to raise the subject at the Porte.[106] So the Italian government handled Halil's ideas gingerly and was reported spending considerable money on various nationalist leaders to discourage demonstrations in Egypt for either the Khedive or the Turks. The German Ambassador at Rome, Johan-

---

[104] C. Snouck Hurgronje, *The Holy War "Made in Germany"* (New York, 1915), p. 57.

[105] Pallavicini to Berchtold #68/p, Nov. 19, 1914, H.H.S.A. Allgemeines Karton 942. The Holy War was proclaimed on November 12, 1914.

[106] Wangenheim to Foreign Ministry, Nov. 3, 1914, A.A. Aegypten #3, Bd. 84, #A92467.

nes von Flotow, telegraphed that the Italians would have taken sterner measures if they had been certain that Constantinople alone was the source of their troubles; but it was strongly rumored that the French were spinning intrigues from Tunis, hoping that they might dislodge Italy from North Africa and cast the blame on Germany and the Turks.[107]

By the end of the year, then, the Triple Alliance was on the verge of dissolution. All of Pallavicini's dire predictions seemed about to be realized, and the Italians could not or would not be satisfied about Turkey's intentions in Tripoli. At one point, Italian policy seemed unreasonably intransigent, because Enver himself intervened to offer Rome some pretty solid guarantees. He suggested that his own brother, Captain Nuri Bey, contact the Sheik of the Cyrenaican Senussi and persuade him to abstain from any assaults on the Italian administration. But Enver required that an Italian cruiser be put at his brother's service, for, he claimed, there was no other way through enemy lines. The Italians declined to release the ship, apparently fearing a confrontation with the Entente fleet.[108] It would admittedly have been difficult to keep Nuri's whereabouts a secret, because the western allies had no lack of information from their missions in Rome, and the search of her ship would have strained Italy's neutrality to the uttermost. Yet in the last analysis no guarantee from the Porte would suffice short of the abandonment of the entire expedition. Turkey could not give up the campaign, for if it repelled Italy, it bound Germany closer by embroiling her with Britain. The desert of Sinai would become still another area where a compromise peace would be shoved farther from reach.

On January 15, 1915, the Turkish Fourth Army began to march toward Egypt. Djemal Pasha eagerly accepted command to offset the rapidly growing popularity of his rival, Enver. He had only 22,000 troops against a British force whose number he set at 185,000 men,[109] but he hoped that the British would be

107 Flotow to Foreign Ministry, Nov. 5, 1914, *ibid.*, #A29571.
108 "Conversation with Enver," Nov. 3, 1914, Jaeckh Papers, Drawer 69.
109 Djemal Pasha, *Memoirs*, p. 155; Girard L. McEntee, *Military History of the World War* (New York, 1937), pp. 250–252. At the Canal, Djemal

able to mass only a small part of their total strength along the Canal and that their lines would remain quite thin. Moreover, he tried to whip up the enthusiasm of his men by turning the whole undertaking into a kind of Islamic crusade, reminiscent of the days of Mohammed the Conqueror, but thoroughly out of place in the conduct of modern war. Despite strenuous German protest, a company of whirling dervishes was attached to the army. Their high conical hats made them excellent targets for the enemy.[110] All Christians and Jews were separated out of the army before it passed south of Beersheba. At Joppa, Djemal had a camel, a dog, and a bull, decorated respectively with the flags of Russia, France, and Britain, driven through the streets. The mob pelted the poor beasts with slop.

The desert was crossed without difficulty and good order and morale maintained. German engineers under an able Bavarian officer, Lieutenant-Colonel Kress von Kressenstein, dug wells along the route, so there was no lack of water. The uniforms, however, were the same dirty issue collected after the Balkan Wars, and not washed since then. Djemal planned to cross the Canal with German steel pontoons, but many of his men were unfamiliar with this kind of equipment and afraid to use it. So the commander assured them that he had bought hundreds of camels from the Arabs. Deprived of water for some days, these would rush into the Canal, drown, and allow the army to advance over their dead carcasses.[111]

In the early morning of February 3, the Turks delivered their attack opposite Ismailia. The half-darkness gave them a certain element of surprise, but their coming was by no means a secret to the British. Their columns had been spotted by aerial observers, and the diplomatic hassle and the antics of the march were themselves sufficient warning to the defenders.[112] One of Djem-

---

faced about 35,000 defenders. The remainder were distributed throughout Egypt.

[110] Wangenheim to Foreign Ministry, Feb. 17, 1915, A.A. Aegypten #3, Bd. 85, #A6799.

[111] Aaronsohn, *Turks in Palestine*, pp. 11–12, 38–40.

[112] Pallavicini to Burian, Beilage #9/p, Jan. 28, 1915, H.H.S.A. Türkei Karton 209.

al's officers says that it was an old Hamidian custom to take
along live chickens on military campaigns to lay breakfast eggs.
The cackling of these, he says, aroused the British who, at any
rate, had their guns quickly in place.[113]

Only one pontoon reached the opposite shore; the others were
shattered by gunfire. Two thousand men were lost and then the
order given to retire. A sandstorm blew up and struck the Turks
in the face. Djemal thought this a sign from Allah that the attack
should not be repeated. If this excuse satisfied his piety, it did
nothing for his pride, and he cursed the Germans throughout the
retreat. At Haifa he compelled the unwilling German consul to
review the beaten army and afterwards he gave a banquet for
Colonel Kress. His intention, far from being generous, was to associate the Germans publicly in the disaster. During the meal,
several of the Turkish officers expressed their fear that Germany
would have later incorporated any territory they might have
won.[114]

In that fear they were not alone. Pallavicini had made the
same observation to Berchtold at the end of December. He furthermore warned that Turco-German activity in Egypt was driving the British to desperation and that they might retaliate with
an attack on Constantinople. He had heard talk from diplomatic
quarters in Athens that a concentration of allied forces at the
Dardanelles was being considered, and he insisted that Berchtold lose no time in warning Berlin. Hohenlohe made these
fears known at the Wilhelmstrasse, but he had the misfortune to
deal with the dauntless activist Zimmermann. Zimmermann
opined that the Dardanelles attack was unlikely and that Pallavicini should not be taken too seriously. Berlin felt that if Britain
felt strong enough to force the Dardanelles, she would do so
whether the Germans moved into Egypt or not. In fact, if they
did not move, the Dardanelles might be threatened all the

[113] Rafael de Nogales, *Memoirs of a Soldier of Fortune* (New York,
1932), p. 312.
[114] Wangenheim to Bethmann, Mar. 4, 1915, A.A. Aegypten #3, Bd. 85,
#A9358.

sooner.[115] Therefore, even after the debacle of February 3, the Austrian Ambassador believed it not out of the question that the Germans would make a second try against the Canal.

To prevent it, he assiduously played upon all the fears and hidden sensibilities of the Turk. While Djemal's troops moved through the desert of El Tih, the Porte sent a certain Batzarian, a Turkish senator of Rumanian extraction, to Bucharest. He carried with him more than a million marks to inaugurate a pro-German press campaign and bring Rumania into the war. But the mission failed, Batzarian returned part of the money to Berlin, and the Turks were harassed by the specter of a flanking attack while they were expending themselves in the Sinai Desert.[116] Pallavicini made much of these grim prospects, omitting no lurid touch in conversation with the timorous Turks. The Ambassador and the Ballplatz also considered ways to challenge a German hegemony in Egypt, should Djemal be victorious despite the obstacles. They had in reserve Djelal Pasha, a son-in-law of the ex-Sultan, Abdul Hamid. The Austrian embassy was ordered to pay regular subsidies to this man and to groom him as a rival claimant, should the Germans eventually try to enthrone Abbas Hilmi as an absolute ruler.[117]

After the repulse at Ismailia there was really little chance of this happening. The disgrace of Turkish arms meant the end of the Khedive's reign and might have meant the end of his life. All along, he had predicted Djemal's failure, not on account of any material inferiority, but because his plans were betrayed to the enemy in the last detail. Abbas accused his relative Said Halim, who had been cut out of the Egyptian succession when inheritance by primogeniture was substituted for the accession of the eldest male. The Grand Vizier had never kept secret his wish to revert to the older practice, which would have brought him a

---

[115] Pallavicini to Berchtold #76/p, Dec. 23, 1914; Hohenlohe to Berchtold #785/8626, Dec. 23, 1914, H.H.S.A. Allgemeines Karton 942.

[116] "Confidential Information," Jan. 21, 1915, Jaeckh Papers, Drawer 69.

[117] Burian to Pallavicini #57/498, Jan. 25, 1915, H.H.S.A. Türkei Karton 208.

throne instead of merely the first office in the Ottoman bureaucracy. According to the Khedive, he had made a bargain with the British to sabotage the expedition in return for his own elevation.

Abbas insisted that the publication of a British white book would bear him out,[118] but these charges, while necessary to insure him the support of the Central Powers and possibly even true, severely numbered his days in Constantinople. He fled to Vienna together with a small circle of Egyptian nationalists and in effect asked the Austrian government to guarantee his life. Otherwise, he feared that Enver and Djemal would depose and jail him to avert public recrimination from themselves for the defeat at Suez.[119]

The auspices were not favorable upon his arrival. Berchtold, who had allowed himself to drift along with the Egyptian expedition, had been replaced at the Foreign Ministry by the Magyar aristocrat Count Stephen Burian. Burian was quite bitter about German insistence that the Austrians be prepared to surrender Trentino to Italy to keep the latter in the Triple Alliance. One of his first official charges was to go to Berlin and remonstrate about the matter. But he got no satisfaction there and, according to associates, returned to Vienna badly disposed toward the German Foreign Ministry and its clients.[120] He turned the Khedive a stony if not completely deaf ear and blandly advised him to make peace with the Porte. This could be done by simply increasing the Sultan's annual tribute. The Ballplatz, in case of need, might even see to it that Abbas was advanced the additional money. This last idea came from Pallavicini and carried

[118] Berchtold to Pallavicini #5258/7128, Nov. 17, 1914, H.H.S.A. Allgemeines Karton 942; Tschirschky to Bethmann, Dec. 30, 1914, A.A. Aegypten #3, Bd. 85, #A188; and Oppenheim to Bethmann, Jan. 22, 1915, *ibid.,* #A12903.

[119] Burian to Pallavicini #1105/969, Feb. 18, 1915, H.H.S.A. Türkei Karton 208.

[120] "Confidential Report," Feb. 9, 1915, Jaeckh Papers, Drawer 69. Humann wrote this after a talk with Austrian embassy counsellor Trautmannsdorff, just returned from Vienna to Constantinople.

strings. It was not to be acted upon unless Austria acquired certain railroad concessions in Egypt to offset Germany's economic preponderance in Anatolia. Burian agreed completely to this stipulation.[121]

At the root of these hypotheses was the feeling that the days of Germany's Turkish ascendancy were numbered. For a month rumors had mounted in the Stamboul bazaars that the life of every German would be forfeit at the first military reverse.[122] The Austrians knew that several provincial governors now opposed the policy of the Committee of Union and Progress, and Burian had certain proof that the Vali of Smyrna, Rahmi Bey, was conniving at Greek intervention to topple the government. Rahmi and the Greek consul in Smyrna hoped to engineer a massacre of Christians in that city which would force Venizelos to dispatch troops. Burian felt that the failure in Egypt would ease their task and enable the Turks to sue for an armistice. He expected to give the Porte his good offices in talks with Russia and secure in return concessions in Egypt and elsewhere.[123] Except for Count Julius Andrassy, the Magyar circle in Vienna believed that Russia would not hold out for the dismemberment of the Dual Monarchy and would abandon Serbia in return for a better position at the Straits. The sole use of all the Tsar's Slavic clients was to force the Turks to grant the Russians more certain egress from the Black Sea. Quick diplomatic action, Burian and Pallavicini believed, could for all time eliminate Russia's problem and avoid a battle at the Dardanelles, where the Austrians felt certain that the Central Powers would be defeated, and the chance for advantageous negotiations lost forever.[124]

Yet despite the rage and frustration of the Turks, there were no Christian massacres and no increase of the Padishah's ene-

---

[121] Burian to Pallavicini #142/1760, Mar. 2, 1915, H.H.S.A. Türkei Karton 208.

[122] Barclay to Grey #10/4026, Jan. 11, 1915, P.R.O., F.O. 371/2479; Elliott to Grey #71/14967, Feb. 8, 1915, F.O. 371/2481.

[123] Burian to Pallavicini #102/1347, Feb. 9, 1915, H.H.S.A. Türkei Karton 208.

[124] Pallavicini to Burian #1/p, Jan. 13, 1915, *ibid.*, Karton 209.

mies. The Greek naval attaché was arrested in the middle of February on the flimsiest charges of spying, and the Greek Ambassador left Constantinople in protest. But Count Quadt got Venizelos to calm down and accept the apologies of the Grand Vizier. The Austrians thought these "insufficient in form," but the Greek Premier was so satisfied that he denounced his man for a precipitate departure and sent back another in his place.[125] Greek intervention at Smyrna never occurred, though the fault was not the Austrians'. They had carefully concealed from their German ally any forewarnings that trouble might be brewing.[126]

The fact was that no influential member of the Committee then wanted negotiations. As a diplomatic factor, the first Suez campaign, despite its unsatisfactory result, might have afforded the Turks a good bargaining position. The very fact that they had brought a force through the desert stood powerfully to their credit and obliged the British to increase their Egyptian garrisons by at least one hundred thousand men. Quite aside from Germany's secret ambitions and the Khedive's family quarrels, the campaign in itself was therefore not a mistake.

In conclusion, it may also be said that the Austrians made out the situation to be worse than it was. Djemal was undoubtedly angry at his allies, but least of all men was he proof against the flattery and blandishments they could work upon him. The German consul at Damascus, Dr. Löytved-Hardegg, paid the Pasha untiring court and praised him as "the Moses of his people." The German embassy spent a great deal of money to quash whatever case the pro-French Syrian newspapers had to make against his dubious generalship. Finally, Kress von Kressenstein replaced all the camels lost in Egypt from the funds of the German military mission.

Djemal always liked a claque, and to all these gestures he responded warmly. He encouraged the establishment of German-language schools throughout Syria, and the sale of German man-

[125] Pallavicini to Burian, Telegrams #129 and 138, Feb. 14 and 16, 1915, *ibid.*

[126] Burian enjoins the strictest secrecy in his dispatch of February 9, 1915.

ufactures rose briskly under his beneficent eye. No one, on the other hand, seemed to take the Austrian merchandisers in the area seriously. The kroner was even refused for payments and exchanged at a very low rate by the moneylenders of Aleppo and Damascus.[127] All in all, the Austrians had to admit that German prestige died hard.

[127] Kastriner to Pallavicini, Feb. 10, 1915, H.H.S.A. Türkei Karton 209, unnumbered. According to Turkish contemporaries, Djemal was very bitter at Kress because the latter had induced him to the Egyptian adventure with promises that Germany would award Bulgaria and Rumania to the Ottoman Empire in return for victory at the Canal (Bayur, III/I, 216–217).

4

Trouble in the Balkans and on the Baghdad Railway

Perhaps nothing better suggests the muddled nature of the German alliance with the Turks than the events of early 1915. At the beginning of the year, after only two months of fighting in the Turkish theater, it became clear that the Sultan's empire could not survive a long war unless available resources, in matériel and men, were carefully preserved and cautiously managed. The entire army command organization had to be tightened up, and the channels of supply from central Europe had to be kept open though none of the Balkan states had yet sided with Germany and Austria. These new conditions revealed Liman von Sanders' unsuitability to direct the Germans in the Near Eastern war. They also emphasized that Austria could not be trusted to get German supplies through to the Ottoman front, much less to enlarge her own aid to the Turks. Finally, the Baghdad Railway proved nearly as unserviceable as the Balkan roads. Men even less than money could not be found for its completion. Many who might have done the job perished in the Armenian massacres.

Breakdown in the Turkish High Command

For Djemal Pasha the fruits of victory could not have been sweeter than those that defeat dropped into his lap. Syria was henceforth administered as an independent pashalik with himself as its lord almost omnipotent. Turkey's allies and the neutral powers reckoned with these new conditions even if they were never officially sanctioned by the Sultan and his masters on the Committee. Wherever Djemal and his retinue came to rest, there existed a nearly sovereign court, not so gilded as the one on the Golden Horn, but more efficient and determined. Consequently, the diplomats accredited to the Syrian area came to be regarded, by themselves and others, as more important than their seniors in Constantinople. Wangenheim was disturbed to learn that Löytved-Hardegg was hailed as "the ambassador at Damascus" by the consular representatives of the other powers, but it was believed he dared not move for Hardegg's reprimand or transfer because the man employed so deft a touch in his dealings with Djemal. The Austrians found the relations between Wangenheim and Hardegg amusing and perhaps eventually profitable: [1] a man not master of his house is hard put to guard against robbers.

An even more serious problem of control touched the position of General Liman von Sanders. It has been shown that he was galled by his lot from the moment of his arrival. He had not been properly greeted at his coming and was thereafter studiously ignored. When he had offered his resignation, Enver had taken him up with shattering alacrity. The German Emperor forbade his removal but hardly restored his prestige. Liman seems to have felt that William added a dose of acidulous comedy to a draught already bitter enough, and he forgot and forgave nothing. Enver was brought to tender the General his apologies. He extolled Liman von Sanders as "the cutting edge of Turkey's sword." But all witnesses concurred that this reconciliation was hollow and left the General no less implacable than before. [2] So matters stood at the opening of 1915.

At this time Liman strove to make himself as uncomfortable as possible to the gentlemen of the Pera embassy. For long stretches he did not speak with them and reduced all contact

[1] Pallavicini to Burian #9/p, Jan. 28, 1915, H.H.S.A. Türkei Karton 209.
[2] Wangenheim to Foreign Ministry, Aug. 20, 1914, A.A. Türkei #139, Bd. 33, #A18066.

with Wangenheim to a few surly and devilishly equivocal notes.
He also shunned the personnel of his own staff, suspecting that
the tactics of the diplomats had drained his office of all real
authority.[3] Though, according to later testimony, Liman was
never regarded at the German War Ministry as the best of generals and was therefore assigned to the inferior Turkish theater of
war,[4] it was quite likely that self-pity and paranoia made up a
large part of his present complaint. Nevertheless, since he persisted in his behavior, his countrymen drew off from him and in
time showed the very ill-will with which Liman had always
charged them. The danger, which Wangenheim quickly spotted,
was that the General spent more and more time in Austrian company. He found the shoulders of Pallavicini and Pomiankowski
ample to cry upon, and Wangenheim feared that he might di-
vulge confidential embassy business to the Austrians.[5]

To stop such leaks, Wangenheim considered the advantages of
associating another officer with Liman's command. To fire the
General outright would have revealed too great a subservience,
on the one hand, to Enver, and to the General himself, on the
other. The name of Field Marshal Colmar von der Goltz, an old
friend and respected mentor of the Turks, was suggested to the
Chancellor, and Bethmann caught instantly at the idea. No difficulties about the appointment were expected from the Ottoman
War Ministry, because Enver had known Goltz longer than
Liman, and his quarrel of the previous summer with the latter
was still lively in everyone's memory.[6]

Enver's reaction radically contradicted his stand of a few
months before. At first he refused even to consider this "act of in-
gratitude" to General Liman.[7] The ethical side of the problem

[3] Wangenheim to Foreign Ministry, Nov. 25, 1914, *ibid.,* #A32246.

[4] "Memorandum on the Turkish Collapse" by von Seeckt, Nov. 4, 1918,
Seeckt Papers.

[5] Wangenheim to Foreign Ministry, Dec. 16, 1914, A.A. Türkei #139,
Bd. 33, #A34944.

[6] Wangenheim to Bethmann, Oct. 31, 1914, *ibid.,* #A2448; Bethmann to
Foreign Ministry, Nov. 3, 1914, *ibid.,* #A2466.

[7] Wangenheim to Foreign Ministry, Nov. 5, 1914, *ibid.,* #A2498.

certainly carried less weight with him than the advice of the
Austrian Ambassador, who counselled strongly against any de-
crease in Liman's power but did not want the German embassy
to know that he had done so. Pallavicini warned the Ballplatz to
conceal carefully his hand in Liman's business and was afraid
that Wangenheim already had more of its scent than he would
have liked. He felt that the despondent and indiscreet Liman
was likelier than the stolid and incorruptible Goltz to do Austria
a good turn one day and should therefore be maintained in his
command.[8]

Consequently, though Enver did not refuse Goltz, he put such
impossible conditions on his reception as almost to destroy its
feasibility. The German embassy was informed that Goltz would
be appointed as general adjutant to His Majesty the Sultan, with
a decisive influence on the conduct of the war and independence
of any Turkish official. In return, Mohammed V expected to dispatch to Emperor William's own retinue Lieutenant General
Zeki Pasha, former inspector general of the Damascus district.
The Sultan especially recommended Zeki for his excellent command of German and warm friendship with many of Liman's
subordinates.[9]

This was more than the Chancellor and Wangenheim had bar-
gained for. The Ambassador was instructed politely to decline
Zeki's appointment because of "lack of space." [10] The real reasons Jagow disclosed at greater length. In his opinion it might be
possible to receive Zeki at General Staff Headquarters, but for
reasons of security his presence in the imperial retinue was unthinkable. To accord such an honor even to Bavarian or Austrian
officers had never been deemed advisable, and the Emperor's
generals would not now entertain such concessions to the Turks.
Jagow stated that Zeki might come to Germany if the Porte in-

[8] Pallavicini to Berchtold #980, Dec. 26, 1914, H.H.S.A. Allgemeines
Karton 942.

[9] Wangenheim to Foreign Ministry, Nov. 18, 1914, A.A. Türkei #139,
Bd. 33, #A31622.

[10] Jagow to Foreign Ministry, Nov. 22, 1914, *ibid.*, #A31850.

sisted on it and could be styled *général à la suite*. He would enjoy all the privileges accorded to the military observers of Austria and the German states, *i.e.*, none at all, but he would be excluded from the Emperor's inner councils, with delicacy or determination as the situation required.[11]

Jagow, however, was clearly aware that he could not proceed too harshly. If he attempted to restrict the activities of Zeki overmuch, the Turks might hamstring or even expel Marshal von der Goltz. Such a development would serve the wishes of General Liman and his covert backers at the Ballplatz. In the end, therefore, Zeki was for some weeks busy at General Staff Headquarters,[12] and the venerable German marshal was treated to the toasts of the pashas at Dolma Bagtché, but each man served to cancel out the threat inherent in the commission of the other. The problem of command at Constantinople was not solved in the least, and Liman was more securely lodged in power than ever before.

This incident was scarcely resolved when Enver announced that the moment had come for a strong drive against Russia. This was the Caucasus offensive, which Pallavicini had deplored some months before. Command of the army was offered to Liman and may have been intended to clarify his position. Yet he turned back the commission as militarily unfeasible and would not reconsider even when reminded of his earlier cravings for action.[13] Since the Caucasus campaign had been discussed in the Turkish cabinet for some time, the inevitable result of this contretemps was that Enver had to assume the task he intended to delegate to another. The War Minister was far from cowardly, but brought little more than innate daring to his office. If, as he once confidentially charged, Liman had little gift for organization,[14] his was even less. His ideas of strategy, as the Caucasus

[11] Jagow to Wangenheim, Dec. 19, 1914, A.A. Türkei #159, No. 1, Bd. 14, #A35399.

[12] Turkish Ambassador Muktar Pasha to Zimmermann, Jan. 2, 1915, *ibid.*, #A178.

[13] Wangenheim to Foreign Ministry, Dec. 6, 1914, A.A. Türkei #139, Bd. 33, #A33710.

[14] Wangenheim to Foreign Ministry, Nov. 25, 1914, *ibid.*, #A32246.

fighting all too soon showed, were those of a prizefighter who strikes out blindly because he has little time to think. Liman knew this and may have wished it so.

Enver's prolonged absence from Constantinople seemed deplorable to Wangenheim. It threatened a revival of the chronic power-jockeying within the Committee membership and could even set off a revolutionary move among the city populace, which was held in check by Enver's charismatic personality. The Ambassador commanded Liman to withdraw his refusal, and when he would not do so threatened him with the mighty intervention of General von Falkenhayn. In the meantime, however, Liman sprang at the very vitals of the German embassy and began to reveal to the Turkish police the names of Wangenheim's secret informants in and near the Union and Progress Committee. One of these men, a German citizen, was roughly handled during interrogation, but the Ambassador did not risk a protest to the Porte and only begged Liman to have greater care of the fatherland's interests. Liman's refusal to accept the Caucasus command stood.[15] On January 3, 1915, Enver's Caucasus army was completely smashed by a superior force of Russians at Sarikamish near Erzerum. The bitter cold, the deep snow, and their totally inadequate equipment made them easy prey for the Russians.

When Goltz arrived at the railroad station, he was handed a letter from Wangenheim excusing his absence from the ceremonies. The Ambassador claimed that his appearance would encourage rumors that he was trying to make a German protectorate out of Turkey and offend the partisans of General Liman. The Sultan's chamberlain, who customarily graced such affairs, also stayed away.[16] Some attempt was made at the German embassy to divide the military mission into factions. Bronsart von Schellendorff was mentioned as leader of a group prepared to

[15] Wangenheim to Foreign Ministry, Dec. 11, 1914, *ibid.*, #A34453. Liman claims that Wangenheim supported his refusal to accept the Caucasus command (*Five Years in Turkey*, p. 49). The German Foreign Ministry documents quoted show just the opposite.

[16] Wangenheim to Foreign Ministry, Dec. 14, 1914, A.A. Türkei #139, Bd. 33, #A34665.

give unqualified allegiance to Marshal von der Goltz.[17] Nothing, however, came of the maneuver, because most of the officers remained aloof and uncommitted, profiting from the fate of the incautious Bronsart, whom Liman packed off to the Caucasus and defeat. When Bronsart returned to the capital at the end of January, his reputation almost as blasted as the health of the frostbitten survivors, Liman tried to have him retired from the army; only the stout intervention of Goltz and Wangenheim preserved this officer's career.[18] Meanwhile Liman requested the War Ministry in Berlin to replace the personnel of the mission with men older or even convalescing from wounds.[19] While thousands of Turks fell in the Caucasus and Egypt, Liman implied that the Turkish theater of war was secure and calm enough to accept the lame and the cast-off of the German military establishment. A few such men were sent down to Constantinople,[20] and if they did not suit the needs of the war, they suited Liman's temperament: they were docile, obedient, and broken.

The danger threatening Wangenheim was an old one and deeply rooted in German history. Bismarck had had to balk the wishes of the elder Moltke and Waldersee to make his foreign policy, but Jagow and the Ambassador in Constantinople could not impose the restraints at the Iron Chancellor's command. Liman sent diplomatic reports to Berlin without their being first reviewed at the Pera embassy, and he advocated courses certain to deepen the Turkish imbroglio and speed it to incalculable disaster. He insisted that all British and French subjects in the capital should be penned in concentration camps. A surprisingly large number of these remained at liberty and admittedly complicated the security problems of the military mission. Moreover, the General would have had shot immediately all Greeks on charges of spying for the Entente. These people bore the Germans no good will, but as Wangenheim pointed out and as

[17] Wangenheim to Foreign Ministry, Dec. 21, 1914, *ibid.*, #A35640.
[18] Wangenheim to Foreign Ministry, Jan. 23, 1915, *ibid.*, Bd. 34, #A285.
[19] Liman to War Ministry, Dec. 6, 1914, *ibid.*, Bd. 33, #B229.
[20] War Ministry to Liman, Feb. 21, 1915, *ibid.*, Bd. 34, #A7080.

Liman most certainly knew, the first Greek so handled would bring the Athens government into the war.[21] Turkey could not afford still another front.

Still the Turks took up Liman's ideas, because they were bolder and clearer than anything from Wangenheim. Their essential foolishness escaped Enver, and he was quite eager to organize concentration camps. Wangenheim observed of this episode that it proved the Turk essentially a barbarian, whose natural lust and sadism would do terrible damage to German prestige and to attempts at a compromise peace.[22]

Wangenheim recommended that a mental specialist be sent down to Constantinople to examine the General. Jagow, however, while recognizing the need of such measures, would not risk public embarrassment.[23] The Ambassador was instructed to accommodate Liman wherever possible, to maintain all conversation with Pallavicini on the least controversial plane, and to acquire new sources of information about Committee sentiments and intrigues. Wangenheim accomplished only the last successfully and put on the payroll a businessman named Wassermann. This man was well known at the city clubs where the Grand Vizier, Talaat, and Djavid came to smoke and take dinner. Wassermann's contacts with Djavid were described as especially close. The Finance Minister was a devotee of poker, while Wassermann was a master at the game. He usually beat the Turk, but often refunded his losses. Such generosity worked and gave the Germans new access to state secrets after Liman's sabotage had closed off the old ones.[24] Attempts to achieve better relations with Pallavicini, on the other hand, were no more than superficially successful.

On several occasions the subject of Trentino came up between the two men. Wangenheim and the entire German Foreign Ministry pounded away at its cession to Italy if the Triple Alliance were to be preserved through the war. Pallavicini retorted that

21 Wangenheim to "Dear Friend," Dec. 30, 1914, *ibid.*, #A46.
22 *Ibid.*   23 *Ibid.*
24 Wangenheim to Foreign Ministry, Mar. 29, 1915, *ibid.*, #A11271.

Germany's argument was a poor one, because she presently occupied Belgium and coveted Egypt for the future. Both measures
had driven Britain into an uncompromising posture toward the
Central Powers and forced promises to the Russian government
inconceivable in her older diplomacy. The Austrian Ambassador
frankly told Wangenheim that Berlin should offer the evacuation
of Belgium to the British cabinet in return for a reasonable ap-
portionment of the Ottoman Empire to the Central Powers. He
believed that Russia had not yet been conclusively awarded
Constantinople because of persistent quarreling between Sazonov and the governments of France and Great Britain. At most,
he hoped that only a protectorate had been contemplated for the
Tsar, so that time was still left for Germany and Austria to make
magnanimous and compelling proposals.[25]

Despite the vehemence of these arguments, there is scant mention of them in Wangenheim's reports to Berlin. The Austrian
viewpoint was known well enough in the Wilhelmstrasse, and
Pallavicini confessed to Burian that Wangenheim was by turns
cold, adamant, and annoyed whenever the subject was brought
up. Burian declared that if Austria could not herself acquire advantages in Egypt, he would sooner see the British fully restored
than the Germans make headway there. The Ambassador replied
that such observations, while completely sound, should be
avoided lest Wangenheim get hold of this correspondence and
show it to the Turks.[26] In the meantime Burian was advised to
consider more generous subsidies to the newspapers of Constantinople to encourage more complete and candid reporting, including defeats like Sarikamish and the Canal. Had the losses on

[25] Pallavicini to Burian #13/p, Feb. 18, 1915, H.H.S.A. Türkei Karton
209. The time for negotiation was in fact fast passing. Sazonov made his
formal demand for Constantinople on March 4, 1915; and Grey accepted
it subject to certain reservations on March 12, 1915 (Robert J. Kerner,
"Russia, The Straits, and Constantinople, 1914–1915," *Journal of Modern
History,* I [1929], 400–415).
[26] Pallavicini to Burian #16/p, Feb. 25, 1915, H.H.S.A. Türkei Karton
209.

the Caucasian front received wider publicity, Pallavicini thought, Wangenheim might have become less smug if not more tractable.[27]

The Problem of Balkan Transport

These disagreements about Trentino and Egypt had a parallel in problems of Balkan transport between the Central Powers. Though Germany's military commitment in the Ottoman Empire was far larger than Austria's, its lines of supply were inadequate and tenuous. Moreover, they were almost completely under the control of the Dual Monarchy and its Balkan neighbors. At the beginning of the war, attempts were made to send supply ships down the Danube, but these were subjected to heavy bombardment by Serbian shore batteries and to the additional danger of mines in the river channel. The Bulgarian government claimed that these mines were a danger to peaceful commerce and demanded that the Russians sweep the river.[28] But the Russians gave no satisfaction, and Sofia was reluctant to press the matter too far. There was already too much suspicion that the Bulgarians, while technically neutral, were serving the interests of the Central Powers.

For much of their information about the Danube route the Germans were dependent on Austrian informants, who emphasized the danger from mines and the additional hazards from Serbian saboteurs and secret agents who combed the region. These reports were in most cases well founded; but on at least one occasion, the German government made queries of its own and concluded that the obstacles were apparently exaggerated at the source. For instance, one Austrian report that mentioned saboteurs was later revised to speak only of the difficulties of navigating through storms.[29] At any rate, Jagow concluded that the dangers of Serbian cannons on the Danube shore were real

---

[27] Pallavicini to Burian #10/p and #16/p. Feb. 4 and 25, 1915, *ibid.*
[28] Michahelles to Foreign Ministry, Dec. 21, 1914, A.A. Weltkrieg #16, Bd. 5, #A35683.
[29] Michahelles to Foreign Ministry, Dec. 24, 1914, *ibid.*, #A36089.

enough and instructed his people to find alternate means of passage.[30]

Bulgaria and Rumania were quick to capitalize on the difficulties of the Central Powers. A glance at the map made it obvious that supplies for the Sultan's armies would have to be transported overland from Hungary through their territories. The Rumanian Prime Minister, Ion Bratianu, declared his country neutral and closed the Rumanian railroads to any military shipments. At the same time, he indicated that he was not above doing the Central Powers some small favors at high prices. He told the German Ambassador in Bucharest that a settlement could be reached if the Central Powers would share the transportation contracts with Rumanian companies instead of awarding them for the most part to the Viennese firm of Schenker and Company. According to Bratianu, Schenker's people were not well liked in Rumania, and indigenous firms could do as good a job or better.[31] This possibility was reported to Jagow, but he commented that no changes should be made that might anger Schenker. Corroborating this opinion was the German Ambassador in Sofia, who thought that Rumanian firms had too little experience in dealing with Turkey and too few contacts in Bulgaria to bring consignments efficiently through that country.[32]

Both men may have been right, but the Rumanian government was quick to feel, or feign, an insult. Bratianu continued to insist that Schenker must relinquish its unreasonable monopoly, but in the meantime did some political horse trading, at which he excelled. He had the German embassy in Constantinople sounded directly, and though the price of cooperation was substantial, Humann and Liman von Sanders recommended that it be paid. The Germans were now assured that war supplies would be passed through Rumanian territory if the Germans paid over quantities of medicines and chemicals that before the war brought

[30] Jagow to Foreign Ministry, Dec. 26, 1914, *ibid.*, #A36229.

[31] Bussche to Foreign Ministry, Dec. 26, 1914, *ibid.*, #A36311.

[32] Michahelles to Foreign Ministry, Jan. 5, 1915, *ibid.*, #A696; Jagow to General Consul, Budapest, Jan. 7, 1915, *ibid.*

high prices in Bucharest. Presumably these commodities would now be given free by the Germans. Rumania would deliver a carefully itemized list that the German government would be expected to fill in a short time.[33]

Jagow decided to give this procedure a trial and on January 9, 1915, twenty-eight truckloads of goods were passed into Rumania and like amounts were delivered in the ensuing weeks.[34] Nevertheless, the Rumanian customs service continued to make all kinds of difficulties, and Bratianu complained that the packing of the supplies was inadequate and compromising. He wanted to pass two truckloads of materials at a time over his southern frontier and not dispatch another pair until it was reported that the first consignment had reached Constantinople. A more rapid rate of delivery, he feared, would be betrayed to the Russians by his police and by the press, which he claimed was uncontrollable.[35]

Rather than slow the rate of delivery, the Germans paid bribes to all and sundry. Bratianu himself does not seem to have gotten any money, though it is possible that some of the fees were passed on to him by the original recipients. The Rumanian Minister of Finance, E. Costinescu, was certainly well paid, as was his secretary, Alexandrini, under whose influence the older, impressionable minister was said to have been.[36] Though the Rumanians professed to be afraid of security leaks, they sent numerous agents, sometimes unnecessarily, to make contact with the Germans in Constantinople and in Berlin. All of these agents expected and were given bribes.[37]

No amount of generosity, however, did anything to achieve a favorable exchange rate of commodities to war matériel. Germany was forced to pay one wagonload of consumer goods for

[33] Humann to Marine and Foreign Ministries, Jan. 7, 1915, *ibid.*, #A866.
[34] Humann to Marine and Foreign Ministries, Jan. 7, 1915, *ibid.*; Bussche to Foreign Ministry, Jan. 9, 1915, *ibid.*, #A1062; and Jagow to Tschirschky, Jan. 10, 1915, *ibid.*, #A1116.
[35] Bussche to Foreign Ministry, Jan. 10, 1915, *ibid.*, #A1198.
[36] Bronsart to War Ministry, Jan. 6, 1915, *ibid.*, #A1466.
[37] Wangenheim to Foreign Ministry, Jan. 11, 1915, *ibid.*, #A1309.

every wagonload of military supplies permitted to cross the Rumanian frontier. Austria was apprised of these terms, but appeared to be as much concerned that Schenker and Company should have a good share of the carrying revenues as that the Rumanians should climb down from their exorbitant demands.[38]

The security problem soon became difficult. The German War Ministry thought that the enemy was well informed and that even the German diplomatic service should be kept in the dark as much as possible about supply shipments to the Ottoman Empire. At various times, Rumanian middlemen were paid in gold instead of commodities, but German diplomatic personnel often did not know the amount of gold paid or the dispatch schedule of the supplies sent down through the Balkan Peninsula to Turkey.[39] At Constantinople, gold for such purposes was kept in the branch of the Deutsche Bank, but the accounts of the bank were closed to Wangenheim and subject instead to the supervision of Marshal von der Goltz.[40] The ambassadors Hilmar von dem Bussche in Bucharest and Gustav Michahelles in Sofia were similarly uninformed, and whenever any of them inquired how Goltz spent his money, the Marshal replied that he was just buying horses for the Turkish cavalry.[41] No inquiries were addressed to Liman von Sanders. Though he was one of the first to press for a deal with Rumania,[42] he was ignored in the subsequent supply transactions.

About January 20, 1915, Schenker and Company, under the prodding of the Austrian Foreign Ministry, agreed to assign some of the carrying business to Rumanian companies. The Rumanians were to handle the traffic on the Budapest-Sofia segment of the route.[43] But subsequent events suggest that the Austrians did not compromise with any good grace. Tschirschky,

[38] Tschirschky to Foreign Ministry, Jan. 13, 1915, *ibid.*, #A1540.

[39] Jagow to Michahelles, Jan. 20, 1915, *ibid.*, Bd. 6, #A2082.

[40] Jagow to Tschirschky, Jan. 18, 1915, *ibid.*, #A2082.

[41] Bussche to Foreign Ministry, Jan. 21, 1915, *ibid.*, #A2587.

[42] Humann to Marine and Foreign Ministries, Jan. 7, 1915, *ibid.*, Bd. 5, #A866.

[43] Bussche to Bethmann, Jan. 20, 1915, *ibid.*, Bd. 6, #A2970.

the German Ambassador at Vienna, had shortly before warned that these supply problems generated considerable resentment in the Austrian capital and that consequently the greatest circumspection must be exercised there. Tschirschky favored putting the business under one supreme coordinating head,[44] and Goltz was given this kind of plenary power.

However, an astonishing revelation came to the attention of the German Foreign Ministry at the beginning of March: Schenker and Company of Vienna, the principal Austrian shipper to the Ottoman Empire, had for some months been sending supplies to the armies of the Russian Tsar. A German agent happened on this information in Genoa, where one of Schenker's men was buying oranges and lemons for shipment to Russia. This man further revealed that he had recently bought large quantities of pepper and coffee for the Russians and was presently scouting about for some medicines needed by the imperial troops. These materials were shipped across Hungary to Rumania and there reloaded by a secret Russian subcontractor. Of the whole enterprise the Rumanian Finance Minister, Costinescu, was perfectly well aware, and, as it turned out, so was the Austrian government.[45]

Before raising an official protest at Vienna, the German government began a private investigation so that as much as possible could be learned before the Ballplatz dropped the curtain of bureaucratic silence. The deposition of a Hungarian customs official was obtained. It carried the additional revelation that Schenker was delivering to the Russians segments of official Austrian army war films, especially those of the less successful field operations. They were shown to the Tsar's troops to instill morale and self-confidence. The exact dates of the shipments to Russia, throughout January and February, were also ascertained.[46] Then Tschirschky addressed himself directly to

[44] Tschirschky to Foreign Ministry, Jan. 11, 1915, *ibid.*, Bd. 5, #A1257.
[45] Deposition to the Hungarian Minister of Justice, March 5 to 18, 1915, *ibid.*, Bd. 6, no number.
[46] *Ibid.*

the management of Schenker and Company, which admitted that it had sent out the contraband but insisted at the same time that the Austrian War Ministry was fully apprised of what was going on. The management assumed, according to Tschirschky, that Vienna had told Berlin.[47] Still later, Ambassador Michahelles learned at Sofia that employees of Schenker in Bulgaria had given Russian espionage agents copies of all their bills of lading. The Russian embassy in Sofia thus knew minutely the nature and the time of everything shipped to the Turks. This information Michahelles judged to be irrefutable, because its source was the Bulgarian Prime Minister, Vasil Radoslavow.[48]

The situation entitled Berlin to raise the stormiest of protests, yet nothing seems to have followed on the private investigations of the German embassy in Vienna, probably for the uncomfortably simple reason that Bismarck had learned long ago: Austria, if not the best of Germany's allies, was often the only one. The German government was therefore reduced to all kinds of amusing and pathetic expedients to avoid calling a sharp halt at the Ballplatz to Austrian machinations. The War Ministry in Berlin considered sending up balloons from bases along the south Hungarian frontier, so that the entire distance to Turkey could be traversed by air. The opinion of Ambassador Michahelles was solicited on this scheme, but he expressed doubts that adequate reception facilities could be built or that the contraptions could stay aloft long enough.[49] Another idea put forth in Berlin was to bring large quantities of German beer on board the supply trains to make the transportation workers friendlier and more circumspect. Tschirschky argued against the beer.[50] Obviously, if too much of it were consumed en route, it would have an effect on the local people just opposite from what the Germans in-

[47] Schenker and Co. to Foreign Ministry, through Tschirschky, Apr. 7, 1915, *ibid.*, Bd. 7, #A12422.

[48] Michahelles to Bethmann, Apr. 19, 1915, *ibid.*, #A13912.

[49] Michahelles to Foreign Ministry, Apr. 2, 1915, *ibid.*, #A11749.

[50] Zimmermann to Tschirschky, April 8, 1915, *ibid.*, #A12302; Tschirschky to Foreign Ministry, Apr. 10, 1915, *ibid.*, #A12556. Some of the barrels were to have contained munitions.

tended. And the authors of the proposal were very naive indeed if they thought that traditional Balkan cupidity could be washed away by even the best of Bavarian brews.

In April all freight rates were raised on Hungarian railroad lines.[51] The move was consistent with Vienna's recent tactics, but may have been a mistake, for this was a public gesture. The crimes of Austrian firms in the Balkans were so far known only to a few highly placed personages, but this latest piece of Austrian obstreperousness was something the general public could comprehend and resent. As such, it was fit material for individual consideration by the members of the Reichstag in Berlin, if not for collective debate by that body. At the request of the German Foreign Ministry, therefore, Matthias Erzberger, a prominent Reichstag leader, left for Vienna and Budapest to interview representatives of Schenker and Company and its associated firms.

On the face of it, the Erzberger mission was superfluous; the guilt of the Austrian ally had already been established, and Erzberger's research would only swell an already heavy dossier. On the other hand, this man's public character, his facility with the pen and easy access to the newspapers were all calculated to impress the Austrians by means denied the professional diplomat. Berlin could hope the Ballplatz might be cowed by the specter of an outraged German public opinion summoned up by the traveling Reichstag delegate.

Erzberger turned up fresh evidence. After a number of interviews with Viennese businessmen, he was able to report that the Austrians were choking off not only Turkish war supplies but also purely civilian products that German industries usually supplied to the East European market. Before the war thousands of shoes and farmers' boots were shipped to Rumania and Bulgaria, and Schenker was awarded much of the carrying business. Erzberger had evidence that now, instead of reaching consignees, the footwear was willfully held up or dumped in Transylvania.

[51] General Consul Fürstenberg at Budapest to Foreign Ministry, Apr. 20, 1915, *ibid.*, #A13694.

In the meantime, the delivery of Austrian shoes was being in every way accelerated to steal the former German market. This information would anger the average German wage earner probably more than Erzberger's other disclosure: Serbia had received foodstuffs and even guns through Schenker since the outbreak of the war.[52]

From a politician's point of view, the results of his trip were thoroughly satisfactory to Erzberger. He suggested to the Foreign Ministry that if he were sent again to Vienna, he would return with still more damning charges against the Austrians. This very self-confidence may in fact explain why, though he was sent back, more was not made of the results of his first and second trips. The documents indicate that at least some of the professional diplomats resented the meddlings of this amateur and begrudged him his influence with Jagow. The Foreign Minister believed that Erzberger's ideas had promise, yet even Jagow must have been aware that the Reichstag deputy would enlarge every little success into a major triumph for himself and his Center party. Apparently Ambassador Bussche in Bucharest intended that this should not happen, because he did his best to belittle the allegations of Erzberger and minimized the losses to German business that the Reichstag deputy ascribed to Austrian intrigue. He went so far as to assert that neither Bulgaria nor Turkey required all the things the Germans were attempting to bring through, even though the Central Powers were hotly entreating a Bulgarian alliance, and the Turks were confronted by a serious Entente attack on the Dardanelles. Michahelles at Sofia sharply criticized these opinions of his colleague to Jagow.[53] They were discounted, but very likely they imposed some restrictions on such future assignments for Erzberger, reduced his credibility somewhat, and certainly revealed how much professional caste consciousness rather than patriotism determined German diplomacy at this and other critical points.

Not much better than Bussche was the German representative

[52] Erzberger to Foreign Ministry, May 14, 1915, *ibid.*, Bd. 8, #A17279.
[53] Michahelles to Foreign Ministry, June 15, 1915, *ibid.*, Bd. 9, #A18942.

in Vienna. He had given Erzberger minimal assistance during his stay in the Austrian capital and on the whole maintained a studied indifference toward the supply problems of the Turkish front. The German War Ministry, continuing to pay dearly in valuable commodities for the dispatch of supplies to the Turks and mindful of Rumanian objections, had taken to concealing war materials between a double wall of specially constructed and allegedly empty boxcars. The purpose of this stratagem was to avoid those compromising incidents that Rumanian customs men were so expert at maximizing and to satisfy the Rumanian King, who had given private assurances of his good will but added that he thought Germany was not always sufficiently careful to guard his government from incrimination. The "boxcar method" had Costinescu's sanction and was possibly concocted by him; but Tschirschky and Bussche collaborated to have one such train stopped and searched at the Bulgar-Rumanian frontier, justifying their actions as proof of Germany's respect for the neutrality of the two Balkan states and for the canons of international law.[54] Against the background of the Dardanelles emergency, such proofs were out of place and extremely perilous.

Reports of this border fiasco soon appeared in the Rumanian newspapers, the Bratianu government naturally denying any complicity in the matter. Within a few days, Matthias Erzberger emphasized to Chancellor Bethmann that this latest incident demonstrated once more the futility of dealing with Rumanian politicians, whose bottomless venality could never be plumbed. Germany's sounder course, the Center leader continued, was to marshal Rumanian public opinion against the Bucharest regime, as earlier he had recommended that German public opinion be used to checkmate Austrian duplicity. On the basis of information gathered during a second tour of the Balkans, Erzberger asserted that a critical shortage of sugar was the weak point of the Rumanian economy. If the Germans were cleverly to exploit that weakness and combine generous allocations of sugar with war

[54] Michahelles to Foreign Ministry, June 18 and 20, 1915, *ibid.*, #A3240, #A3268.

materials for the Turkish forces, the Rumanian people would assault any of their bureaucrats who attempted to stop the supply
convoys in their passage south.[55]

This kind of blackmail had mildly revolutionary overtones. It
was the sort of thing to which the German government would
have recourse later in the war, but for which, at this earlier
stage, it had no stomach. Furthermore, Germany was not Rumania's only source of plentiful sugar; as Erzberger knew, Austria had begun filling up the gaps from her own resources.
Bussche, when the Erzberger memorandum was referred to him
as the man best able to gauge Rumanian opinion on the spot,
scoffed at the proposal and described the Rumanians as so dull
and long-suffering as to be able to do without sugar indefinitely, and without much else besides. He thought Erzberger too
sanguine and prone to exaggerate.[56] The Ambassador may very
well have been right, but one suspects that it was Erzberger's
lower-middle-class, equalitarian touch as much as any lack of
cool reason that denied his ideas serious consideration at the
Wilhelmstrasse.

The hostility of Jagow's department agreed, moreover, with
the opinions of German banking circles. Arthur von Gwinner,
director of the Deutsche Bank, advised against any attempts to
go over the heads or behind the backs of the Rumanian cabinet.
Such maneuvers might prejudice these men against German enterprise after the war. Gwinner himself had no aversion to such
dealings with the men in Bucharest and, in fact, he was prepared to use his contacts to supply Costinescu with certain types
of machinery of great value and highly technical design. The
Rumanian Finance Minister could then sell these himself, acquir-
ing an attractive private income and coverage against a future
election reverse.[57]

[55] Erzberger to Bethmann, June 22, 1915, *ibid.*, #A19606.
[56] Bussche to Foreign Ministry, June 23, 1915, *ibid.*, #A19828.
[57] Deutsche Bank to Foreign Ministry, May 1, 1915, *ibid.*, Bd. 7,
#A15029.

The longer this huckstering continued, the greater became the danger not only to Germany's material and money reserves but also to her prestige in the Balkan Peninsula. Germany had so far acquired no new allies in that area but rather, according to a report from Athens, was in danger of clashing with a new enemy. The German embassy reported that the Greek ministers and the Greek people were intently watching the course of the Dardanelles fighting and thought the stories of German transportational difficulties offered new proof of the imminent fall of Constantinople. There was talk of a revival of the Byzantine imperium, and the German Foreign Ministry was urged to stop such rumors and stem their deleterious effect on Turkish morale.[58] At this report, Jagow was so disturbed that he flatly told the Pera embassy that all German attempts to bolster Turkish armaments substantially had failed, and no more could be undertaken for fear of compromising diplomatic ramifications. The Ambassador was instructed to inquire of the Turkish government whether it had exhausted all means to produce its own munitions and medicines.[59] Of course, the German Foreign Minister knew the answer and, without saying so, was throwing up this whole business, which had obliged him to annoy the members of his department and to call in persons whom they declined to regard as other than trespassers.

However, the Balkan tribute did not stop, because Erzberger, intervening for the last time in the supply question, instilled yet a little more fight into the German Foreign Minister. The Catholic Center leader reported to the Wilhelmstrasse that, according to his own confidants, the Rumanians were so disturbed at Greece's new aggressiveness and the realignment of Balkan frontiers it might entail that they had come to their senses and would cease to make difficulties.[60] Ambassador Bussche, on the

[58] Mirbach to Foreign Ministry, July 12, 1915, *ibid.*, Bd. 9, #A21352.
[59] Jagow to German Embassy, Constantinople, July 12, 1915, *ibid.*, #A3675.
[60] Erzberger to Bethmann, July 22, 1915, *ibid.*, #A3832.

other hand, declared that there were no grounds for such optimism, that Erzberger got most of his information "from Jewish
vegetable peddlars," and that he should keep his fingers out of
Rumanian politics.[61]

Nevertheless, the efforts of the German military mission at
Constantinople seem to have corroborated Erzberger's opinion
rather than that of the German representative in Bucharest. Marshal von der Goltz sent Bronsart von Schellendorff on special
mission to the Rumanian capital, and he was there able to arrive
at an arrangement whereby small arms and medicines would be
sent down to Turkey in diplomatic dispatch bags of one hundred
kilograms capacity each. While the amounts thus conveyed
would be much smaller than those trucked into Turkey, the Rumanian government guaranteed that they would not be tampered with or in any way impeded. Significantly, Bronsart observed in his report to General Headquarters that the packing of
such dispatch cases should always be done under the supervision
of army personnel and absolutely without the interference of the
German diplomatic corps.[62]

Costinescu and Bronsart had agreed that a maximum of
thirty-six dispatch bags could cross Rumanian territory per week.
This privilege was understood to extend also to Austrian diplomatic personnel. Though it was assumed that they would make
as full use of their diplomatic immunity as their German ally,
later evidence shows that Austrian diplomatic couriers rarely
transported the maximum numbers of cases and did not fill them
with the requisite materials.[63] When challenged about these de-
ficiencies, Vienna professed alarm at reports that Russia was preparing to bombard the Rumanian port of Constantza in retalia-
tion for the Britianu ministry's willful violations of its neutrality.
The pessimistic Bussche reported that the British Foreign Office,
through its missions in Bern and at The Hague, was also keeping

[61] Bussche to Foreign Ministry, July 25, 1915, ibid., #A3880.

[62] Bronsart to War Ministry, July 17, 1915, ibid., #A22102.

[63] Bussche to Foreign Ministry, Oct. 17 and 30, 1915, ibid., Bd. 10,
#A30149, #A31485.

a careful tally of these violations and sought to deepen the apprehensions of his chief as to London's purpose.[64]

The supply problem was not definitely settled until the Central Powers had overwhelmed Serbia in the campaign beginning October 6, 1915. With Bulgarian collaboration, confirmed by the military convention signed at Pless on September 6, they drove the Serbian defenders back into Montenegro and Albania by November 24. The artillery barrage mounted by the Serbs on their shore of the Danube River was destroyed before that, and on October 29, a Hungarian steamer arrived at Widdin by the river route. Emperor William sent his congratulations to Chancellor Bethmann and commended the "valor" of the Bulgarians in throwing their lot with the Austro-German coalition. With the success of the negotiations with the Sofia government, in the Emperor's opinion, "wonderful prospects open out before us." [65]

Before concluding this discussion of the transportation problem, it would be well to observe that these prospects might have dawned much sooner. General Erich von Falkenhayn formulated plans for an offensive against Serbia as early as November 14, 1914. When Austrian forces were repulsed by the Serbs in the following month, Falkenhayn offered three German divisions to the chief of the Austrian General Staff, Franz Conrad von Hötzendorf, to implement his Serbian proposals. However, Conrad was cool toward any allocation of manpower to break down the Serbian barrier to Turkey. He argued that it was useless to beat the Serbs as long as they could tap the resources of an unvanquished Russia. The main thrust should therefore go against the Tsar's troops and any available German manpower should be

[64] Bussche to Foreign Ministry, Aug. 13 and 16, 1915, *ibid.*, #A23902, number obscured.

[65] Emperor William to Bethmann, Oct. 31, 1915, *ibid.*, #A31556. Michahelles estimated that about six hundred tons of supplies for Turkey would then begin to travel the Danube daily (Michahelles to Foreign Ministry, Oct. 31, 1915, *ibid.*, Bd. 11, #A31598). A notice of the *Frankfurter Zeitung*, December 28, 1915, shows that the problem was still not completely solved. The paper complains that transport rates were still too high in Austrian territory. It urges the Vienna government "to make sacrifices for the common war effort."

assigned to this effort. Conrad was also afraid that the Serbs would retaliate with a drive on Budapest for any renewed Austrian pressure on their lines. Finally, he warned that unless Russia was knocked out of the war, neutral Italy and Rumania would swing over to the Entente side. If the last happened, Conrad held, it would be immaterial whether or not the Turkish front was adequately supplied. Later the General changed his mind, but the Germans felt that he had forced them earlier in the war to protracted, exasperating, and expensive solutions of their supply difficulties.[66]

Until the documents for this period are released by the Ottoman Archives, there will be no way of gauging fully the Turkish reaction to their political and military extremities of early 1915 or the extent to which they were aware of the recurrent clashes between their allies. Western evidence indicates that the Turks were not satisfied with the efforts made in their behalf and secretly suspicious that the Central Powers had not done their utmost. The sacrifices of the Dardanelles oversensitized a Turkish nationalism and already keen racial pride, and even the Germans admitted that the supplies brought to Constantinople were indecisive, almost pitiable. They were mostly medicines, of small bulk but of great ultimate value. Yet they were not the guns or heavy shot needed to repulse the Entente ships pressing the Dardanelles and win a battle whose loss would mean the end of the Ottoman Empire.

Among the common people there was little disposition to commend German efforts. The wrangling in Bucharest and Sofia was unknown to them, food prices were high in the bazaars, and the behavior of some of the German soldiers was unbearably arrogant in the streets. German merchants in the capital began to send their families home, and the military mission ordered its

[66] Carl Mühlmann, *Das Deutsch-Türkische Waffenbündnis im Weltkriege* (Leipzig, 1940), pp. 39, 40–49. For Conrad's argument, see Franz Conrad von Hötzendorf, *Aus meiner Dienstzeit 1906–18* (Vienna, 1923–1925), V, 310, 818–821, 850–853.

men to doff their uniforms when not on duty.[67] The Porte itself
was only icily correct toward General Liman, because some of
his officers, when on furlough in Germany, expressed contempt
for the Turks and referred to the country as "louse land." To another sobriquet, "Enverland," the Grand Vizier also took exception, perhaps less because it was inaccurate than because it
seemed a painful personal insult.[68]

The Austrians chose this time to make demands that could not
but appear extortionate. For some months they had been concerned about the fate of Roman Catholic endowments in the Ottoman Empire, and Pallavicini took at face value every rumor
that the Young Turks intended to confiscate them. From sources
at the Vatican, he was informed that even if the Turks did not
go so far, they would reconstitute the Catholic Church on a patriarchal basis after or even during the war. As Pallavicini described it, this plan would have created a council of Catholic
laymen empowered by the Turkish government, though not of
course by the Roman Papacy, to elect a patriarch. The patriarch
would then appoint his suffragan bishops and lay down general
jurisdictional rules for them. The entire establishment would
tender the Pope only the loosest obedience, and the primacy of
secular control inherent in the scheme brought down the wrath

[67] Bax-Ironside, British Minister in Sofia, to Grey #125/40782, Apr. 7,
1915, P.R.O., F.O. 371/2487.
[68] Wangenheim to Foreign Ministry, May 11, 1915, A.A. Türkei #139,
Bd. 35, #A15741. This kind of barracks-room sarcasm spread as far as
France, where it was quoted by *Le Matin,* much to the mortification of the
Ottoman embassy in Berlin, which promptly registered a protest. The Imperial German government tried to reprimand the personnel involved, but
in some cases was unsuccessful because they were Bavarian subjects. The
War Ministry in Munich jealously guarded its prerogatives against Berlin,
and no stiffer punishment than a change of assignment was given. The case
of Bavarian Captain Franz Endres, a member of the staff of Kress von
Kressenstein, was typical. He publicly ridiculed the defenses of the Dardanelles and the Sultan, but Wangenheim, much to his perturbation, was
unable to do much about it. See a considerable correspondence about this
and similar incidents in *Geh. Staatsarchiv München,* File MA95027, especially #14191, #41002, #15752 for April–May, 1915.

of the Papal Delegate in Constantinople. This was Monsignor Angelo Dolci, who spurred Pallavicini to interrogate the Grand Vizier on the matter and warned the Austrian Ambassador that the Porte intended to act quickly and by surprise.[69]

Quite apart from the Papal Emissary's fears, the Austrian government had long cherished hopes of supplanting France as the paramount protector of Catholic interests in the Near East. Such a religious policy would be the natural complement of an economic ascendancy that Pallavicini hoped to build up by increasing railroad connections to Turkey via Bulgaria. These lines were to be built with Austrian capital and were speculated upon before Dolci interjected his own fanatic zeal and frenzy.[70] Therefore neither man was disposed to doubt that grounds existed for rumors of a new governmental anti-Catholic policy, and Said Halim got nowhere when he denied these allegations in answer to Pallavicini's official protest. The Austrian representative implied that no more material aid would be forthcoming if the government ignored a question so close to the Habsburgs' Catholic conscience. Before he left the Porte, he had extracted from the Grand Vizier an official order to all the *valis* cautioning them against any damage to Christian property and a personal promise to have the patriarchal project shelved in the Committee of Union and Progress.[71]

Beyond question, the Grand Vizier conceded in an ill humor. He hardly understood the point at issue, but was certainly right in considering it inappropriate to conditions of a military emergency. The sum total of this Austrian move was to spread Turkish demoralization from the popular level to the higher echelons of Turkish bureaucracy. In these it had never entirely been absent, and the conspiracy of Rahmi Bey has already been mentioned. Dissatisfaction now spread as far east as Baghdad, and the American consul in that city was approached by the provin-

[69] Pallavicini to Burian #21/p, Mar. 18, 1915, H.H.S.A. Türkei Karton 209.
[70] Pallavicini to Burian #9/p, Jan. 28, 1915, *ibid.*
[71] Pallavicini to Burian #21/p/b, Mar. 18, 1915, *ibid.*

cial governor-general, who offered to reveal the Committee's secret code and use his resources for a revolution against the Sultan's ministers. The police of the Mesopotamian area were
described as thoroughly disaffected and unlikely to quell any
popular insurrection when it was once sparked from the outside.
Morgenthau was quite excited at the news and believed that the
Baghdad malcontents should be encouraged and pushed on-
ward.[72]

The American Ambassador had apparently had a change of
heart. It will be recalled that before the war he was anything
but interventionist. He might have restricted German maritime
ascendancy in Turkish waters during the previous autumn and
encouraged the pacifists in both Berlin and Constantinople, yet
he had done nothing and interpreted his government's neutrality
in the most modest and unimaginative manner. Now he recommended a forward policy because, by their own admission, the
Germans had overplayed their hand. While they were tolerated
in the capital, their lives were imperiled as soon as they moved
into the country districts. Morgenthau was struck by the hostility
of the provincial administration to the foreign policy of the central government and found at every hand proofs of divergence
between the *valis* and the Committee. This cost the Germans
dearly. Their paper money was accepted in Stamboul, but hard
cash was required of them for everything on the march. With
one hand they gave gold to the Turks while with the other, as
Morgenthau probably did not know, they dropped it into the
pockets of Costinescu and his Rumanian cohorts. The same
conditions prevailed along the line of the Baghdad Railway as in
the provincial markets, and the workers, refusing anything but
gold, had thrown down their tools and left construction at a
standstill.[73]

Everything reported by Morgenthau is corroborated in the
German dispatches. The American may even have gotten his in-

[72] Morgenthau to Secretary of State, Feb. 10, 1915, D.S., #867.00/741.
[73] Morgenthau to Secretary of State, Enclosure from Charles Brissel, Consul in Baghdad, Feb. 24, 1915, *ibid.*, #867.00/751.

formation from German embassy personnel, with whom he remained at all times cordial. Between the threats of the Austrians and the chronically dangerous antics of Liman von Sanders, a government more united than the Turks would have had no choice but to work for a separate peace. Abundant discouragements existed before the Dardanelles attack and only multiplied during that engagement. The difficulties of supply turned into the worse horrors of heavy casualty losses. The Turks blamed these on the chief of the German military mission, because however much he was later admired from the outside, those close to his staff felt that he had hindered as much as helped the final repulse of the Entente. When the advance of the Entente ships toward the Straits was first reported, Liman remained curiously unperturbed and would not recommend a regrouping of the troops in the capital district.[74] He instead left too many men in the Adrianople theater and obliged Bronsart von Schellendorff, as Enver's chief of staff, to recall these forces on his own authority. Bronsart was immediately charged with insubordination because, though Enver's second, he was also subject as a German officer to the head of the military mission. Enver, however, thoroughly vindicated his conduct and once again recommended the recall of Liman.[75] By one account, he did even more and contrived a plot against the German general's life.[76] Whether or not this particular allegation is true does not matter so much as the pervasive bitterness which the odd conduct of Liman von Sanders only served to spread.

Neither the temper of the times, given the military situation, nor the behavior of the man, given his past performance, is then

[74] Wangenheim to Foreign Ministry, Mar. 2, 1915, A.A. Türkei #139, Bd. 34, #A7636.

[75] Enver to Emperor William, Mar. 2, 1915, enclosed in Wangenheim to Foreign Ministry, same date, *ibid.*, #A7708.

[76] Robert Rhodes James, *Gallipoli* (New York, 1965), p. 254. James states that Enver had Liman given poison, which seriously sickened but did not kill him. Thereafter, Liman used his own cook to prepare all his meals. During his internment on Malta of 1919, Liman purportedly told all this to the British authorities. I have not found any further documentary evidence for the incident.

really so striking as the ease with which German diplomacy adjusted to both. If Wangenheim's conduct is an accurate indicator, the German embassy shared the pessimism of the Turks and would have helped it to its natural conclusion. Whether he had the sanction of Berlin for his conduct is not clear from the evidence, but British documents show that the German Ambassador made a move for peace in late January, 1915. He sent Paul Weitz, no stranger to such commissions, to interview Mr. Arthur Nias, director general of the Imperial Ottoman Bank at Constantinople. Nias was a British subject, but despite the outbreak of war, had not had his personal liberty curtailed in any way. His experience was not atypical and says much about Turkey's weak security control, in which Germany acquiesced until the end of the fighting. Weitz detailed the feud between General Liman and Wangenheim and vividly emphasized the vexation of the German Ambassador. Wangenheim was quoted as saying that the Germans had "mismanaged" the situation, that only 5 per cent of the Turks were Germanophile, another 5 per cent professed to be but lied, and 90 per cent of the Turks frankly hated the Germans. Mines and ammunition were perilously short at the Straits, other supplies were bogged down in Rumania, and even the rudder of the *Goeben* was so corroded that it could not much longer remain dependably in use.[77]

What Weitz said subsequently became a minute for the inspection of the British cabinet. Lord Grey, the Foreign Secretary, was much interested in its contents and used them to initiate discussions with the Russians and French. All parties, however, handled the Nias-Weitz disclosures cautiously, because materials of this kind were always suspect at the source and because, in this case, they seemed to cross with other peace overtures transmitted from Athens. Prime Minister Venizelos reported himself in possession of several pledges from members of the Turkish parliamentary opposition that Turkey would get out of the war if her empire was left "unimpaired." Grey believed

[77] Cabinet Minute by Oliphant #19780, London, Feb. 16, 1915, P.R.O., F.O. 371/2481.

that this qualification about Ottoman territorial integrity also covered the German bid and, as he noted in the margin, was in that case inadmissible because of previous promises to the Russian government. Grey would entertain a solution that did not require the "complete disappearance" of the Ottoman Empire, but he was firmly resolved that Russia must be awarded the dominant position at the Straits. The French Foreign Office, apprised of this latest news from Constantinople, concurred in Grey's decision, and even the Greeks, not to speak of the Russians, would have opposed any attempt to accept the Turco-German offer as it stood, or was believed to stand. Venizelos, while transmitting these peace bids, had expressly added that he did not support them in any way.[78]

This was not the end of Wangenheim's peace feelers, as it might have been had the Ambassador suspected that Sazonov, in some final observations on the Nias-Weitz incident, was demanding not only the Straits but the entire eviction of Turkey from Europe for all time. One more effort was made under his auspices, for about March 12, 1915, the British ship *Euryalus* entered the harbor of Smyrna and received on board emissaries from the incorrigible intriguer Rahmi Bey. About a month earlier, the Vali had made stabs at an armistice, known to the Austrians and favored by them with a discreet silence. Now he made a second attempt with German approval and protection.

The conference between the British officers and the Vali's men had scarcely begun when a Turkish torpedo boat came into sight and anchored so close that its all-German crew was easily seen. Neither the Turkish nor the British vessel made any attempt at attack, and the American consul who observed the whole encounter concluded that it was prearranged. The presence of two

[78] Grey to Buchanan #206/14967, Feb. 10, 1915, *ibid.;* Buchanan to Grey #225/24844, Feb. 27, 1915, *ibid.* It should be pointed out that while the parliamentary opposition, the provincial bureaucracy, and the German embassy, each by a different approach, seemed ready to work for peace, the Porte and Enver would not likely have cooperated. With the defeats at Sarikamish and Suez so fresh, the Turkish government *per se* was in no position to achieve decent terms, as has been previously mentioned.

belligerent ships was probably intended as a kind of counter-guarantee, and Consul Horton was not far wrong when he suggested that the British had deliberately let the torpedo boat out of the Straits. It signified German approval of Rahmi's proposals. These were that the Vali should be proclaimed Sultan in return for surrendering his province to the Entente.

However, the British were not willing to go so high with the Turk. They offered him considerable money and a "high office," but they did not propose to liquidate the House of Osman. Furthermore, they would not engage in another conference until all foreign military personnel had been expelled from the Ottoman Empire. In other words, the good offices of the Germans were not to be recognized, much less rewarded. Consul Horton had all these details from the German consul at Smyrna, who seemed informed of the plot at every stage.[79]

Though the negotiators aboard the *Euryalus* were unable to reach an agreement, the conversation was not entirely unsatisfactory from the German point of view. Wangenheim's embassy had been able to enlist the benevolent actions of Morgenthau and his staff in the cause of a mediated peace, and the evidence indicates that the American Ambassador was sincerely grateful to his German colleague for efforts the latter made to secure an asylum in Turkey for refugee Jews from Russia.[80] As long as he held his post in Constantinople, Wangenheim was quick to use the Zion-

[79] Consul George Horton in Smyrna to Morgenthau, Mar. 12, 1915, D.S., #867.00/753; Horton to Secretary of State, Mar. 13, 1915, *ibid.*, #867.00/-755. In many of his speeches, Talaat throughout the war continued to refer to Rahmi Bey as his "most trusted friend." Such expressions would seem to indicate that Talaat either did not know of Rahmi's intrigues or, if he did, approved of them. It is furthermore likely that Djavid was behind some of these moves. Djavid recalled later that about March, 1915, he was approached in Berlin about a separate peace by persons from the staffs of A. Briand and T. Delcassé. He informed Jagow and Zimmermann, both of whom were described as "enthusiastic," to follow up these leads, though Zimmermann expressed some doubts about Delcassé's reliability (Bayur, III/I, 294; III/II, 159–161).

[80] Wangenheim to Foreign Ministry, Jan. 17, 1915, A.A. Türkei #134, Bd. 33, #A2047. Apparently, this activity had been continuing for some time.

ist question to prod the American, who, if not as anti-German as
he later made himself out to be, was not by nature an assertive
or hard-working diplomat.

A month later, the British in Egypt used American diplomatic
personnel to transmit peace feelers to Djemal Pasha in Syria.
These hinted strongly at a partition of the Ottoman Empire,
with Djemal enthroned as king of an independent Syria.[81] The
implication might further have been intended that Smyrna,
though not the entire Ottoman Empire, might pass to Rahmi
Bey. If the second assumption is correct, it would indicate that
the British regretted and were ready to revise the adamant position taken aboard the *Euryalus*. Confirmation of the Straits to
Russia was, of course, still assumed at London, but the creation
of a confederacy of militarily weak Ottoman satrapies would not
have prejudiced the Tsar's interests at all.

But of their primary aim the *Euryalus* conversations failed.
Peace was no nearer in sight. The natural consequence was to
discredit those persons in the German government who believed
that the allies were tractable. Their opponents could now even
argue that negotiations would prove fruitless until the British
were more fully convinced of the magnitude and reality of German control over the Ottoman Empire. In the ensuing months,
especially in the matter of the Baghdad Railway, the Berlin government attempted to widen and deepen its commitments in
Turkey. Its purpose, on the one hand, was to help prosecute the
war; but on the other hand, it intended as fully to convince the
allies that it had something really valuable to give away at the
negotiating table.

The Baghdad Railway

With such an aim ultimately in view, the Wilhelmstrasse took
up the problems of the Baghdad Railway. As originally planned,
the line from Constantinople to Baghdad was to be 1,255 miles

[81] J. W. Oman, Commanding Officer, U.S.S. *Carolina*, to Secretary of the
Navy, Apr. 6, 1915, D.S., #867.00/758.

in extent. It was to be built by two German concessionaires, the Anatolische-Eisenbahn-Gesellschaft, organized in 1888, and the Baghdad-Eisenbahn-Gesellschaft (1903), both owned by a financial syndicate whose controlling member was the Deutsche Bank. As the war approached, there were some signs that investors had lost interest in the project. It proved impossible to sell out an issue of Ottoman government bonds, intended to raise 119 million francs, on the European market. Future construction on the line was thereby put in doubt, and at the outbreak of war only 867 miles of track had been laid down and not even all of these were in consecutive stretches. There were very long breaks all along the line, and the road segments, of questionable military utility at best, were so bad that not even civilian traffic was possible upon them. The two greatest obstacles were the mountain chains of the Taurus and the Amanus. These had not yet been cut by tunnels, and supplies were slowly and arduously transported over them by trucks and draught animals. The trip from Baghdad to Constantinople took at least twenty-two days under these conditions, and unless German engineering could correct them, supply and conveyance to the Syrian and Mesopotamian theaters would remain minimal.[82]

A solution for these difficulties should have been sought at the earliest possible moment or, barring it, the war should not have been allowed to ramify into Anatolia and the Syrian littoral. Persons who had travelled the terrain and knew the problems at firsthand stressed this to the German General Staff. Professor Ernst Jaeckh told General von Falkenhayn that the line must be in first-class working order for the Egyptian campaign to succeed. But until the end of 1914, Falkenhayn did not believe that the condition of the lines would necessarily exclude a victory at the Suez Canal. In fact the General raised the old argument, which provoked him when expounded by others, that the war

[82] McEntee, The World War, pp. 144–145; Mühlmann, Deutsch-Türkische Waffenbündnis, pp. 184–187; and Ulrich Trumpener, Germany and the Ottoman Empire 1914–1918 (Princeton, 1968), pp. 285–286.

would be won on the Russian front and that the outcome of the Canal venture, one way or the other, would not be decisive.[83] Only when there was no immediate strategic objective in sight did the General worry about the ramshackle condition of the Constantinople-Baghdad line.

Professor Jaeckh put the problem in a new light. Recognizing that the events of early February had made it impossible for Germany to annex the Canal in the immediate future, the professor still insisted that a good railroad connection with Syria and the Sinai Peninsula would become a means of threatening the British at the peace conference and bringing them there sooner. If Germany clarified and intensified her threat to the Canal, the British would be more willing to award the Germans "a free passage" from Berlin to Constantinople via the Danube River. While bright prospects beckoned to German enterprise in the Ottoman Empire, somewhat less glamorous but ultimately more secure opportunities lay in the Balkan Peninsula. To realize these, the German government must get a firm hold on the Rumanian railway system and prevent the recurrence of the congestion of the Danube from which the war effort suffered so expensively at just that time. Jaeckh contended that the Wilhelmstrasse must be prepared to make significant exchanges with the Entente powers to forestall their objections and compensate them for any territories the Germans might pick up.[84] For while he mentioned only Rumania specifically, he implied that German aspirations would not end there but might also engross Serbia in some way and require the end of international control of Danube navigation.

Jaeckh believed that he had made a tremendous impression at General Staff Headquarters. Falkenhayn was quoted as saying that he had been given "a new historical insight," and the professor also named General Helmuth von Moltke and Emperor William as converts to his thesis. The Emperor supposedly had

[83] Ernst Jaeckh, *Der goldene Pflug, Lebensernte eines Weltbürgers* (Stuttgart, 1954), pp. 220–227.

[84] Jaeckh's résumé of a conversation with Falkenhayn, for Zimmermann, Feb. 13, 1915, A.A. Türkei #152, Bd. 79, #A5647.

promised to order personally the acceleration of construction on the Baghdad line, even though the effort might be financially disadvantageous for his government.[85] In the meantime, the professor was kept on call for more high-level consultations. His advice, his books, and even his personal maps of the Turkish area were solicited by German political and military leaders. But the very fact that the Foreign and War Ministries did not have accurate maps [86]—and we have Jaeckh's word that they did not—portended that in the end the professor's fervency would remain frustrated and unharnessed. While the conviction that Turkey was not primarily a military problem gave Jaeckh no difficulty, the generals were not comfortable with the idea that the Ottoman Empire was more a diplomatic chess piece than a battlefield challenge. This idea hampered both their diplomatic and military planning.

Falkenhayn seems to have been the first to recover from his novitiate's enthusiasm. While the thought of a Balkan ascendancy, as painted by Jaeckh, had definite allure, the costs of tunneling through the Taurus and Amanus mountains repelled him the more he thought them over. Of these doubts he never really divested himself, but in the meantime he was willing to turn over Jaeckh's schemes to the inspection of other professionals. Marshal von der Goltz read them and returned a nearly ecstatic opinion. The Marshal urged the speediest completion of the Baghdad line, not only to make Balkan blackmail but to reach India itself. Goltz deplored the professional and public skepticism toward the idea and put himself on record as holding a march to the Indus Valley as completely within the range of sober possibility. He cited the careers of Alexander the Great, of Tamerlane, and particularly of the Persian Nadir Shah, who had conquered India with 100,000 men in 1739, and advanced from Afghanistan to Delhi in less than three months. Goltz concluded that a modern power like Germany could do it again with as few men and in as little time. If the costs mounted higher than planned, they would still be less in the long run than maintain-

[85] *Ibid.*   [86] Jaeckh, *Der goldene Pflug*, p. 228.

ing a state of constant preparedness in Germany against Britain's world dominion. That dominion turned on the control of India, where alone, the Marshal concluded, it could be decisively broken. German troops need not actually penetrate the subcontinent; even to approach it closely would force the British to the conference table.[87]

In a somewhat lower key, even General Liman von Sanders concurred. Construction of the Baghdad line should be resumed at once and at a brisker pace. Like the Emperor, he held that costs did not matter. Until all branches of the line attained perfect working order, the General would have commandeered every vehicle in the Ottoman Empire and with these hurled another army against the Suez Canal.[88]

The only dissenter, not surprisingly, was Ambassador von Wangenheim. He estimated that three years would be needed to tunnel the Taurus Mountains, though he thought the Amanus tunnel could be ready by the beginning of 1916. Both jobs, however, would depend on the availability of labor and might deny manpower to the fighting lines.[89] Of this latter possibility, his chiefs in Berlin were apparently not afraid; or considering the source, they were inclined to minimize it. In the middle of April, the General Staff had the Pera embassy informed of its formal approval of the intensive tunneling of the Taurus and Amanus mountains. The imperial government was prepared to advance the Porte a subsidy of forty million marks, which the Turks were expected to match or exceed. Their best financial expert, Djavid Bey, was invited to Berlin to conclude a formal agreement.[90]

The Turkish cabinet agreed in principle to accept the German subsidy as the basis of serious negotiations, and Djavid Bey arrived in Berlin on schedule.[91] Though in his discussions with the

[87] Memorandum on the Baghdad Railway, Feb. 26, 1915, A.A. Türkei #152, Bd. 79, #A8560.

[88] Comment on the Baghdad Railway, Feb. 20, 1915, *ibid*.

[89] Wangenheim to Foreign Ministry, Mar. 16, 1915, *ibid*., Bd. 80, #A9556.

[90] Foreign Ministry to German Embassy, Constantinople, Apr. 17, 1915, *ibid*., #A10398.

[91] Wangenheim to Foreign Ministry, Apr. 23, 1915, *ibid*., #A14009.

representatives of the Imperial Treasury, the Reichsbank, and the Deutsche Bank, he gave no hint of future difficulties, he was scarcely out of the capital when Wangenheim reported him moving to lay down a long train of petty traps and snares.[92] A dispatch from Vienna confirmed Wangenheim's suspicions: the Turk, en route through that city, told the German Ambassador, Tschirschky, that his government would match the subsidy only if the tunneling were completed in six months. It could not, given the exigencies of the war, tie up its funds for any longer period. Djavid claimed to have heard the Germans themselves suggest the six months' term in Berlin, but Tschirschky thought such an allegation scarcely credible.[93]

From one brazen act, Djavid glided swiftly to another. He departed Vienna for Rome. Italy was not yet at war with the Central Powers, and the Turkish emissary could discuss at leisure the financial problems of the Baghdad Railway with a number of Italian bankers. Several French bankers apparently joined the discussion, and Wangenheim was amazed to learn that Djavid had inquired their terms to complete the Baghdad line after the war.[94] A personal reprimand from Enver, issued at Wangenheim's request, ended Djavid's dalliance with the French. The financier was ordered to return to Berlin and make himself more tractable to the Germans.[95] Having returned, he proved no more agreeable, and Arthur von Gwinner, the head of the Deutsche Bank with whom he spoke, described their interview as thoroughly unsatisfactory. Djavid indicated that Turkey would meet her share of the costs, a sum equivalent to approximately forty million marks, but thereafter would expect the Germans to pay all freight charges for equipment shipped on the line. The Porte would further require an additional subsidy of 250,000 Turkish pounds to replace the funds allocated for the railroad.[96]

Djavid knew that however obnoxious he became, he had sub-

---

[92] Wangenheim to Foreign Ministry, Apr. 30, 1915, *ibid.,* #A14840.
[93] Tschirschky to Foreign Ministry, May 1, 1915, *ibid.,* #A14943.
[94] Wangenheim to Foreign Ministry, May 3, 1915, *ibid.,* #A15122.
[95] Wangenheim to Foreign Ministry, May 4, 1915, *ibid.,* #A15169.
[96] Gwinner to Anatolian Railway Company, May 4, 1915, *ibid.,* #A15176.

stantial backing in the Committee of Union and Progress. In supporting the Germans in this matter, Enver stood almost alone. Talaat, who as Minister of the Interior was entitled to be consulted on the project, opposed the completion of the line on any but Turkey's terms. He held that the additional subsidies were fully justified because the railroad was contributing to German strategical aims rather than Turkish ones. In Vienna, Ambassador Tschirschky declared that there was something to the Turkish argument. He personally believed that Djavid was a man of integrity, well versed in his calling and fair in his conduct of the negotiations with the Deutsche Bank. Unfortunately, he informed Djavid of his high esteem, and this disclosure did nothing to diminish the rapacity of Turkish financial demands.[97]

Both Gwinner and Karl Helfferich, Secretary of the Imperial Treasury, reminded Djavid that the troops to be carried on the Baghdad Railway would be Turkish.[98] Djavid nevertheless remained unabashed, and the German government once more crumpled under the brunt of Turkish effrontery. Jagow, for the Foreign Ministry, recommended to Emperor William that almost any Turkish demands should be conceded. Whether or not a second Canal campaign was mounted, the railroad had to be turned as quickly as possible into a substantial menace so as to "be a trump for us in negotiations with England." [99]

Chancellor Bethmann ordered Helfferich to be more accommodating to the Turkish demands. The banker was informed that the Baghdad Railway question was not, and never had been, simply a financial one. It had "the greatest value for negotiations." Germany must therefore be ready to settle with the Turks at low rates of interest and, if necessary, renounce the sums advanced forever.[100] Helfferich, in polite but definite language, was being told to hold his temper during his next meeting with Djavid Bey.

[97] Tschirschky to Foreign Ministry, May 5, 1915, *ibid.*, #A15273; Wangenheim to Foreign Ministry, May 12, 1915, *ibid.*, #A15851.
[98] Helfferich to Foreign Ministry, May 16, 1915, *ibid.*, Bd. 81, #A16269.
[99] Jagow to Emperor William, June 19, 1915, *ibid.*, #A19323.
[100] Bethmann to Helfferich, June 19, 1915, *ibid.*, #A19323.

Translated into money, these directives meant that the Germans tacitly agreed to assume the cost of construction. The promised forty-million-mark subsidy grew to payments of 360 million marks for Baghdad projects before the war was over. On the other hand, the Turks produced only 41,000 Turkish pounds by way of a Baghdad subsidy on one occasion, in 1916. Even this was not their own capital but rather money drawn from a series of low-interest German loans.[101] Essentially, the Turks contributed nothing to the transportation problem except their own obstructionism. They agreed to supply laborers and to begin the recruitment at once, but despite their pledged word and the excellent terms that the skill and persistence of Djavid Bey had extracted from Berlin, the new laborers were not forthcoming and those already on the job continued to desert. The engineers of the Baghdad Railway Company reported that they were disappearing into the Mesopotamian wilderness in increasing numbers, a sign believed to portend still heavier demands from the Porte.[102]

Because once again no unified control was exercised over German policy, and because so many German leaders set a high diplomatic value on the Baghdad Railway, little could be done to guard against future Turkish extortions. Jagow instructed the Treasury Secretary to put aside as much as 500,000 marks to cover unforeseen expenses and the possibility of total disavowal of its commitments by the Turkish government.[103] Jagow scented sabotage but had no answer except to attempt to buy off the saboteurs.

As soon as they had initialed the agreement, the Turks pressed for the appointment of one of their own people as chief revenue collector for the Baghdad Railway Company. The company re-

[101] Agreement between Djavid Bey and the Baghdad Railway Company, July 24, 1915, *ibid.*, Bd. 82, #A22227. For total German payments and Turkish reactions, see Trumpener, *Germany and the Ottoman Empire, 1914–1918*, pp. 303–304; 316.

[102] Baghdad Railway Company to Foreign Ministry, June 24, 1915, A.A. Türkei #152, Bd. 81, #A20936.

[103] Jagow to Helfferich, Sep. 28, 1915, *ibid.*, Bd. 82, #A28045.

jected the demand as inconceivable. Yet it was never possible to
convince the Turks that they had gone too far, because they
were encouraged by members of the German military
mission.[104] Wangenheim hounded Berlin to harden its line toward Djavid Bey, but the Ambassador was ignored. Bethmann
and Jagow held that any sacrifice could be justified as a military
necessity, an opinion which they took from the War Ministry
and Liman's entourage, who in turn had done much to instill it
into the Turkish leadership. With German opposition so weakened by recurrent internal dissension, it was no wonder that the
Turks began to talk about nationalization of all railroads after
the war. The appointment of a native collector of revenue was
seen by them as a preparation for this process.

Six months after Djavid had signed the subsidy agreements in
Berlin, the progress of the railroad was at a virtual standstill.
The important trunk line to Egypt, from Aleppo via Damascus
and Jerusalem, consisted of long stretches of track broken by still
longer stretches of land. The main line through Asia Minor had
moved no farther east than Ras-el-Ain. Lack of money was then
not so much the reason for the delay as lack of labor.[105] Of this
the government in Berlin had become increasingly aware as it
tried to dispose of the financial details with Djavid. For on the
normal losses due to desertion, the Turks imposed the casualties
of the Armenian massacres of 1915 and beyond. The victims of
these horrors were often laborers along the Baghdad line. With
their deportation or execution at the hands of the Young Turks,
the Germans saw shrink rapidly an already insufficient manpower reserve.

The Armenian Massacres and a Peace Move

The Armenians attained notoriety in Hamidian times as the
bankers, industrialists—and martyrs—of the Ottoman Empire.

[104] Baghdad Railway Company to Hohenlohe-Langenburg, Temporary
Ambassador to the Porte, Sep. 1, 1915, *ibid.*, Bd. 83, #A29586; Wangenheim to Foreign Ministry, Oct. 21, 1915, *ibid.*, #A30534.

[105] "Review of Progress in Building the [Baghdad] Railway," Jan. 15,
1916, *ibid.*, Bd. 84, #A1766.

The great wealth and influence enjoyed by the prominent members of the race undoubtedly aroused the jealousy of the poor, average Turk and put him squarely behind the gory pogroms of Sultan Abdul Hamid II. The sensationalism of these horrors tended to make the average European observer forget that not all Armenians were rich and that for as many Armenian pashas and politicians as fell afoul of the Sultan's wrath, there were thousands more of that race, humble hucksters or day laborers, who were just as wretched and desolate as the Turks or Arabs. The German diplomat Friedrich Rosen, traveling the Baghdad line in 1902, observed that most Armenians were not rich and many earned a meager living in various jobs connected with the building and administration of the Baghdad Railway. Rosen believed that the Armenians accepted such jobs to demonstrate their loyalty to the Sultan's regime.[106] However that may be, their presence on the line was considered vital by the Germans. The slightly educated Armenians made reasonably energetic laborers, and the better-schooled members of the race were excellent foremen and supervisors. Their gift for European languages made them easier to get on with than any other Near Eastern people whom the Germans encountered.

Thus, it is not likely, as the Entente propagandists frequently charged, that the Germans originated and actively abetted the wartime Armenian massacres. Germany's guilt, and that is heavy enough, lay in not restraining her ally more decisively and more firmly. Many humanitarian and religious groups within Germany wanted the government to do just this, but such steps as were taken remained of a private, diplomatic nature, and were no more pushed to the extreme than the economic and financial demands referred to above. However, the little that was done was regarded by the Turks in 1915 as a serious infringement of their sovereignty. They were roused to countermeasures, which satisfied the racist aspirations of the Committee and weakened the Germans who, the Committee feared, were best in a position to overwhelm its rule.

[106] Rosen, *Diplomatischen Wanderleben*, p. 72.

The war cut off the Armenians from outside help. The agreements of early 1914, in which Wangenheim had played a conspicuous part and which led to the appointment of two European commissioners to safeguard Armenian rights in eastern Anatolia, were nullified when the belligerent alignments were formed. The commissioners were given six months' salary as terminal pay and then dismissed from the Ottoman service. Wangenheim protested this decision to Talaat, whom he tried to impress with the bad publicity that would come of the episode. But the Minister of Interior would tolerate no foreign interference with Turkish internal affairs and expressed the hope that the German Ambassador would not soon again subject them to mutual embarrassment.[107]

For such efforts the Wilhelmstrasse earned the mounting resentment of the Turks and no lasting gratitude whatever from the Armenians. Even before Turkey entered the war, the Armenian community protested the conscription of its men into the Turkish ranks and blamed the order on the German military mission. The belief that the Germans were responsible was cultivated by the British and French consular services and by American missionaries, if German reports can be believed.[108] Wangenheim, however, would have preferred to exempt the Armenians from active service because he had a low opinion of their fighting caliber and realized that they served German interests best in their traditional railroad occupations. He was unable to advance this opinion among the Turks, who retorted that if the Armenians demanded rights, they must also recognize that they had duties toward the State.

The Ambassador did seek an interview with the Armenian Patriarch and assured him that Germany regarded the European reform program for Armenia as only postponed, not terminated forever. When hostilities ceased, Germany would be the first to

[107] Wangenheim to Bethmann, Feb. 2, 1915, A.A. Türkei #183, Bd. 36, #A5043.

[108] Consul Rössler at Aleppo to Wangenheim, Oct. 16, 1914, *ibid.*, #A28983.

take up the work again. The Patriarch in his turn declared that all intelligent Armenians wanted to continue under Turkish dominion, that few really preferred annexation by Russia, and that, if anything, he and his hierarchy wished that Germany might take special charge of the Armenian people in the future. He pointed out to Wangenheim that any preference for the Entente shown by the Armenian came of the fact that French was taught in the schools. He urged the Ambassador to use diplomatic pressure on the Porte to have German substituted for French throughout the Ottoman Empire and promised to recommend the German language to his compatriots. To that end, he hoped that the German government would subsidize a patriarchal newspaper to support this and similar projects.[109]

The Ambassador favored such a newspaper, but there is no evidence that he expended embassy money on it. He interviewed the Patriarch again in February, 1915, informing him that German soldiers had been instructed to protect Armenian interests whenever there was occasion to do so. Under embassy auspices a number of German Protestant deaconesses were sent to Armenian settlements in Anatolia. The Patriarch had commended their work the previous year, especially because they made no attempt to proselytize their own religion.[110] The introduction of the deaconesses nevertheless led to trouble with Djemal Pasha, who was not so sure that their work was nonsectarian or that their coming was not intended by the Germans as a censure of the cruel and arbitrary behavior of Turkish troops in the Armenian districts.[111]

Clashes between the races multiplied rapidly in early 1915. The defeat of Sarikamish had much to do with them. Though the government managed to conceal the enormity of this loss from the Ottoman Empire as a whole, the Armenian provinces knew better than any other the true outcome of the battle. The cold, ragged, and maimed Turkish columns, retreating from the Caucasian

---

109 Wangenheim to Bethmann, Dec. 29, 1914, *Ibid.*, #A388.
110 Wangenheim to Bethmann, Feb. 22, 1915, *ibid.*, #A7681.
111 Wangenheim to Bethmann, Apr. 3, 1915, *ibid.*, #A12287.

front, filed through the Armenian villages, and in some cases were indifferently and even extortionately treated by the local inhabitants. The vanquished commander, Enver, assembled some Armenian notables at Konia and praised the loyal service of their countrymen in combat against the Russians, but the Turkish recruits did not agree with him and were in any case anxious to wreak on the Armenians the destruction spared the Russians.

In truth, Enver's remarks could not be trusted. His sentiments at the moment were generous, but they did not accord with the platform of the Young Turk Party enunciated in 1911. At that time, the membership had assured to all races of the empire the free practice of their religion, but the suppression of all language enclaves other than Turkish was even then adumbrated.[112] It was an offense to the Committee that Armenian was anywhere spoken, and the kind of cultural renaissance envisioned by the Patriarch under German benevolence was absolutely intolerable to it. Sooner or later, Enver would give clear proofs of that fact.

At the beginning of March, the Turks apprehended near Adana some espionage agents whom the British had landed from submarines off the Syrian coast. Wangenheim was unable to learn the number of persons involved, but he commented that the government would magnify the danger and cite it to justify an intensification of the Armenian persecutions. Even though actual collusion between the British and the Armenians could often not be proved, the Turkish authorities contended that the Armenians had not revealed the presence of the enemy agents and to that extent had given them aid and comfort.

The German Ambassador thought that British espionage was no great military threat and preferred to keep out of the business, but the Patriarch and a number of prominent Armenian laymen immediately sought his protection and mediation. They told him that persecutions had been least severe wherever German consuls were in residence—a fact that German apologists were later to emphasize—and they begged Wangenheim to in-

[112] Johannes Lepsius, *Deutschland und Armenien, 1914–1918* (Potsdam, 1919), pp. xvi–xvii.

crease their number at once. Germany could and must now assume the role of Britain and Russia in Armenia after the Congress of Berlin. With even more regret than embarrassment, this
group was politely turned away from the German embassy. Yet
their rejection was not unequivocal. Had German policy been so
clearcut, it would have taken less of a toll of Wangenheim's
nerves. Rather, as he described it to Chancellor Bethmann, his
task was to keep such pro-German sentiment lively and yet restrained and, at the end of the war, to summon it up full-blown
against the Turks.[113]

   Dr. Johannes Lepsius, a German authority on Armenia who excoriated his government for inhumanity and Wangenheim for almost criminal negligence after the war, implies that Enver knew
the spirit if not the substance of the German embassy's policy.
Lepsius believed that the Turks were anxious to consummate the
liquidation of the Armenian race before Germany was able to
conclude a military convention with Bulgaria. This would bring
that country into the war, release supplies in quantity, but also
raise the possibility that German troops would arrive in strength
to bar the Turks from their murderous designs.[114]

   The German government did not of course go so far. It was
unable to muster more than a series of bland reprimands against
the Turks. Yet the Committee could not be sure that the urgings
of Christian conscience would not impel the Wilhelmstrasse further. And if not conscience, then material interest, because, the
Turks were fairly certain, if Turkey ever became "the German
Egypt," then the Armenians would deputize for the Germans in
the governmental bureaux, on the provincial and municipal
councils, and at the humblest stations of the Baghdad Railway.

   Therefore the pace of destruction quickened. It was intended
to erase the shame of Sarikamish and eliminate enemies from the

113 Wangenheim to Bethmann, Apr. 15, 1915, A.A. Türkei #183, Bd. 36,
#A13922.

114 Lepsius, *Deutschland und Armenien*, p. xxvii. Lepsius puts the number of German officers in Turkey at 75; of enlisted men, at 150. He says
there were none at all in Central Anatolia. This estimate seems too low,
even for early 1915.

rear as the Ottoman Empire made its major effort at the Dardanelles; but as much as either of these, it would secure Turkey's postwar future against both Armenian and German infiltration. Enver appointed one of his brothers-in-law, Djevdet Bey, Vali of Van. Shortly after the arrival of this official began a series of incidents between the Armenian residents and the Turkish police. Djevdet suggested a conference between himself and leaders of the Armenian community to thrash out the problems, but having lured three of the latter outside of Van, he immediately put them to death. These executions were followed by an assault of Turkish troops on Armenian houses in Van. About April 22, 1915, the whole city rose up against the Turks, more in self-defense, it would seem, than at the instigation of British or Russian agents.

The Turks later justified their action by insisting on the danger of Russian espionage; and Van did indeed rise a second time on May 10, when Russian troops advanced toward the city. This second insurrection was more bloodily suppressed than the first one. But the April bloodshed had only the slightest military justification. Nothing of the April massacres appeared in the Constantinople press, and because of this about six hundred of the capital's Armenian intellectuals were taken completely by surprise, rounded up, and put under arrest on April 25.[115]

Lest other Armenians of the Ottoman Empire attempt to imitate the insurrectionaries of Van, Enver decided to suppress all Armenian schools and newspapers. Wangenheim regretted these orders as both morally and materially deleterious to Germany's cause. He made a feint at protest, but warned Berlin that the Turks would use all kinds of diplomatic and financial extortion at the slightest cross word. Projects like the Baghdad Railway would suffer.[116] Nevertheless, the Ambassador instructed his consuls to collect any kind of information that would show that the Germans had tried to alleviate the lot of the Armenians. These

[115] *Ibid.*, pp. xiv–xv, xix.

[116] Wangenheim to Foreign Ministry, May 31, 1915, A.A. Türkei #183, Bd. 36, #A17493.

notices were to be published in a white book in hopes of impressing Entente and German public opinion.[117]

The last found a powerful voice in Dr. Johannes Lepsius. The
son of a famous archeologist and himself a noted traveler and
writer on the Near East, Lepsius was delegated by various Protestant Evangelical societies to enter Armenia and verify at firsthand the atrocity stories. Wangenheim did not want the professor to come. He was as certain that the Turks would charge the
Germans some sort of retribution for causing them this embarrassment as that not a single Armenian life would be spared because of Lepsius' endeavors.[118] But Lepsius convinced the Wilhelmstrasse that his intention was not to pressure the Turks but
instead to argue the patriarchal entourage into greater loyalty toward the Ottoman regime. Alleging this as his reason, he got as
far as Constantinople, where the Armenian Patriarch acclaimed
him but Talaat refused him permission to travel into the interior.
He had badgered Wangenheim unmercifully with letters, and
the Ambassador described his reaction to Lepsius' proposals as
something between amusement and contempt.[119] Yet Lepsius
emphasized an argument to which the Ambassador was always
open: the liquidation of the Armenians would seriously and perhaps irreparably diminish the prospects of Germany's ascendancy in Turkey after the war.

When Lepsius returned to Germany, he devoted himself to
keeping the German public unsparingly informed about the Armenian massacres. Though the German newspapers were not as
chary of this news as might have seemed desirable in the interests of the Turkish alliance, the professor still preferred to make
his disclosures in the journals of Basel and Zürich. What he
wrote was not always up to date or unbiased. Much of it came

[117] Foreign Ministry to German Embassy, Constantinople, July 4, 1915,
ibid., Bd. 37, #A20525.

[118] Wangenheim to Foreign Ministry, June 9, 1915, *ibid.*, #A18287.

[119] Zimmermann to Wangenheim, June 6, 1915, *ibid.*, #A17493; Lepsius
to Foreign Ministry, June 22, 1915, *ibid.*, #A19605; and Wangenheim to
Foreign Ministry, June 24, 1915, *ibid.*, #A19783.

from Armenian informants in the Turkish capital, and a large source, reworked with many variations, was given him by Ambassador Morgenthau at the time of his visit to Constantinople in July, 1915. Morgenthau showed him a collection of American consular reports detailing the atrocities and suggested that the Armenians be removed from the Ottoman Empire and resettled in the American West. Lepsius took up that idea enthusiastically and, while in Switzerland, asserted that it had significant support in the German diplomatic corps.[120] No individual was named in this connection, but Wangenheim forced the Porte to receive Monsignor Dolci when that prelate bore to the Turkish government a handwritten note from the Pope begging that the Armenians be spared or transported to some nonstrategic region under neutral supervision.[121] Wangenheim's action was the more noteworthy because Pallavicini, to whom Dolci usually turned, deliberately made his own protests less forthright than those of his German colleague.[122]

In all his Armenian endeavors, Wangenheim sought the close cooperation of Henry Morgenthau. It is quite possible that he needed not so much the American's help as someone to conceal Germany's hand in the business or to share the brunt of Turkish recriminations, should these become really serious. At any rate, the Foreign Ministry approved the Ambassador's suggestion that the Armenian question be linked with the Jewish one. Wangenheim was ordered to tell the Grand Vizier that it was feared that Jewish properties were being rifled during the Armenian disturbances. If such outrages continued, the Ambassador was to point out, Germany's alliance and America's neutrality might both become impossible to justify because of the influence of

[120] Brackolin, German Consul in Basel, to Bethmann, Sep. 22 and Oct. 7, 1915, *ibid.*, Bd. 38, #A27810, #A29234.

[121] Wangenheim to Foreign Ministry, Oct. 13, 1915, *ibid.*, #A29776.

[122] Pallavicini to Burian #37/p, May 20, 1915, H.H.S.A. Türkei Karton #209. According to this dispatch, Pallavicini declined common action with both the German and American ambassadors. For the Austrian attitude, see also Trumpener, *Germany and the Ottoman Empire, 1914–1918*, pp. 208–209, 213, 229.

Jewish international opinion. The Wilhelmstrasse requested that relief supplies purchased by American Jewish societies be admitted from American ships calling at Syrian harbors and hoped that no difficulties would be made about applying some of these to Armenian relief also.[123]

Whatever else may be said about Germany's Armenian policy, it did have the effect of dividing the Young Turk leadership. None of these men wanted to add America to the ranks of the Sultan's enemies, and with sizable quantities of money and goods being dispensed in relief, the prospects of loot were manifest. From British documents, it appears that Djemal Pasha was prepared to concede Armenian autonomy as the basis of an immediately negotiated peace in May, 1915. The Armenian state was to be governed by a Christian prince, his administration staffed by European experts. Over this whole organization Djemal, proclaimed Sultan by the Entente, would exercise only the most nominal suzerainty. He would exact no tribute because the real basis of his authority would be a Kingdom of Syria enlarged to include Palestine, Mesopotamia, and Arabia. Finally, the Ottoman Empire would forever renounce Constantinople and the Straits, which would presumably pass under the jurisdiction of the Russian Tsar or an international commission.[124]

Next to the cession of Constantinople and the Straits, the most astonishing aspect of this separate peace maneuver was the prominent part played in it by the Armenians. Djemal used them as his emissaries to Copenhagen and Stockholm, where contact was made with British agents. At the same time, the Pasha made himself responsible for the safety of the Armenian race, interdicting his own troops from further persecution in return for the payment of large fees by wealthy Armenian leaders. Until the final peace was signed, Djemal would receive from the outside and then distribute to the Armenians materials for their relief.

123 Zimmermann to Wangenheim, Oct. 24, 1915, A.A. Türkei #183, Bd. 38, A30496.
124 "Copenhagen: Miscellaneous" #69757, May 29, 1915, P.R.O., F.O. 371/2489; Cabinet Memorandum #200744, Dec. 29, 1915, F.O. 371/2492.

Though he would reserve a great deal for himself in the process, the price did not seem too high to either the Armenians or to two members of the Entente. For the first would have security of person and property; the second, entrenchment at the Straits with the minimum amount of international commotion.

The British Foreign Office was quite excited by these soundings from Djemal. At least some of the king's ministers believed it possible to turn the Fourth Army against the Young Turk government and to send it to Constantinople reinforced by British units from Egypt.[125] No resistance was expected from the Germans, because they were numerically weak in the area and were reported by Djemal's people as discouraged by the losses at the Dardanelles and anxious to avoid a recurrence of the allied drive at any cost. If Djemal surrendered to the Entente, it was prearranged that the German military mission would be withdrawn in protest. But it was understood that the German officers were eager to go, lest they pay with their honor or their lives for some overwhelming Turkish defeat of the near future.[126]

Unfortunately, the British documents do not tell which officers and which ministers were ready to implement Djemal's plot, though the intrigue apparently had support in both the German War and Foreign Ministries. That nothing came of it may mean in part that only a few German subalterns and chargés were prepared to collaborate. In any event, the French Foreign Ministry protested strongly against the whole affair. It reminded London and St. Petersburg that Syria and Cilicia should not be auctioned off to Djemal but more fittingly reserved to France, which had been active in that part of the Ottoman Empire since the sixteenth century.[127]

The French declaration brought an end to further dealings with Djemal. The Russians were considerably embarrassed by the obdurate attitude of their ally, the more so as they had not

[125] Grey to Buchanan #3123/201112, Dec. 29, 1915, *ibid.*

[126] "Copenhagen: Miscellaneous" #69757, May 29, 1915, P.R.O., F.O. 371/2489; Cabinet Memorandum #200744, Dec. 29, 1915, F.O. 371/2492.

[127] Nicolson to Grey #201112, Dec. 29, 1915, *ibid.*

anticipated it at all. Sazonov spluttered unconvincingly that the business had never left the talking stage and that there had been no intention of cheating a faithful comrade-in-arms. But the French remained petulant and implied that Sazonov's sins, bad in themselves, were the outgrowth of covert encouragment from Grey, whose final aim was to confront France with a *fait accompli*.[128]

This charge was probably unfair, but the necessities of war did not allow Grey to argue against it at length. The British Foreign Secretary instead attempted to prove his good faith by holding the Russians as much at arm's length as the Turks. He had the Russians told that Djemal's proposals could be considered only if Basra were excluded from the new sultanate. The Turks could not be permitted to govern there again or forbid Britain a free approach to India through the Persian Gulf. Moreover, the boundaries of Djemal's kingdom could not engross lands already marked out for the Arab nationalist leader, Sherif Hussein of Mecca.[129] The British had been negotiating with the Sherif since October, 1914, but possibly would have jilted him for immediate peace on the Turkish front if France had not made a fuss.

George Buchanan, the British Ambassador at St. Petersburg, described Sazonov as unsettled and even somewhat humiliated by the affair. The Russian minister believed that the attitude of France might put in question all the promises made to him about the disposition of Constantinople. It seemed to condemn Russia to a needless prolongation of war against the Turks, bleeding her to a point where her representations at the peace conference would be ineffectual and unregarded. Sazonov therefore began to insist that the Russian government had never taken Djemal seriously. To the reservations of the British and French it intended to add its own provisos about the Holy Places in Jerusalem and Bethlehem. In a manner evocative of 1853, Sazonov averred that these could not be surrendered to other than Rus-

---

128 Buchanan to Grey #1999/201528, Dec. 31, 1915, *ibid.*
129 Grey to Buchanan #209/34, Dec. 31, 1915, *ibid.*, F.O. 371/2767.

sian auspices. Djemal would have to admit both towns as extraterritorial enclaves, though they belonged logically in the Syrian Kingdom and one, Jerusalem, frequently served as Djemal's wartime headquarters. However, Buchanan believed that Sazonov would drop this demand as soon as France renounced her lien on Syria and Cilicia.[130] But France, the ensuing months proved, was unwilling to do this much, and the Russian government in its turn denied credence to all further missives from Djemal.

It is quite possible that Enver Pasha knew what was being done behind his back. Certainly he behaved as if he had discovered still another ground for objection to German diplomacy and was more than ever deaf to any rational discussion of the Baghdad Railway and the Armenian persecutions. On one occasion, when the Germans pressed him too hard, he retorted that he intended to replace every German in Turkey except General Liman.[131] As prospects of a negotiated peace faded, the Wilhelmstrasse strove to exploit the recent turn of events in Greece. There the King had finally dissolved the ministry of Venizelos, putting in its place a cabinet led by D. Gunaris. Though he was publicly committed to maintaining the country's neutrality, the German government believed it might be possible to league Gunaris with the Central Powers. To do this, Wangenheim moved to persuade Enver to make timely concessions. He had in mind the cession to Greece of the Dodecanese Islands and of all Turkish claims in Albania. But Enver refused and instead proposed in the Committee that Turkey's war aims be formulated and published.[132]

[130] Buchanan to Grey #2003/68, Dec. 31, 1915, *ibid.*

[131] Wangenheim to Foreign Ministry, July 15, 1915, A.A. Türkei #139, Bd. 36, #A21466. According to this dispatch, Enver had begun to earmark a number of German officers for reassignment outside the Turkish theater. Wangenheim believed the decision might indicate greater Turkish confidence in their own technical grasp of the war, but otherwise had no explanation. Enver's plans were particularly curious since the Dardanelles fighting was then at its height.

[132] Wangenheim to Foreign Ministry, Mar. 14, 1915, A.A. Türkei #168, Bd. 13, #A9339; Mirbach to Foreign Ministry, Aug. 3, 1915, *ibid.*, Bd. 14, #A23201; and Neurath to Foreign Ministry, Nov. 12, 1915, *ibid.*, #A5653.

In the midst of the Dardanelles fighting, such a step was at best premature. It was a heady but irresponsible proclamation, delivered to the Germans and to the Entente alike, that Turkey expected to win the war and would oppose as treason any shuffling of her provinces as the Germans were then doing in the daylight and in the dark. The permanence of the present frontiers was affirmed, and the Greeks were served notice that the Porte intended to gather in all its former Mediterranean islands. To be sure, one or two might be reserved to the Athens government if it were willing to write a military alliance with Constantinople and actively assist the Turkish war effort. But with so much withheld and with the little proffered left discouragingly vague, it is difficult to see how the Greeks could have brought themselves to do any such thing.

Greek affairs once before had almost cost Wangenheim his position. In the autumn of 1915 they returned to baffle, plague, and finally kill him. The health of the German Ambassador had deteriorated rapidly during the year, and in July he had been given a recuperative leave of absence from Constantinople. The holiday had done him no good, and when he returned in October, Pallavicini thought he looked worse than ever.[133] He interviewed Enver and chided him for the enormity of his war aims. But the Turk, who had always been respectful even when he disagreed with his German mentors, this time refused to listen to advice. He admitted that the full reincorporation of Albania into the Ottoman Empire might not be practicable, but he demanded of Wangenheim a promise that the Central Powers would support the installation of an all-Turkish bureaucracy in that country after the war. The German Ambassador indicated that even so much was not possible for him. He did, however, consult Pallavicini on the point after his conference with the War Minis-

---

The last dispatch was written by Wangenheim's chargé after the Ambassador's death and may be taken to summarize the advances to the Greek government.

[133] Chargé Trautmannsdorff to Burian #83/p, Oct. 9, 1915, H.H.S.A. Türkei Karton 209.

ter. The Austrian then told him that Vienna rejected such a scheme categorically. Albania was not negotiable. If Austria could not have it, it should be offered to Italy to induce her to leave the war, or to Serbia, to dissuade her from any "Great-Slav" propaganda after the peace had been written.[134]

As a last resort, Wangenheim appealed to Said Halim, the Grand Vizier. He was always known for a moderate and had no interest in the war beyond securing his Egyptian estates prosperous and intact. Said Halim declared that he did not support Enver's aggressiveness and believed he could force the War Minister to back down by disputing with him in the Committee. But on October 22, 1915, the ambassadors of the Central Powers were abruptly informed that the Grand Vizier had been relieved of the Foreign Ministry and was to be replaced by Halil Bey, president of the Ottoman Chamber of Deputies. This man had no experience in statecraft, knew hardly any French, and in fact was to prove little more than Enver's clerk. According to Pallavicini, his career was one of lifelong xenophobia, though the German embassy discounted rumors that Turkish diplomacy would be fundamentally altered.[135] Nevertheless, within two days of Halil's appointment, Wangenheim died of a stroke.[136]

---

[134] Pallavicini to Burian #797, Oct. 20, 1915, *ibid.;* Tschirschky to Bethmann, Nov. 14, 1915, A.A. Albanien #1, Bd. 18, #A33160. Tschirschky here gives an account of Wangenheim's difficulties as he had it from Hilmi Pasha, the Turkish Ambassador in Vienna. The Austrian view about Albania is also given in some detail in Pallavicini to Burian #40/p, May 31, 1915, H.H.S.A. Türkei Karton 209.

[135] Pallavicini to Burian #89/p, Oct. 22, 1915, *ibid.*

[136] Pallavicini to Burian, no number, Oct. 25, 1915, *ibid.*

5

Wolff-Metternich, Kühlmann, and the Lure of Partition

The last quarter of 1915 saw the appointment of a new German Ambassador to Constantinople and the emergence of new problems to confront him. In this period the Turks brilliantly fought their way to victory at the Dardanelles and compelled the Entente to withdraw their forces from that area at the beginning of the next year. This victory caused a tremendous rise in self-confidence and chauvinism among the Turks and led them to disagree increasingly with German attempts to develop grand strategy in the Near East. The areas where the allies clashed were Tripoli and Persia, where the Germans planned to weaken Italian and British strength respectively, and Egypt, where Falkenhayn proposed to renew the attack on the Suez Canal.

In none of these areas did Berlin and Constantinople achieve a real compromise. In fact, the Turks became so bitter that they demanded important concessions from the Germans as evidence of good faith. These entailed the abrogation in 1916 of certain nineteenth-century treaties that had safeguarded European interests in the Ottoman Empire. To achieve their ends, the Turks brought various kinds of diplomatic blackmail to bear on the Wilhelmstrasse. Toward the solution of all these problems, Austria made no constructive contribution. Instead, at the end of 1916, the new Austrian Foreign Minister, Count Czernin, advanced proposals that nearly splintered the alliance of Turkey and the Central Powers.

Wolff-Metternich, the Man and His Environment

The selection of Wangenheim's successor developed into a question of the first magnitude in Berlin. Despite considerable thought and argument, the solution proved unsatisfactory in the end. For the Foreign Ministry, the problem would have been fairly routine, but the General Staff insisted that the new man must have a grasp of the military as well as of the political situation, must possess the confidence of the German Emperor, and, above all, must enjoy the esteem and support of the ruling circles in the Reich.

Wangenheim had not really had all these qualifications. His approach to politics was often deft and penetrating, but it was rarely farseeing and comprehensive. Perhaps that was due to the peculiar nature of the Turkish alliance, rather than to any shortcomings in the Ambassador. He did not believe in the military value of the Turks from the beginning, and in a few months wanted to shake them and the war entirely. Thus, he gained a posthumous reputation for carelessness and defeatism, though the end of the war proved him to have been right all the time. More importantly, his detractors overlooked his fine sense of humor, professional flexibility, and manly candor. Though his political relations with the Porte and even with Enver were hopelessly bad at the end of his career, there is little evidence that the Turks ever came to dislike him as a man. Humann probably put his finger on it when he said that Wangenheim was the true bohemian, never taking himself seriously and never standing on ceremony. Whatever diplomatic turns he propounded, whatever intrigues he dabbled in, these traits at least remained constant and recommended him to the Young Turks.

It was unfortunate that Humann, who knew how to describe Wangenheim's qualities so well and engagingly, was not able to collaborate more effectively in the choice of his successor. In that critical autumn of 1915, he may have been blinded by personal ambition or overborne by a real ground swell of public discontent with the German Foreign Ministry.[1] It would be easy to overestimate the pervasiveness of the criticism of the Wilhelmstrasse—the mind of the German people at large was not really exercised by the Turkish diplomacy or the men who made it—but it was real and destructive enough. Its exponents, relatively few in number, were high in social rank and loud in complaint. Behind them were several army generals and the head of the General Staff, Erich von Falkenhayn himself.

By this time, General von Falkenhayn was thoroughly disgusted with what he called the pacifism and treason of the diplomatic corps and certain of the large German newspapers. He believed, and disclosed these suspicions to the court party and the Junker aristocracy, that all these weaklings and backsliders had the secret help and encouragement of the Chancellor, Bethmann-Hollweg. Bethmann-Hollweg, it was held in some quarters, had been throwing out peace feelers almost since the first engagements of the war, and the farther the mission or consulate from Berlin, the more probable was it, in the General's eyes, that the Chancellor was there pursuing his devious purposes.[2]

The vacancy at the Pera embassy therefore triggered an amount of activity out of all proportion to the importance of even that post. Falkenhayn demanded that the most extraordinary care and forethought be used to select the new incumbent. In fact, the ranks of the junior diplomats and even of the army itself should be closely scanned with a view to replacing not only Wangenheim but also every one of his colleagues in all the major capitals. Falkenhayn wanted a thorough housecleaning, a total overhaul. To support so drastic a step, the General charged the older diplomats with all sorts of major failures. He was particularly disturbed by their handling of American neutrality and stated that if the Foreign Ministry had not blundered, German-

---

[1] Colonial Secretary Solf to Jagow, Feb. 22, 1916, A.A. Deutschland #135, No. 1, Bd. 1, #A660. Solf here charges that Humann misrepresented Metternich to have him recalled.

[2] Grumme-Douglas to Seeckt, Dec. 28, 1915, Seeckt Papers.

American sentiment could have been exploited to force President Wilson to join the Central Powers or at least to abandon his policy of covert assistance to the British. The Irish question, he also claimed, might by that time have been brought to a head so that the British war effort would be lamed by a bloody civil conflict. Lastly, the neutrality of Spain was regarded by Falkenhayn as an inexcusable irritant, which could have been eliminated by timely inducements to Madrid. Promises in Morocco and at Gibraltar were mentioned by him and his circle; that they had not been moved officially and energetically in the Wilhelmstrasse was taken by these people as certain evidence of treason. What was needed was a sure, strong, and ruthless hand.[3]

It did not seem too outrageous to Falkenhayn and his supporters that his should be the hand to coordinate all these enterprises as Chancellor. An assignment to Constantinople might supply the political experience that some objected must complement the General's purely military training. If he were accredited to the Porte, so the argument further ran, the Balkan neutrals would know that Germany meant business and would swing into line behind her. And if Rumania and Greece declared for the Central Powers, Holland and the Scandinavian nations, so the Falkenhayn circle professed, could not long withhold their adherence. On the other hand, if at this critical moment the qualifications of the General were overlooked or ignored, then, to Germany's peril, none of these things would happen.[4]

Though the affairs of the Pera embassy were far from satisfactory and imminent doom was descried by some observers in that and other quarters, Falkenhayn was of course passed over

[3] *Ibid.* At this time, there seems to have been fairly wide speculation in Germany that Spain would eventually declare for the Central Powers. High hopes were held of the Spanish intellectuals, among whom all sorts of pro-German demonstrations and rallies were encouraged. See *Frankfurter Zeitung*, December 24, 1915.

[4] Treutler, in the Emperor's Retinue, to Foreign Ministry, Feb. 27, 1916, A.A. Deutschland #135, No. 1, Bd. 1, #A751; Bethmann to Foreign Ministry, Aug. 29, 1916, *ibid.*, #A3068. These two documents indicate that Falkenhayn twice applied for the Constantinople post, the second time when Metternich was recalled.

and never became either German Chancellor or Ambassador to Turkey. The political narrowness of the man, his rough arrogance and humorless earnestness, portended, if applied to Turkish business, political disasters as great as any Germany might suffer on Near Eastern battlefields. Had he been appointed, there is reason to believe that Falkenhayn would seriously have pressed the emigration of German-Americans and Irishmen to Mesopotamia on the Turkish government.[5] This sort of project and its author the Turks would not have abided for one moment. It had neither finesse nor common sense, would never have been espoused by Marschall and Wangenheim, and ought not to have been entertained by anyone designated to assume their heritage. Bethmann and the Emperor William must have felt something like this, because they faced up to the army and appointed a professional, civilian diplomat as their emissary to the Sultan. He was Count Paul Wolff-Metternich. From the start of his mission, he was dogged by ill omens and never gained the position his predecessors had achieved.

In the first place, Metternich was not of their stature. He had intelligence and cultivation and, throughout his long career, became known as a man of reasoned and well-articulated views. Before the war, he was an eloquent advocate of better relations with Britain and, as was well known, counted the period of his London embassy as the happiest time of his life. This taste for things English, badly concealed, even flaunted to his associates, was incidentally one of his greatest crimes in Falkenhayn's eyes. But the Metternich of 1915 was not the man who had worked and written so well in the twilight of the world's peace, but rather an elderly, phlegmatic, and even peculiar gentleman who regarded Constantinople not as the great culmination but instead as the crowning annoyance of his service. These views he did not trouble to conceal from the Sultan's court. He could not curb his distaste for socializing nor be affable at soirées and receptions. Instead the Count preferred to seclude himself with old magazines on the topmost story of his embassy or to putter

5 Grumme-Douglas to Hans von Seeckt, Dec. 28, 1915, Seeckt Papers.

about the embassy garden shaded by a bizarre and floppy hat.[6]

An old hand like Pallavicini naturally knew this man and his weaknesses quite well and moved quickly to point them up to the Turks. Wangenheim was scarcely buried in the summer embassy garden at Therapia and his successor not yet arrived when the Austrian sought an interview with Talaat Pasha. He came bearing medals and decorations for the Minister of the Interior, for Halil Bey, and for various other Committee dignitaries. He was obviously concerned to stand not merely well, but even better than his new German colleague, with the membership of the new cabinet.

Having dispensed his Austrian decorations, Pallavicini regretted to Talaat that a higher German nobleman had not been named as Wangenheim's successor. The candidacy of Prince Ernst Hohenlohe-Langenburg, who had served as interim Ambassador during Wangenheim's convalescence of the summer before, was raised by Pallavicini as especially appropriate. On the other hand, the appointment of a mere count somewhat slighted the Sultan's august position. Then the Austrian Ambassador pointed out that the Committee, reputedly now so hostile to foreigners, need never fear the Austrians, because they had no large navy and could neither aspire to nor maintain large colonies overseas. The obvious comparison with Germany, with her strong naval arm, was not lost on Talaat. But the Interior Minister was unconvinced by this line of argument and coldly observed to Pallavicini that the Turkish leadership must be alert against all threats to the country's independence, whatever their source.[7]

Pallavicini was so startled that he forgot himself enough to threaten that "Turkey would never come to anything without Austria." Talaat went away angry from this interview, but within a few weeks became even angrier with the man from Berlin. In

[6] The above Grumme-Douglas letter contains such details, as does Rosen, *Diplomatischen Wanderleben*, p. 76.

[7] Pallavicini to Burian #90/p, Oct. 25, 1915, H.H.S.A. Türkei Karton 209.

the passage to Constantinople, Metternich's baggage was lost. Consequently, the Ambassador was for some time without his dress uniform and refused to be presented to the Sultan until it arrived. The first audience with Mohammed V was therefore delayed more than two weeks, during which the ruler and his ministers became increasingly annoyed, and Metternich amused himself by dropping snide and superior comments about Turkey and the Turks. Pallavicini seems to have had a fairly detailed catalogue of these and probably broadcast them more than was the intention of the German Ambassador. Before long, he could report that the Turks did not like Metternich.[8]

Metternich told Pallavicini that Berlin was disgusted with the financial extortion of the Turks and their arrogant claim of being indispensable to the Central Powers. The recent performance of Djavid Bey in the Prussian capital had turned even the last few die-hard partisans of the Turkish alliance against it, and among these, Metternich frankly asserted, he had never counted himself. He had been charged to tell Halil, among other things, that the German government could not agree to the entire abrogation of the capitulations, which a Turkish law of October 1, 1914, had proclaimed, and would now seek clear legal substitutes for the privileges withdrawn from the foreign community. Metternich observed quite correctly that even Wangenheim had agreed only to assist in the gradual removal of the capitulations and had never sanctioned their immediate nullification.[9]

While all this was true, the time was hardly right to urge the point on the Turks. Their own disgust with the situation was as strong as Metternich's, and all around him the German Ambassador could see proofs of misery, war-weariness, and hatred for the German military mission. Meat had become critically short in Constantinople. The government had organized the butchers into a rationing agency so that available supplies might be fairly distributed, but there was simply not enough to go around, and charges of bribery and black-marketeering were heard every-

8 Pallavicini to Burian #103/p, Dec. 18, 1915, *ibid.*
9 Pallavicini to Burian #97/p, Nov. 20, 1915, *ibid.*

where. Metternich soon learned that it was believed in the city
that too many cows and sheep were being shipped off to Germany, resulting in meager stocks and high prices. After some
soundings, he ascertained that these allegations were grossly exaggerated and that the real culprits were operators in the Committee selling at a personal profit. He tried to persuade the newspapers to clarify the situation in Germany's favor, but they were
immovable. In fact, it was completely in the government's interest to cultivate every such lie. It had recently suspended subsidy
payments to soldiers' families and so made the most of the shortages to blame everything on the Germans.[10]

The capital police were said to be thoroughly in sympathy
with the people and instructed to arouse them against foreigners.
Metternich no longer regarded them as a reliable means of protection and, under the circumstances, became keenly disturbed
by talk that the Germans would be dealt with like the Armenians.
This threat of course never materialized, but the Turks even
before the death of Wangenheim began to give evidence that
they would dare anything just short of it. The Austrian embassy was several times rifled during the spring of 1915, and Pallavicini's dragoman and a few of his clerks held, on the slimmest
charges, by the Turkish police. The Austrian Ambassador was
obliged to swear that none of his people had had any traffic with
Armenian revolutionaries or Russian expionage agents, as was
charged.[11] The experience must have been exceptionally painful
for him because he had notably lagged behind his German colleague in protests about the Armenian question. But the Turks
were less concerned to make these fine distinctions than to impress upon both of the Teutonic powers that neither was im-
mune. Metternich, by no means as ingratiating as Pallavicini,
could not be sure that his turn was not next.

Metternich was not alone in his apprehensions about what the

[10] Metternich to Bethmann, Jan. 17, 1916, A.A. Türkei #134, Bd. 35,
#A1840.
[11] Pallavicini to Burian #47/p, June 24, 1915, H.H.S.A. Türkei Karton
209.

Turks might next do. An agent of the Committee approached Ambassador Tschirschky in Vienna and warned him that in view of the hostile mood of the Turkish people, some lavish gesture by the German government might now be necessary. This man, the merchant Bondy Bey of Adrianople, had in mind the installation of municipal lighting systems and trolley lines throughout the Ottoman Empire at German expense. Tschirschky attempted politely to dismiss the suggestion as inconceivable as long as the war lasted, but he was unable to convince Bondy Bey, and the higher powers undoubtedly behind him, that the money was not available. The Turks contended that the recent end on January 8, 1916, of the Entente attack on the Dardanelles would release many resources for use elsewhere. Since they were chiefly responsible for the enemy's repulse, they arrogated to themselves the privilege of saying how and where such resources should be applied.[12]

This argument was senseless and irresponsible, but directly in line with Enver's intention to liquidate German control in the Ottoman Empire. The bills to be presented to Berlin would be made so high that the Germans would not care to prolong their stay. In the Armenian and Baghdad Railway imbroglios, the hand and mind of Enver were everywhere apparent. Should the new German Ambassador forget that, the Ottoman War Minister detailed new grounds of complaint shortly after his arrival.

Grand Strategy: The Question of Tripoli, Afghanistan, and Persia

Like all the Young Turks, Enver Pasha was a vigorous Pan-Islamite. He hoped to bring the greatest number of his coreligionists under the Sultan's direct political dominion and in the meantime to strengthen his religious authority as Caliph. He was thus acutely sensitive to competitors in the frontier provinces of the Ottoman Empire and in areas that, for one reason or another, had fallen away from it. In late 1915 he began to charge that the

[12] Tschirschky to Bethmann, Jan. 15, 1916, A.A. Türkei #134, Bd. 35, #A1538.

Germans were active in Tripoli, Mesopotamia, Persia, and Afghanistan beyond military necessity. While Enver agreed that the Senussi tribesmen had to be thrown against the Italians in Tripoli, from the beginning he preferred, and later demanded, that these operations be left entirely to his office. He viewed it as an excellent opportunity to develop a Moslem community of interests.[13]

On the other hand, the supplies and credit Enver could extend to non-Turkish combatants were always severely limited, and the Germans were quick to make up the difference, whether for their own benefit or for that of their ally was not always clear. On November 7, 1915, Enver became so alarmed at the German subsidies disbursed to the Sheik of the Senussi and the German industrial agents at work in the Tripolitanian area that he cabled the Berlin Foreign Ministry that 150,000 Turkish pounds was being shipped to the Sheik, making all further foreign payments unnecessary. He warned that deepening German commitments would lead to a conflict of jurisdictions in the area and therefore must be curtailed at once.[14]

But the German Foreign Ministry, probably spurred by the criticisms of the army, was not ready to make a clean finish in Tripolitania. It was rumored that France was prepared to make over the Fez area to Spain, while Britain was supposed to be willing to relinquish Gibraltar in return for a Spanish declaration of war against the Central Powers. These reports were scarcely corroborated, but the Germans wondered whether they might hold out Tripoli to the Madrid government to confirm its neutrality or win it to their side.[15] To achieve these ends, Turkey's claim to Tripoli had to be ignored and German influence increased in the area, however great the irritation of Enver Pasha.

A similar problem, though of a much more serious nature, was presented by the Persian-Afghan expedition. Most German par-

---

[13] Neurath to Bethmann, Oct. 28, 1915, Jaeckh Papers. The industrialist Mannesmann was reconnoitering among the Senussi tribesmen.

[14] Neurath to Foreign Ministry, Nov. 7, 1915, Jaeckh Papers, #A32296.

[15] Neurath to Foreign Ministry, Nov. 7, 1915, Jaeckh Papers, #A32261.

ticipants in this expedition state that its impetus came from Enver himself.[16] In conception the expedition violated a principle of Bismarckian diplomacy, which assigned Persia unalterably to Russia and Britain. Emperor William confirmed this principle by the Potsdam Agreement with Russia of 1911.[17] Enver, however, espoused enthusiastically an attack on Britain in India. A march would be staged eastward through Persia, with an important diversionary thrust through Afghanistan.

The German War Ministry sent twenty-five officers to Constantinople to reconnoiter the ground and make an alliance between the Central Powers and the Emir of Afghanistan. In the interests of secrecy their party was gotten up as a circus as it passed through the Balkans. Yet apparently even as few as twenty-five men were more than Enver contemplated. He complained that the men were of the lowest caliber, loud, lazy, and almost constantly drunk. Many were the sons of rich families that contrived to have them sent to less dangerous zones of the war. They were openly contemptuous of Turkey and had several times to be tossed out of the cafés because they gave such offense to public propriety. Enver charged that their drunken ravings had destroyed whatever secrecy was attached to the mission and intimated that he was ready to have it recalled to Germany.[18]

This did not happen, but Enver gave the expedition no help. He had obviously changed his mind about its necessity and suspected that its membership had ulterior motives. This distrust was an important reason for the expedition's ultimate failure. It was also plagued by problems of internal command. The two German leaders, Wilhelm Wassmuss and Oscar von Niedermayer, both knew Persia at first hand and refused to submit to

16 Oskar von Niedermayer, *Unter der Glutsonne Irans* (München, 1925), p. 16; Ulrich Gehrke, *Persien in der deutschen Orientpolitik während des Ersten Weltkrieges* (Stuttgart, no date), p. 23.

17 Bradford G. Martin, *German-Persian Diplomatic Relations, 1873–1912* (S-Gravenhage, 1959), pp. 201, 206.

18 Hans Lührs, *Gegenspieler des Obersten Lawrence* (Berlin, 1936), p. 22. Christopher Sykes, *Wassmuss the "German Lawrence"* (London, 1936), pp. 47–50.

one another's decisions. Wassmuss, a former German consul at Bushire, insisted that he could not be expected to share authority with Niedermayer, a geologist with some field experience in Persia but no diplomatic service. The two men argued the point at some length, and Wassmuss finally quit the expedition at Baghdad in February, 1915. Travelling alone, he moved toward the Persian Gulf shore and there worked to rouse the tribes against the British.[19]

Wassmuss' choice of an operational theater may in itself have been unfortunate. The tribesmen of the Persian Gulf were notorious separatists and frequently rebelled against the jurisdiction of the Persian government in Teheran. Wassmuss' association with them cannot have predisposed the Persian government to any larger military collaboration with the Central Powers. It was not entirely clear to some of the Persian ministers whether the Germans were getting ready to deliver an attack against the British or the Persian Shah.[20]

Enver did not approve of Wassmuss' separate tack. Nor could he agree with the German expedition about other points of common planning. Neither Wassmuss nor Niedermayer had been enthusiastic about his plan to blow up the British oil refineries at Abadan and sink a ship in the Shatt-el-Arab to prevent the British from bringing up relief forces from the Persian Gulf. Enver queried the German Foreign Ministry about this proposal, but Berlin answered that it would be better to capture rather than destroy Abadan to keep its facilities intact for postwar exploitation. Enver ignored this German viewpoint and had a tramp steamer sunk in the Shatt-el-Arab anyhow. The British promptly raised the vessel and the episode was of no importance to the prosecution of the war save as an instance of Enver's defiance and determination.[21]

Without the Turkish documents, no complete analysis of Enver's policy is possible. It seems safe to speculate, however, that he wanted to make sure that the Germans would not simply contrive to make themselves heir to British and Russian economic

[19] *Ibid.,* p. 57.   [20] *Ibid.,* p. 58.   [21] *Ibid.,* pp. 52–53.

enterprises in Persia and Afghanistan after the war. Perhaps, by preserving intact such enterprises for the Entente, the German government awakened suspicions in Enver that it was attempting to use these as the basis of a separate peace with the Entente. Whatever his motives, Enver declared shortly after Wassmuss left the expedition that all its personnel were to be subject to the over-all command of a Turkish officer, Rauf Bey. The Germans were to put on Turkish uniform immediately or surrender their stores and return to Constantinople.[22]

Niedermayer was still at Baghdad when he received this order. Rather than obey it, he decided to push on to Afghanistan beyond the reach of Enver's authority. Henceforth it was not clear under whose command he was working and with what charge. According to the American consul at Baghdad, Niedermayer carried one million marks for distribution to various Persian and Afghan officials. It was his intention to bribe the Swedish officers and men who formed the leadership of the Persian gendarmerie.[23] With their support, the Persian government might be pressured into cooperating with the Central Powers. But the American consul also reported that the Germans had given money to hundreds of British Indian refugees congregating around Baghdad and east of the city. Baghdad was in the Ottoman Empire, and the Turks insisted that they alone should offer any subsidies in the area, especially when their own citizens were sometimes the recipients. The British Indians they dismissed as "plants" and spies of the Entente.[24]

As in Tripolitania, these German gestures to which the Turks so objected made no real contribution to the war effort. Moreover, though Niedermayer reached Afghanistan, he found Emir Habibollah Khan to be diplomatically unpliable and "no nigger chief who could be swayed with glass pearls." The Emir would not even consider a military operation with Germany unless he

[22] Niedermayer, *Unter der Glutsonne Irans,* pp. 26–27.
[23] Charles Brissel to Secretary of State, Apr. 9, 1915, D.S., #867.00/785.
[24] Charles Brissel to Secretary of State, July 17, 1915, D.S., #867.00/-776.

were assured money, arms, and a political guarantee against the retribution of the vice-regal government of India. Niedermayer was not empowered to give any of these guarantees, and his mission collapsed. His embarrassment was the greater because Kabul was full of Austrian prisoners of war escaped from Russian camps. These Austrians refused to have anything to do with the Niedermayer party and, when challenged for assistance, claimed that they had converted to Islam and taken Afghan citizenship.[25] Niedermayer left Afghanistan on May 21, 1916.

In Persia, German efforts for an alliance met with similar failure. On August 24, 1915, the German Ambassador, Prince Henry Reuss, offered the Persian ministry a money, munitions, and territorial integrity guarantee. The Austrian Foreign Ministry, however, while not flatly withholding its concurrence, observed that the Central Powers should not seek to establish large commitments in Persia. Burian felt that since Russia seemed unlikely to capture Constantinople, the Tsar should be left the possibility of a warm-water port on the Persian Gulf. Austria therefore recommended disengagement from the area. Nor would Burian permit the recruitment of Austrians in Persia, escaped from Russian prison camps, for the purposes of German policy.[26]

In the end, however, it was the arrival of a Russian army at Teheran in late November, 1915, which scattered the plans of the German Ambassador, along with many members of the Persian ministry and parliament, to the winds. Reuss fled to Kermanshah, and the adolescent Shah, who remained in Teheran, was put under close Russian surveillance. As late as October the Shah had still not given his signature to the pact that his ministers had formulated with the Germans. Reuss is said to have tried to force the ruler's hand by bribing his bodyguard, but the Russian advance curtailed the attempt. Some details of the plot were in any case leaked to the Shah's entourage, and therefore

[25] Niedermayer, *Unter der Glutsonne Irans,* pp. 156, 159, 161–168.

[26] This paragraph is a summary of the conclusions, based on German archival material, of Gehrke, *Persien in der deutschen Orientpolitik,* pp. 57–59, 172–177, 180–181.

the German Ambassador made his withdrawal in bad odor and
unregretted. Berlin relieved Prince Reuss on December 18, 1915,
officially for reasons of health.[27]

Further discussion of the Afghan and Persian imbroglios
would be beyond the scope of this study, but enough has been
said to suggest how complex was the legacy that Metternich in-
herited from Wangenheim, both on the borders of the Ottoman
Empire and within it. Wangenheim's merit was to have treated
the Turks as equals; Reuss, and even Wassmuss, handled Moslem rulers in a rough and extortionate manner not excluding
blackmail.

Reuss was relieved just when Metternich was settling into his
new embassy. His colleague's fate must have had a depressing
effect on him and helps explain why he was so remiss in fulfill-
ing those social functions normally expected of a German ambassador. Pallavicini reported that Metternich cut even the gala receptions and musical evenings of the Austrian embassy, though
the donations taken were to be turned over for war relief to the
Turkish Red Crescent. According to the Austrian Ambassador,
the Turkish newspapers commended his charitable activities
warmly but completely ignored the German Ambassador or mention of German news generally.[28] The matter evidently gave
some concern to Berlin, because Metternich dutifully reported
that he had had ninety Ottoman notables to dinner since his
arrival.[29]

But this was not enough to put the Turks in a better mood or
erase their resentment. The Turks increased the annoyances and
insults to German and even Austrian consular personnel in the
provinces. In the Baghdad area, scores of Christians and Jews
were arrested and shipped out for internment in Anatolia by the
Turkish police. An Austrian query elicited the charge that these
persons were British spies, but in many cases the Austrians knew

[27] Dagobert von Mikusch, *Wassmuss der deutsche Lawrence* (Leipzig,
1937), pp. 184–185.

[28] Pallavicini to Burian #2/p, Jan. 8, 1916, H.H.S.A. Türkei Karton 210.

[29] Solf to Jagow, Feb. 24, 1916, A.A. Deutschland #135, No. 1, Bd. 1,
#A702.

they had dealings with themselves and the Germans. The Austrian consul at Baghdad argued for their release, but he was refused, and Austrian shops in Baghdad were subsequently looted. Pallavicini decided against further protest.[30]

Under these circumstances Metternich recommended that Germans be discouraged from travelling in the Ottoman Empire. Their concession-hunting offended the Turks, and they were suspected of plotting with Armenians and other political pariahs.[31] In Palestine it was reported that German enlisted men were deliberately denied wine and fresh fruit by merchants on orders of the Committee. Civilians could not expect better treatment, and the German business community in Jerusalem was already in the process of pulling up stakes.[32] Emperor William sought some redress for these grievances by flattering the Sultan: Mohammed V was presented with the baton of a German marshal.[33]

But the cure was not to be found in the mood or caprice of one man. More fundamental to the solution of the problem were the legal safeguards to which Europeans were entitled under Ottoman law. What these safeguards were had not been clear since the abolition of the capitulations in October, 1914. Wangenheim had not succeeded in getting any substitute for the old code, and Metternich was instructed to adjust the situation as soon as possible. In light of the hostility of Turkish public opinion and the series of harassments just described, it was with some surprise that the German Foreign Ministry received a Turkish proposal to assign German advisers to the principal departments of the Sultan's administration. The departments of Interior, Finance, Marine, Agriculture, Commerce, and—most important of all—Justice were named.[34] In the Justice Department, a German judge

30 Pallavicini to Burian #4/p and #9/p, Jan. 13 and 29, 1916, H.H.S.A. Türkei Karton 210.

31 Metternich to Bethmann, Jan. 30, 1916, A.A. Türkei #134, Bd. 35, #A3142.

32 Consul to Schmidt to Metternich, Jan. 9, 1916, *ibid.*, #A2905.

33 Pallavicini to Burian #60, Jan. 28, 1916, H.H.S.A. Türkei Karton 210.

34 Notice of Turkish Embassy to German Foreign Ministry, Nov. 13,

was to be appointed to the Supreme Court at Constantinople, and German judges were also to be associated with all provincial appellate courts. In every commercial court, a German official was to be available for consultation by Europeans, and all of these men, above the commercial system, were to be recompensed at the rate of not less than 2,000 Turkish pounds annually.[35]

The Turks declared that they were ready to implement the program as soon as the Germans made their appointments. They urged that the appointment of the Germans be widely publicized.[36] Humann was inclined to take their offers at face value, but Metternich wanted to go slowly and ponder the Turkish motives at greater length. This attitude raised a storm of protest, disgruntled German businessmen now joining the military party to demand the Ambassador's recall for incompetence and lack of initiative.[37] Nevertheless, Metternich contended that the Turks were not acting in good faith. Their willingness to receive German advisers simply did not tally with the hostility shown to the Germans in the provinces.

Furthermore, it was not in keeping with the Turkish character to turn reasonable when the military situation of the Ottoman Empire was improving. The Turks were beating back the Entente at Gallipoli and on November 22, 1915, in the Battle of Ctesiphon repulsed a British advance on Baghdad. The British were thrown back and practically encircled in Kut-el-Amara, where after a long bombardment General Charles Townshend and all his men surrendered on April 29, 1916. Against this military background, Metternich pointed to one Turkish condition that the military and commercial enthusiasts were inclined to overlook. This was the requirement that all German advisers

1915, A.A. Türkei #139, Bd. 38, #A32981; Comment by German Foreign Ministry, Dec. 10, 1915, *ibid.*, #A35740.

[35] Deliberation of the Ottoman Cabinet, no date, *ibid.*   [36] *Ibid.*

[37] Humann to Jaeckh, Jan. 28, 1916, A.A. Deutschland #135, No. 1, Bd. 1, #A379.

transact their business in the Turkish language, not in German or
even in French. The Ambassador estimated that most Germans
would need several years to master the Turkish language and
until they did could exert only a very slight influence on the
Ottoman bureaucracy.[38]

On the basis of the available evidence it is not possible to say
whether or not the Turks were sincerely ready to admit German
advisers into their administration, nor to judge the motives behind the project. However, it is worth recall that peace moves
were being made in Constantinople at the time. Henry Morgenthau was proposing that the British and Germans submit sealed
copies of their minimum war aims to President Wilson in Washington. These would be examined in the strictest secrecy to see
whether a basis for further discussion existed, and if it did not,
Wilson promised to destroy the correspondence to avoid embarrassment to either side. Morgenthau indicated that Pallavicini
was interested, though he had no instructions from Vienna, and
Metternich even more so. The German Ambassador stated that
prospects for negotiations seemed favorable because Britain had
lost no territory as yet but had added Egypt and Cyprus to her
colonial empire.[39] But the Sublime Porte could not accept the
loss of Egypt as final. Possibly to persuade the Germans against
doing so, it raised hopes in Berlin that extensive German penetration of the Turkish bureaucracy would be encouraged.

Humann advised the German government to ignore Morgenthau's proposals and criticized Metternich for his gullibility. He
did not believe that the American Ambassador had sufficient authorization from President Wilson behind him.[40] Moreover, Falkenhayn staunchly opposed taking up the Morgenthau proposals.
He asserted to Emperor William that the British could be driven
completely out of Mesopotamia and urged the recall of Metter-

[38] Metternich to Bethmann, Dec. 4, 1915, A.A. Türkei #139, Bd. 38,
#A35811.

[39] Morgenthau to Secretary of State, Dec. 1, 1915, D.S., #867.00/799.

[40] "Strictly Confidential" Memorandum by Humann, Dec. 4, 1915, Jaeckh
Papers.

nich for his pessimism and lack of circumspection.[41] Humann
went even further and suggested that as a prelude to more intensive campaigning, not only Metternich but also Liman von Sanders should be replaced and the military mission reorganized
under Bronsart von Schellendorff.[42]

Neither of these things happened, but no peace bids were
given to Henry Morgenthau, and fifteen Germans were nomi-
nated by Berlin for appointment to the major Ottoman bureaux
in February, 1916.[43] On so slim a basis as this, Entente propagandists fulminated about a German protectorate,[44] though the
arrival of the advisers in Constantinople was really meaningless
because of the reasons that Metternich had correctly apprehended. Morgenthau, however, was annoyed that his peace efforts had been rebuffed. During an interview with Halil Bey, he
warned the Ottoman Foreign Minister that the Germans would
not rest content with the assignment of their nationals to Turkish
courts. If they won the war, they would assert their control everywhere and annul any concessions they had ever made to the
Turks.[45] In the books he wrote after his service, the American
Ambassador encouraged the fiction of overriding and all-pervad-
ing German control, ascribing to German advice some of the
more atrocious Turkish policies during the war.[46]

Despite the failure of the Metternich-Morgenthau encounter,
it is not likely that Turkish fears of a separate peace were stilled.
Pomiankowski, the Austrian military attaché, said the Turks
fought the first years of the war for their existence, the latter

[41] Humann to Jaeckh, Jan. 28, 1916, A.A. Deutschland #135, No. 1, Bd.
1, #A379; Metternich to Foreign Ministry, Jan. 10, 1916, A.A. Türkei
#139, Bd. 39, #A950.
[42] Humann to Bethmann, Feb. 18, 1916, A.A. Türkei #139, Bd. 39,
#A4890.
[43] Foreign Office Recommendations to the Ottoman Embassy, Berlin,
Feb. 9, 1916, *ibid.*, #A3361.
[44] See, for instance, André Mandelstam, *Le Sort de l'Empire Ottoman*
(Paris, 1917), pp. 171–172; E. F. Benson, *Crescent and Iron Cross* (New
York, 1918), p. 143.
[45] Morgenthau to Secretary of State, Dec. 22, 1915, D.S., #762.67/ 1/2.
[46] Morgenthau, *Morgenthau's Story*, p. 49.

years for their independence. According to a remark of a Committee member to Pomiankowski, all classes of the Ottoman Empire were bent on guarding their independence against Germany
as well as against the Entente.[47]

If Pomiankowski's information was correct, it suggests a motive for a somewhat astonishing offer that Enver made to
Falkenhayn about February 27, 1916. Hitherto, the talk in Constantinople had been all of shortages and straining available resources to the farthest limit. Now, however, the Ottoman War
Minister proposed to lend Turkish troops for service on the
Western Front.[48] Falkenhayn professed his warmest thanks, but
he tried to decline the offer with the observation that the experience of the Turks was not appropriate to the conditions of the
western campaign. Nevertheless, Enver pressed his offer with
such vehemence that Falkenhayn had to yield in the end. By the
autumn of the year, seven Turkish divisions were placed in Galicia, Rumania, and Macedonia.[49] They were clothed and supplied better than their comrades on any Turkish front, and
withal gave the Germans no cause for honest complaint. At the
same time, they enabled Enver to argue that he had troops to
spare and would need no further foreign reinforcements.

The number of German troops in the Ottoman Empire at the
beginning of 1916 was only about 5,500,[50] yet the evidence suggests that Enver thought this number already presented a serious
problem of German infiltration and control. Metternich reported
that the Ottoman War Ministry seemed to be doing its best to ir-
ritate and discredit German officers by transferring them to posts
where the Turks had done poorly.[51] Furthermore, Enver
dropped hints that he planned to send away the German military mission after the war and make major armaments purchases

[47] Pomiankowski, *Ottomanischen Reiches,* pp. 183–185.

[48] Treutler of the Imperial Retinue to Foreign Ministry, Feb. 27, 1916,
A.A. Deutschland #135, No. 1, Bd. 1, #A751.

[49] Mühlmann, *Deutsch-Türkische Waffenbündnis,* p. 120.

[50] Pomiankowski, *Ottomanischen Reiches,* p. 184.

[51] Metternich to Foreign Ministry, Feb. 24, 1916, A.A. Türkei #139,
Bd. 39, #A5105.

outside the German market. The German High Command immediately protested this kind of wholesale change and persuaded
Enver to promise that a German officer would always be appointed as chief of the Turkish General Staff as long as the Committee remained in power. Even then, Enver emphasized, this officer would not be allowed to hire German personnel at will and
would be obliged to open vacancies to the best-qualified appli-
cants, whatever their nationality.[52]

Interestingly enough, the German embassy believed that the
Austrians would have a clear edge on all other competitors
under such circumstances and were assiduously playing up to
the Turks to make the most of it. Austrian units began to display
their heavy guns on the street corners of Constantinople and,
whenever they paraded, handed out small wooden models of
these guns to the city children. The Austrians also established a
very popular clinic in the heart of the city, where Turks lined up
for blocks to receive free medical attention. Metternich became
so annoyed that he told Enver it was to be hoped that no German loans to Turkey would be used to make purchases in
Austria.[53] But the Turk made no commitment and to the end of
the war continued to play off one ally against the other.

The Second Canal Campaign: Germany's
Motives and Aims

About the time that Enver forced the use of Turkish troops in
the western fighting and spoke of changes in the organization of
the German military mission, the German General Staff became
interested in a second offensive against the Suez Canal. The project had never been dead but only slumbering since Djemal's unsuccessful campaign of February, 1915. The failure of Entente
arms at the Dardanelles had naturally encouraged the Central
Powers. But Falkenhayn might not have recommended an operation that experience showed to contain so many difficulties and

[52] Military Attaché Lossow to War Ministry, Nov. 19, 1916, *ibid.*, Bd.
42, #A185.
[53] Attaché Renner to Bethmann, Apr. 22, 1916, Jaeckh Papers.

which had once failed had not Enver threatened to get rid of the
Germans and so increase his own contributions to the war effort
that his claims could not be denied at the peace conference. A
major effort on the Egyptian front, however, would make unlikely any further deployment of Turkish troops in Europe. In
addition, the Germans might yet find in Egypt those economic
opportunities from which an unmanageable Turkish nationalism
was threatening to debar them elsewhere.

For this new Egyptian operation, the Germans revived their
contacts with the Khedive Abbas Hilmi. Since his deposition by
the British in 1914, the Khedive had been wandering around Europe. He attempted a reconciliation with London and offered to
use his influence for the creation of a British protectorate in
Syria to be joined to the Egyptian protectorate after the war.
But the British War Minister, Kitchener, opposed any further
dealings with Abbas Hilmi, would not guarantee his restoration,
and at best would consider only some office for the Khedive's
son.[54] However, German reports indicated that Kitchener was at-
tracted by the idea of a dual protectorate and regretted that he
got little Cabinet support for a British landing at Beirut instead
of at Gallipoli.[55]

Thus, no agreement was reached between the British and the
Khedive. To make absolutely certain of the fact, the German
Ambassador to Switzerland, Conrad Romberg, arranged the ri-
fling of the correspondence of the Khedive's French mistress,
with whom Abbas Hilmi was living in Switzerland in the winter
of 1915–1916.[56] As an additional precaution, the Germans
began to cultivate the circle of Egyptian nationalists living in
exile in Switzerland. Ferid Bey, one of the leaders of this group,
promised to accept German patronage in return for a ministerial
emolument.[57]

As in 1914, the Germans were woefully short of factual infor-

---

[54] Hindenburg to Foreign Ministry, Nov. 29, 1915, A.A. Aegypten #3,
Bd. 87, #A35058; Kühlmann to Bethmann, Dec. 3, 1915, *ibid.*, #A35113.
[55] *Ibid.*   [56] Romberg to Bethmann, Dec. 13, 1915, *ibid.*, #A36467.
[57] Consul Rössler to Bethmann, Dec. 17, 1915, *ibid.*, #A36671.

mation about the enemy in Egypt. They believed in the immi-
nence of a revolution against the British and badly underesti-
mated British troop strength.[58] They did not know, furthermore,
that General John Maxwell had laid out considerable defensive
works east of the Canal and had put into service many miles of
pipeline to bring fresh water to troops fighting in the Sinai
Peninsula.[59] Instead, the German army and Foreign Ministry relied on stories picked up by their agents in the rumor mill of
Switzerland. There it was held that Kitchener was desperately
concerned about troop shortages and the decline of morale in
units already organized. The British War Minister was reported
to have pled at least twice for the dispatch of an Italian relief
force to Egypt, but on both occasions, he was turned down by
General Luigi Cadorna, the Italian Chief of Staff. Cadorna
thought that all manpower needs could be satisfied by drawing
off reinforcements from the Gallipoli and Salonika fronts.[60]

All this misinformation was similar to the illusions of 1914, but
a new element was the conviction with which it was held not
only by German diplomats and army generals but also by some
leaders of the German business community. Neutral correspondents of Fritz Thyssen and Company, travelling in Egypt, circu-
lated the notion that sentry duty along the Canal was being performed negligently if at all, allowing the Egyptians to carry off
hundreds of guns and much ammunition. The same sources insisted on the existence of a simmering feud between Australian
and English regiments which would boil into a mutiny under the
pressures of a Turco-German attack. Matthias Erzberger was
particularly enthusiastic about this possibility.[61] Finally, these

[58] Romberg to Bethmann, Dec. 9, 1915, *ibid.*, #A35965.

[59] By way of comparison, it might be pointed out that the Entente knew
as little about Gallipoli as the Germans knew about Egypt. See James, *Gallipoli,* pp. 53–54.

[60] Romberg to Bethmann, Dec. 20, 1915, A.A. Aegypten #3, Bd. 87,
#A37079.

[61] Erzberger to Jagow, Jan. 13, 1916, *ibid.*, #A1239. The *Frankfurter
Zeitung* carried numerous assurances of this kind (Dec. 1, 4, and 5, 1915).
It reported the comments of missionaries returned from Egypt, which held
that the people were just waiting to be armed to attempt a revolution. The

commercial pundits believed that neutral Dutch sea captains, whose vessels normally used the Suez Canal, could be induced to sink these at both canal entrances to inhibit the arrival of British relief convoys from the Mediterranean or the Red Sea.[62]

While these reports were being sifted in Berlin, Metternich at the Pera embassy tried to persuade Enver Pasha to bribe Sherif Hussein of Mecca to furnish cavalry support to the Turco-German army in Egypt or at least to keep his tribesmen neutral during its offensive.[63] Hussein of course had years of treasonable dealings with the British behind him by 1916, but the Germans believed he had still not adjusted every question outstanding between himself and London. The British were reportedly refusing to restore to the Sherif all the income of his Egyptian estates, and the Germans wanted to make counterproposals before the argument was amicably settled. But Enver vetoed the payment of any money to Hussein and warned the German Ambassador not to pursue the matter again.[64] He did not do so.

Enver's decision was a critical factor in the Ottoman collapse; in a few months, the Sherifian forces went over openly into the Entente camp. Yet it did not come as a complete surprise, because in the affairs of Tripolitania and Persia, Enver had already shown that he did not like German monies being paid out to Moslem peoples. However, there were more basic reasons be-

British were reported so frightened that they even supervised services in the mosques, lest any pro-German utterances be made. But the same paper insisted that the whole campaign should aim to bring Britain to the peace table, since "she must now realize that any further fighting would put her deeper into America's financial debt and undermine European culture." *Frankfurter Zeitung*, Dec. 25, 1915, recommended such negotiations as fully in the spirit of Bismarckian diplomacy.

[62] Report of the Political Section, General Staff to the Foreign Ministry, Feb. 13, 1916, A.A. Aegypten #3, Bd. 87, #A4119.

[63] Metternich to Zimmermann, Jan. 28, 1916, A.A. Türkei #165, Bd. 38, #A2610.

[64] Confidential Situation Report by Humann, Jan. 16, 1916, Jaeckh Papers. Britain had already pledged her support of Arab independence in the agreement of October 23, 1914, between Hussein and Sir Henry McMahon, but subsequent events showed that Hussein considered himself bound by it almost as little as the British. See Edward M. Earle, *Turkey, The Great Powers, and The Bagdad Railway* (New York, 1924), p. 284.

yond Enver's opposition that led the German government to curtail further approaches to the Arabs. These reasons emerge from
an analysis of the Arab question prepared for the German Chancellor before Hussein's assistance became important. The author
was Metternich's dragoman, Fritz Schönberg, and his opinions
were supported by the Ambassador and the principal chargé,
Neurath.

Schönberg argued that Germany would knock Russia out of
the war and deprive her of Finland, Poland, Ukraine, and the
Transcaucasus at the peacemaking, but in the spirit of Bismarck,
all Germany's gains from the war should be framed by the older
ideal of the Russo-German alliance. Germany should help re-
juvenate the Russian market because it had been, and would
again become, a good customer. She should assist in keeping
open Russia's channels of export so that the Russians could earn
foreign exchange. In order to relieve the traditional Russian pressure on the Straits and its consequent threat to Balkan Europe,
Schönberg suggested that the Tsar be helped to an egress into
the Arabian Sea. The Russians should be permitted to build a
railroad to some terminus on the Persian Gulf and assured the
right to exploit any areas touching on it. Oil deposits alone
would be capitalized and worked jointly by a consortium of the
Teutonic powers and Russia. While Schönberg admitted that
in the process Germany might suffer some economic disadvan-
tages, he insisted that these would be more than offset by the
chance to pit Russia against Britain on the frontiers of India.
Clearly, therefore, nothing in the area—neither money nor land—
should be promised to the Arabs which would later undermine
an agreement with Russia.[65] Metternich himself came to dismiss
Hussein as a politically negligible robber chieftain, too fanatical
to work with the infidel British, and easily removed by assassination if he became difficult. The last expedient had been recommended by Enver.[66]

In retrospect, Metternich's superficial contempt for Arab na-

[65] Neurath to Bethmann, Enclosure, Sep. 16, 1915, A.A. Türkei #165,
Bd. 37, #A27847.
[66] Metternich to Bethmann, Jan. 22, 1916, *ibid.*, Bd. 38, #A2528.

tionalism seems incredible, but it must be remembered that the Ambassador had no firsthand Near Eastern experience and was heavily dependent on his dragoman. These old Near Eastern hands were highly regarded in the service, and Schönberg's ideas about a negotiated peace roughly corresponded with the Ambassador's own. The memorandum also apparently found favor with the German Chancellor, because in February, 1916, he sent a special emissary to Constantinople to encourage Metternich to explore possibilities for a separate peace even while the buildup for the Canal campaign continued.

This emissary was Reichstag deputy Matthias Erzberger. He arrived in the Turkish capital on February 5 and, according to Pallavicini, came not as a mere private citizen but rather as Bethmann-Hollweg's personal representative. Erzberger's remarks and actions, therefore, were quite likely covered by a mandate from the top echelon of the German civilian bureaucracy, though it is less certain that the military leadership approved all the ideas he put forward in Constantinople. To Pallavicini, he declared that everybody in Germany was sick of the war and revolted by the Armenian persecutions. The Emperor, at the urging of his wife, was ready to shake the Turkish alliance and would already have done so, except for the noxious influence of Falkenhayn.[67] Erzberger himself loathed the Turks and, after an interview with Talaat Pasha, was more than ever sure that the whole race was unregenerate. During this interview, which occurred shortly after the deputy's arrival, Erzberger demanded that the Armenian persecutions immediately cease and the victims be paid compensation by the Ottoman government. Furthermore, he wanted as many Armenians as possible to be settled along the route of the Baghdad Railway, where they would be under German supervision and care. Finally, he insisted that Talaat incorporate his agreement to the demands in duplicate memoranda, to be filed with the German Foreign Ministry and with the Sublime Porte. Talaat, however, refused to sign anything,

[67] Pallavicini to Burian #13/p, Feb. 11, 1916, H.H.S.A. Türkei Karton 210.

nearly exploded at Erzberger's boldness, and dismissed the Reichstag deputy in a towering rage.[68]

In the next few days, Erzberger, still in a vengeful frame of mind against Turkey, outlined to Pallavicini his ideas for a reasonable peace settlement in the Near East. Metternich attended some though probably not all of these talks. Both men agreed that the masters of the Ottoman Empire were without either integrity or ideals. Their rule of force, they thought, would eventually alienate even the docile and long-suffering Turks and ignite a revolutionary upheaval if Turkey did not first succumb to British and Russian attacks. It was no longer possible for the Central Powers to hold the Ottoman frontiers intact, and in any event, Egypt, Arabia, Mesopotamia, and Armenia always hung only loosely to the center. The Austrian Ambassador flatly stated that somebody had to pay the cost of the war, and Turkey might best do it by ceding her outer provinces to the Entente with German and Austrian approval. In these conversations, none of the participants claimed Ottoman territory for their own governments. Pallavicini specifically remarked that the Dual Monarchy was neither sufficiently industrialized nor commercially adept to make significant profits for itself so far from home.[69]

But the Austrian Ambassador did indicate that his government would probably wish to acquire control of the network of French religious elementary schools set up in Turkey before the war. Erzberger agreed to this idea and commented that the teaching of German would make splendid progress among younger Ottoman students.[70] However, when he got home, he found that these educational schemes were opposed by Turcophil professors like Ernst Jaeckh and Geheimrat Schmidt of the Turkish Educational Ministry. They did not like the Austrian initiative nor the concentration on younger students, holding that

---

[68] Pallavicini to Burian #14/p, Feb. 14, 1916, *ibid.*

[69] Pallavicini to Burian #14/p, Feb. 14, 1916, *ibid.*; Metternich to Bethmann, Jan. 25, 1916, A.A. Türkei #179, Bd. —, #A357. In the latter, Pallavicini stated similar views to the German Ambassador.

[70] Pallavicini to Burian Telegram #85, Feb. 9, 1916, H.H.S.A. Türkei Karton 210.

all such efforts were most successful at the university level. Nevertheless, the Austrians anticipated a favorable outcome and had large donations taken in the archdioceses of Vienna and Gran in Hungary. The Cardinal of Cologne was also an important donor.[71]

Before Erzberger left Constantinople, he was accorded an interview by Enver, possibly with the hope of erasing the bad impression made by Talaat. Enver promised that the Armenian exiles would be settled in carefully guarded areas, though apparently not contiguous to the Baghdad Railway. He also spoke of permitting religious freedom and of eventually reopening the Armenian Christian seminaries. However, in his final report to the Chancellor, Erzberger damned those assurances as insufficient and recommended that Germany herself assume responsibility for the Armenians. In the meantime, German investors should be warned off Turkey.[72]

Precisely what form of protection Erzberger had in mind for the Armenians is not clear, though Metternich before his Constantinople visit had proposed an Armenian protectorate.[73] This was a return to the old Wangenheim scheme, but mention of it may not have been made to Pallavicini during the Erzberger discussions. In any event, after the return of the Reichstag deputy,

[71] Matthias Erzberger, *Erlebnisse im Weltkrieg* (Berlin, 1920), pp. 65–67, 69. It is interesting to recall that Gustav Stresemann, speaking for his National Liberal party, took up the question of the dissemination of the German language in the Ottoman Empire in a long Reichstag speech of March 1, 1917. While he admitted that it was humiliating for Germans in Constantinople to have to speak French, he concluded that the situation could not be changed. He declared that the Turks could be better impressed with German medical science than with any sort of educational scheme and called on the government to subsidize the dispatch of a large corps of doctors to the Ottoman Empire. See *Stenographische Berichte über die Verhandlungen des Reichstags, 1914–1920* (20 vols.; Berlin, 1917–1920), Bd. 309, 85 Sitzung, p. 2474.

[72] The conversation with Enver took place on February 10, 1916. It is described in Erzberger's report, "My Travel Impressions of Turkey," dated February 25, 1916, in A.A. Türkei #158, Bd. 14, #A5281.

[73] Metternich to Foreign Ministry, Dec. 21, 1915, A.A. Türkei #183, Bd. 40, #A36794.

Johannes Lepsius, who had been in bad odor with official circles for over a year, was briefly rehabilitated to organize a movement to send an expedition of doctors and nurses to the Armenian villages of Syria and Mesopotamia.[74] This move was not without political overtones, because, as Lepsius pointed out to the Chancellor, if Germany popularized herself in Turkish Armenia, the Russian Armenians would be more likely to put themselves under German protection after the war.[75]

However, Jagow seems to have scotched these schemes as too expansive. He advised the army that his secret information indicated that Russia was now set on having a position on the Persian Gulf. To lead to it, the Russians intended to create a corridor of land under their jurisdiction from Trebizond to Alexandretta and Baghdad. Jagow commented that he did not think that the Russians would attempt to dislodge German businesses from the area, and in the spirit of the Schönberg memorandum, he recommended that Germany use any control she acquired in the Armenian districts only to barter it away to Russia in exchange for a timely peace.[76]

Austro-German Commercial and Cultural Rivalry and Turkey's Reaction: The Treaties Question

Until the Bolshevik Revolution took Russia out of the war in a manner that few Germans could have foreseen, many government departments in Berlin continued to propound this scheme of buying her out at Turkey's expense. The diplomatic correspondence indicates that besides the Wilhelmstrasse, the Chancellor's office, the Navy Department, the Colonial Secretariat, the Roman Catholic Episcopate, and the German academic community favored what amounted to a betrayal of the Ottoman ally.[77] Yet hardly were such sentiments born when military devel-

---

[74] Erzberger to Foreign Ministry, Mar. 7, 1916, *ibid.*, Bd. 41, #A6225; Lepsius to Bethmann, Mar. 10, 1916, *ibid.*, Bd. 42, #A8626.

[75] Lepsius to Bethmann, Apr. 17, 1916, *ibid.*, #A9943.

[76] Jagow to General Staff, May 10, 1916, *ibid.*, #A12323.

[77] Pallavicini to Burian #14/p and #19/p, Feb. 14 and Mar. 2, 1916, H.H.S.A. Türkei Karton 210.

opments dampened and destroyed them. Even before Erzberger conferred at the German and Austrian embassies in Constantinople, the Russians were reorganizing their Caucasus command and bringing it under the aggressive and relatively young
General Nikolai Yudenitch. On January 17, 1916, Yudenitch ordered his troops to advance on a broad front against the Turkish
Armenian city of Erzerum. This attack was swift, effective, and
profited magnificently from the element of surprise. The Turks,
who had believed that the bitter winter cold put any change of
the battle lines out of the question, were rolled back distances of
from fifty to seventy miles. Erzerum was occupied on February
16, and Yudenitch and his senior commander, Grand Duke Nicholas, confidently projected a march to Erzincan, the Plain of
Sivas, and the edge of the great Anatolian grain-growing district.

The Russians had thus taken in the field what the German diplomats proposed to bargain away over the conference table. The
new situation in the Caucasus reinforced the objections of the
German General Staff and justified their contention that a negotiated settlement was not possible. Furthermore, the Austrians
proved unable to pull together with the Germans for more than
a few weeks, and the cooperation between Erzberger and Pallavicini soon gave way to the older habits of deception and petty
rivalry. The Turks did their best to sow dissension and possibly
knew a great deal about the opinions exchanged between the
Reichstag leader and the ambassadors. Pallavicini reported being
approached by a Committee agent, who told him that the government was tired of cajoling the Germans and anxious to confer profitable concessions on the Austrians. The Ambassador was
invited to have engineers sent down from Vienna to prospect for
oil in Syria and assured help of every kind from the commander
in the area, Djemal Pasha. Pallavicini commented in his report
that the Turks were trying to set Vienna and Berlin at loggerheads, but he could not resist the additional advice that Djemal's
move be cautiously followed up.[78]

[78] Pallavicini to Burian #13/p, Feb. 11, 1916, *ibid.* On the other hand,
Talaat was reported to have promised Metternich that the Turkish govern-

On March 10, 1916, a more powerful bid for Austrian support was made by the Sublime Porte. The ordinarily xenophobic Foreign Minister, Halil Bey, summoned Pallavicini to his office and told him that the Committee no longer regarded an Ottoman restoration in Albania as in the best interests of the Turkish state. Instead, the government would be content to see the country pass under Habsburg rule, whereby the security of both Moslems and Christians would be effectively safeguarded. Halil disclosed that he was still being badgered by fanatical Islamic nationalists from Tirana and Durazzo, but he swore that these were being discouraged by all means at the Committee's disposal. Some of the firebrands had even been put under protective custody in Turkish jails, and if necessary the Young Turks would proceed still more stringently to prove to Vienna that their movement no longer harbored any threat against Austrian predominance in the Adriatic Sea.[79]

Halil's pledge thawed the ice that had fallen upon Austro-Turkish relations since Erzberger's arrival in Constantinople. The Austrians were persuaded or frightened into believing that they had most to gain from direct deals with the Turks rather than from conspiracies with the Germans. They refused therefore to set any modest limits to their enterprise in advance or to associate themselves with any attempts to dragoon the Ottoman ally. The Germans, on the other hand, went ahead ruthlessly and in the midst of the Turkish defense of Erzincan attempted to deprive the troops of money and supplies. Speaking in the name

---

ment was prepared to cede "half of Jerusalem" to the Germans if they faithfully represented Turkey's interests at the peace-making. The consent of the Moslem clergy was supposed to have been assured beforehand, but later the Porte declined to go through with the transaction because of the outbreak of the Arab revolt. It was alleged that the deal would lay the Turks open to Arab charges of impiety and sacrilege. The author has found no document in which Talaat's promise is mentioned. This information, deriving from the recollections of Turkish military personnel, is found in Bayur, III/III, 209–210.

[79] Pallavicini to Burian #21/p, Mar. 10, 1916, H.H.S.A. Türkei Karton 210.

of the German Foreign Ministry and of the Imperial Ministry of
Finance, Berlin's delegate to the Ottoman "Dette Publique," Ru-
dolphe Pritsch, told Talaat that it would be impossible to sanction a loan for the defense of Anatolia unless the government immediately paid up the kilometric guarantees covering the
completed sections of the Anatolian and Baghdad Railways. Pallavicini had never seen Talaat so angry; he charged that the demand was unreasonable and roundly accused the Germans of
sabotage. He came to blows with the German bureaucrat, and
the situation would have degenerated still more dangerously had
not the Deutsche Bank relented and the Austrians come through
with a loan of their own.[80]

Talaat swore to Pritsch that the Committee would never forget
the incident and that Germany would now have its unending
hatred. The threat was not idle. The Armenian proscriptions increased, and in the holocaust of destruction, no distinction was
made between Armenian and German businesses. Metternich
protested, but Halil ignored him and coolly added that the Porte
would not later entertain any German demands for indemnity.
He made no attempt to deny the vandalism, but instead described it as merely incidental to the victorious prosecution of
the war. Moreover, he suggested with simple irony that Berlin
should itself be happy to make good all damage suits.[81]

In this argument between Halil and Metternich, the German
army found in favor of the Turk. It interposed to put an end to
further talk about peace at Turkey's expense in 1916. The General Staff had Field Marshal August von Mackensen sent to Constantinople as Emperor William's personal representative. He
carried with him a bejeweled marshal's baton to be conferred on
Mohammed V and publicly commended the wisdom of the Committee's policies when he arrived on March 5. Pallavicini believed that Mackensen did not fully succeed in restoring the

[80] Pallavicini to Burian #19/p, Mar. 2, 1916, *ibid.* The kilometric guarantees are described in Earle, *Bagdad Railway,* p. 81.

[81] Metternich to Bethmann, Apr. 3, 1916, A.A. Türkei #183, Bd. 42,
#A9024.

confidence of the Turks in the German alliance, but he did give the Committee the satisfaction of Metternich's almost public humiliation.[82] In every speech and on every state occasion, the Marshal stressed the importance of Turkey's victories and Germany's continuing need of them. He held all contact with the German embassy down to an embarrassing minimum, and when Metternich attempted to modify or deny his sanguine appraisals, he found the army telegraph station closed to the transmission of his dispatches. After Mackensen left, practically all the Ambassador's reports were censored before relay to the Wilhelmstrasse. When he complained, he was informed that the volume of correspondence had become so large as to impair Enver's unrestricted communication with the German War Ministry. In the interest of victory, the General Staff had found it necessary to impose an order of priority.[83]

Had the army had its way, it would also have imposed Metternich's replacement. This was not yet possible, because the Ambassador still had the support of certain political and religious factions within Germany. This was what the Turks meant when they described Count Metternich as "trop Catholique." [84] On April 28, 1916, about fifty Reichstag deputies arrived in Constantinople, their mission to encourage the German Ambassador, to soothe the nationalistic Halil, and finally to evaluate on the spot Turkey's strength as an ally. Among the most important members of the delegation were Count Kuno von Westarp and Herr Ernst Bassermann, the Conservative and National Liberal leaders respectively.

The Reichstag delegation was received by the Sultan and tendered a sumptuous dinner by the Committee of Union and Progress. During this banquet, however, it was easily observed that Halil was intractable and the Turks only superficially cour-

[82] Pallavicini to Burian #26/p, Mar. 31, 1916, H.H.S.A. Türkei Karton 210.

[83] General Staff to Bethmann, Mar. 16, 1916, A.A. Deutschland #135, No. 1, Bd. 5, #A7198.

[84] Pallavicini to Burian #76/p, Oct. 7, 1916, H.H.S.A. Türkei Karton 210. The remark was made by Prince Said Halim.

teous to their guests. The Ottoman Foreign Minister made a
rapid speech in his own language reviewing the course of the
war and the reasons for Turkish intervention. He emphasized,
the Germans thought too much, that the decision was taken to
destroy for all time Russia's expansion towards the Straits and,
by omitting any other reasons, implied that it had nothing whatever to do with the financial, economic, and military help the
Germans had poured into Turkey since Abdul Hamid's reign. Indeed, Halil praised the Germans specifically only for approving
the abolition of the capitulations, distorting an issue that his lis-
teners would have preferred not be brought up at all. The German deputies believed that Halil was trying, as politely as possible, to insult them.[85]

For their own part, they gave insults too, though mostly unin-
tentional and adolescent. They cut the heir to the throne, being
unaware of exactly who he was, and ate the Turkish viands with
a little too much occidental disdain. In making so much over the
unresponsive Halil, they completely ignored his predecessor at
the Sublime Porte, the Grand Vizier, Prince Said Halim. The
Prince was in fact no longer important and, since the portfolio
for foreign affairs had been taken from him, was like some exotic
oriental bird from which the talons had been drawn in the Committee's zoo. Nonetheless, the Germans should have guarded
against giving him offense, for the sensitive aristocrat went immediately to Pallavicini and proposed that Austria mediate a
peace with Russia. The terms to be held out to the Tsar, which
Said Halim claimed many of the Turkish parliamentary opposition leaders approved, were that the Straits would be kept open
unconditionally to Russian commerce even if the Sultan were at
war with a third power. Though there would be risk for the
Turks, it was intended to be offset by a powerful submarine fleet
guaranteed to them by treaty with the Entente powers. The
Grand Vizier hinted that Austria might build the submarines.[86]

[85] Metternich to Bethmann, Apr. 28, 1916, A.A. Türkei #158, Bd. 15,
#A11453.
[86] Pallavicini to Burian #36/p, May 6, 1916, H.H.S.A. Türkei Karton 210.

The Germans could not allow such an arrangement. The spring and summer of 1916 were spent feverishly in cultivating new commercial contacts with the Ottoman Empire and in renewing the old ones. Despite the skepticism of men like Erzberger and Metternich regarding the prospects for foreign business, a heavy traffic of German salesmen streamed into Constantinople as soon as the Reichstag delegation had left. This was partly matched by the arrival in North Germany of various Turkish trading missions which scouted for new products and low prices. The Turks were repeatedly assured that Britain would lose control of the world textile market through an upsurge of nationalism in Egypt and India, and advised to sign contracts to assure themselves of high quality German substitutes. Chambers of Commerce in cities like Bremen, Hamburg, and Mannheim stood the Turkish missions most of their travel expenses, and the General Staff ordered the Prussian Ministry of Transportation to concede half-fares to them and to German salesmen travelling in the other direction. Undoubtedly, the army believed in the utility of all these measures even more than the industrial representatives who got cheap excursions to southeastern Europe under its auspices.[87]

At the same time, similar efforts, again under the aegis of the army and of its impulsive amanuensis, Professor Ernst Jaeckh, were made to reach the average Turk through the media of mass entertainment and the fine arts. However, this venture miscarried and showed almost comically how little Jaeckh and the generals understood the temperaments of their own artists and of the people to whom they were trying to present them. It proved very difficult to find enough musicians and actors to make the trip to Constantinople. Most had sufficient work at home and doubted that they could recover the costs of travelling to a foreign country. To meet this objection, the price of conveyance was cut to a minimum, but by and large only a number of court musicians, whose princely employers guaranteed them against loss, were at all enthusiastic about the invitations. The concerts of German

[87] Metternich to Foreign Ministry and Enclosure, June 2, 1916, A.A. Türkei #158, Bd. 15, #A14578.

music went off tolerably well, and possibly the articles about the differences between German and Latin (i.e., French) harmony, which Jaeckh had written up and Metternich was obliged to put in the Turkish newspapers, had something to do with the success.[88]

But the presentation of German drama, which Jaeckh extolled as not only diverting but also morally elevating, was a ridiculous fiasco. The sacred texts of Goethe and Schiller must not be tampered with, much less translated into Turkish or French. Consequently, nobody except the German diplomats and soldiery, together with a sprinkling of the more cosmopolitan representatives of the Sublime Porte, knew what was going on. The performances had to be held indoors, an insufferable handicap as the balmy Turkish spring gave way to sticky summer heat. Though performances for upper-class ladies were organized separately from those for men, they still excited the opposition of the Stamboul crowd, which resented and vilified so many women showing themselves off in one place. The city's German merchant community virtually boycotted the travelling theater. They hated Jaeckh for his frequent and voluble depictions of a golden Turkey, which they had come to know as a hellhole. Moreover, as they rudely pointed out to him, the German classics were boring enough in Berlin; why bring them down to Constantinople? The money would have been better spent to build a German community hall in the city.[89] These beery barbs tell much about the average Germans in Turkey. They were a loud, vulgar, and bustling lot, who would have ruined efforts more sensibly conceived than those of the naive and pretentious Jaeckh.

Nonetheless, the attempt to "sell German" was broken neither by the failings of the Professor nor of the German expatriate bourgeoisie. The timing was bad; the Turks had too much else on their minds to be amused. On April 18 the Russians captured Trebizond and, though the large Turkish garrison escaped, there-

[88] Metternich to Bethmann, June 2, 1916, *ibid.*, #A14937.
[89] The actor Schueler to Jaeckh, June 2, 1916, *ibid.*, no number.

after cut up the southern coastal traffic of the Black Sea, which had brought coal and grain into the capital. Pressing his advantage, Yudenitch then besieged Mush, Bitlis, and Erzincan. He took all three by the beginning of August and triggered a panic in Constantinople exceeding what accompanied the first Entente bombardment of the Dardanelles forts.

Like some great apocalyptic tide, thousands of deserters and refugees receded from Armenia across Asia Minor, committing every horror of pillage and pogrom on the way. No distinction of sex, religion, or race was made, and indeed there seemed no motive behind the slaughter at all. Armenian and Turk, Greek and Kurd, all joined frantically in what seemed the carnival of the condemned. The disaster was blamed on the German advisers and on the Committee. The Germans were quietly issued hand grenades to defend themselves against food rioters, and Talaat was forced reluctantly to schedule more frequent meetings of the entire C.U.P. membership. Though the party chief believed he had already conceded enough, he was not spared the discovery of a plot to take his life and those of Enver and Djavid. The leaders were army officers of the middle ranks, men of Talaat's age who had mounted the ladder of political conspiracy with him but had been left far behind in the ascent. They were all said to have engaged in terrorist activities against the cronies of Abdul Hamid in the old days, and the Interior Minister was reported, probably correctly, as completely shattered that necessity forced him to liquidate his former friends.[90]

The inner Committee leadership decided that something had to be done to popularize the party and the war. For the moment, it increased the salaries of all civil servants to discourage disaffection and sabotage. A number of modernist decrees, quite wrongly ascribed to German influence, like the subjection of the Sheik ul Islamate to the Ministry of Justice and the streamlining of the female frock, were delayed and sent back to committee. But continuing bread riots, in which even Enver's wife was re-

[90] Pallavicini to Burian #71/p and #76/p, Sep. 15, 1916, and Oct. 7, 1916, H.H.S.A. Türkei Karton 210.

ported to be playing a leading part, showed the ministers that the public expected them to do more.[91] In Pallavicini's language, they had to be shown that they were getting "something solid" out of the fighting and the alliance with the Central Powers.[92]

Through the office of Halil Bey, the Turks proposed their solution: the abrogation of the Paris Treaty (1856), the London Treaty (1871), and the Berlin Treaty (1878). All three documents infringed upon Turkey's sovereignty over the Straits, and the Berlin Treaty, in two of its paragraphs, allowed for foreign protectorates over Armenia and the more vaguely described "Christian communities." Since Turkey had long ago repudiated the treaty privileges of the Entente powers, the latest rumpus could only be construed as directed against the Germans.[93]

About September 5, Halil departed for Berlin to argue the treaty problem with the Wilhelmstrasse. Enver left for General Staff Headquarters at the same time, to press the Turkish case on the military establishment. Both men met with the stiffest resistance, though the army gave way first. The Austrians refused to cooperate at all. The Ballplatz pretended to deplore the Turkish actions and scored them as arbitrary and deceitful. However, Burian gave play to his temper mostly in private and at this time secretly instructed the Austrian consuls to do everything to accommodate the Turk. He had become interested in Pallavicini's scheme of a Habsburg protectorate over the Ottoman Catholics, and was convinced that nothing should be done to spoil the prospect of a definite settlement with the Porte.[94] Burian promised the Wilhelmstrasse that he would consider a separate dec-

[91] Chargé Radowitz to Bethmann, Oct. 24, 1916, A.A. Türkei #134, Bd. 36, #29078.

[92] Pallavicini to Burian #71/p, Sep. 15, 1916, H.H.S.A. Türkei Karton 210.

[93] Metternich to Foreign Ministry, Sep. 5, 1916, A.A. Türkei #204, Bd. 1, #A24061.

[94] Burian to Pallavicini Telegram #4890/4885, Oct. 4, 1916, H.H.S.A. Türkei Karton 208.

laration of protest, but Berlin clearly felt that this would never materialize.[95]

More disheartening were the diverse pressures brought to bear by the Turks. These had been allowed to accumulate over several months, so that in the end the Germans found them irresistible. Halil reminded his allies that the Baghdad Railway had not been coming along at all well. The delay had now become particularly insupportable, because the Turks had captured Kut-el-Amara on April 29, 1916, and argued that they needed only better transportation and more supplies to push the British back to the Persian Gulf and out of Mesopotamia altogether. They had done less spectacularly in the Caucasus, but that was all the more reason, according to Halil, for rushing in reserves of matériel and manpower to stem the Russian advance. The Ottoman Foreign Minister demanded that the Germans at once resume building of the tracks between Ras-el-Ain and Nissibin. If they did not, the Turks would finish the job themselves. Furthermore, they would expect the German government to assume half the construction expenses as a "war cost," though this flagrantly contradicted earlier Baghdad Railway conventions, wherein Turkey paid all the charges by various methods of delayed financing.[96]

Metternich advised the Wilhelmstrasse to hold firm, but Jagow backed down as soon as he learned that members of the German army had themselves put the Turks up to their current stand. The chief engineer of the Baghdad Railway reported that German officers coached both Halil and Enver in the arguments now being brought forward and assured the Turks that even the threat of nationalization would not be overstepping the mark. These outrageous maneuvers were said to have been sanctioned by General Otto von Lossow, military attaché of the Pera em-

[95] Zimmermann to Constantinople Embassy, Nov. 6, 1916, A.A. Türkei #204, Bd. 1, #A29872.

[96] Metternich to Foreign Ministry, Apr. 6, 1916, A.A. Türkei #152, Bd. 86, #A8992.

bassy. And Lossow took his orders from Falkenhayn.[97] Both men appeared to have no higher motive than to disgrace Metternich and to usurp from the Foreign Ministry all control of the Turkish diplomacy.

Lossow declared that the Turks were in deadly earnest and quite prepared to wreck cheerfully twenty-five years of German railroad imperialism. No act of the Committee's would be better calculated to recover popularity and make the crowd forget the danger along the Caucasian ramparts of the empire. The attaché recommended any concessions to save the situation and charged that those who minimized the potential danger did not really understand the Near East.[98] During his visit to Berlin, Halil made sinister reference to a provisional law that had been tabled in the Turkish cabinet. It called for the expropriation of several short lines: Smyrna-Aidin, Smyrna-Kassaba, and Mudanya-Brussa, formerly under French management. Lossow cited this law as a portent of still worse to come. On the other hand, Metternich dismissed the provisional law as just so much negotiating tinsel and was supported in that view by Liman von Sanders.[99]

Liman believed that the Turks were still too intellectually backward to know what to do with the railroads even if they got hold of them. As a military solution, he would have satisfied their arguments by relinquishing a broad belt of Caucasian territory to the Russians rather than channeling in more resources for its defense. He told Enver that there was little risk of Yudenitch pressing much farther, because his logistical problems were already immense, and the Russian would not want to risk what he had already taken. But Enver refused to listen to this advice, perhaps suspecting it as part of a higher plan to buy a Russian peace with Turkish land. He told Liman that under no circumstances would he countenance the transfer of units from the Second and Third Caucasian Armies to the Sixth Army operating

[97] Metternich to Bethmann, May 1, 1916, *ibid.*, #A11772.

[98] Jagow to Imperial Treasury, Apr. 7, 1916, *ibid.*, #A8992.

[99] Constantinople Embassy to Bethmann, Sep. 21, 1916, *ibid.*, Bd. 90, #A26134.

around Kut-el-Amara.[100] Thus, the Anatolian grain country was neither successfully defended—the Bolshevik Revolution simply removed the Russian threat—nor the advantages of the capture of Kut fully achieved. Instead, while the Germans quarreled among themselves, the Turks were allowed to throw away a victory and blackmail an ally to no clear purpose.

Yet if the purpose was not always clear, the instinct was sound. The Turks could sense that the Germans were ready to give Mesopotamia to the Entente, especially to Russia. That much had been in the air since Erzberger's visit to Constantinople. They could not be blamed, therefore, for attempting to set their own price on the transaction. Some Germans suspected that Enver did not really want to push on beyond Kut-el-Amara, whatever his claims, and had given secret orders that the victory be used to fraternize with Townshend, the defeated British commander. It was thought that the Turks wanted to contact Townshend's superiors in London by extending him every courtesy and comfort in captivity. The Germans were scandalized by the freedom allowed the distinguished prisoner and cursed the Turks when they were evicted from their quarters to make room for Townshend's staff. Many transferred immediately to other theaters of fighting, but could do little more because the senior German officer at Kut, Marshal von der Goltz, had died of typhus during the siege. His successor was a Young Turk chauvinist who ignored their pleas, kept them inactive, and constantly humiliated them.[101]

There was no question that Turkish diplomacy was as active in other areas as it was in Berlin under Halil's personal direction. While he negotiated the future of the three great treaties governing the Straits, he and his cohorts sought to provoke new enemies to overcome German intransigence. Since his arrival in the German capital, he contended that international protectorates over the Ottoman Christians only encouraged them in treason

100 Liman to War Ministry, Oct. 26, 1916, Seeckt Papers.
101 Adolf Friedrich, Duke of Mecklenburg-Schwerin, to Seeckt, Aug. 8, 1916, *ibid.*

and seditious localism. As he spoke, a new wave of Armenian brutalities set in along the Baghdad Railway route, and still more ominous, the Turks contrived to reopen the Greek question. Reports reached Berlin of horrible massacres of Greek villagers all along the Black Sea coast to Trebizond. Halil was furnished with Enver's intelligence reports claiming that the Russians were distributing guns to the victims. Enver also personally assured the Pera embassy that nothing more terrible was happening than putting the Greeks on short rations and water. The Germans, however, knew that much worse was true and that they could do little to stop it. Liman von Sanders, whose Fifth Army command covered the Greek districts, sternly forbade his troops to take any part in the bloodletting, but this did not exclude the dangerous prospect that the news from the Black Sea might force the Greek government to intervene in the war.[102]

Greek intervention for the Entente did not materialize until June 29, 1917, but the events would have justified Venizelos' declaration half a year earlier. More immediately, the Greek persecutions worried the Germans about what new crimes would be held to their account and shortened their patience when they confronted Halil. The Pera embassy tried to persuade the American Ambassador to mediate the argument between the Greeks and the Turks, but Henry Morgenthau was unfortunately recalled at this time. His departure was attended by much talk that he had offered to buy Palestine for his Zionist associates and offended the Committee in the attempt.[103] Nonetheless, the German embassy believed that the Sultan's government was by no means as insulted as was made out. In fact, the Turks were reported ready to haggle about a price with the new American Ambassador, Abraham Elkus, as staunch a Zionist as his predecessor.[104] It is almost certain that the Germans overesti-

[102] Kühlmann to Bethmann, Dec. 11, 1916, A.A. Türkei #168, Bd. 15, #A34108.

[103] Elkus to Secretary of State, Nov. 17, 1916, D.S., #867.00/802-2.

[104] Kühlmann to Bethmann, Jan. 20, 1917, A.A. Türkei #190, Bd. 2, #A2615.

mated Turkey's willingness to parley, but concern still lingered that the Porte was trying to introduce a new factor into the situation. In previous German schemes of partition, the United States of America had never had any place.

With all these threats—Greek, Zionist, and nationalist—the German Foreign Ministry was forced to allow the nullification of the treaties of 1856, 1871, and 1878. The most the Wilhelmstrasse could do was to argue that it had been caught by surprise. Halil for a time went along with this subterfuge and wrote the Pera embassy that the Porte would never have brought up the treaty matter if it had anticipated offense to the Teutonic allies. Nevertheless, there was no going back. The Turkish papers exulted over the news, and Halil claimed that Turkish public opinion had never given him any real room to negotiate.[105] A few days later, he wanted to include reference to the affair in the Sultan's speech from the throne. Mohammed V was to say that the nullification of the treaties had the warm support of both Germany and Austria, but this declaration was struck out because of strong German protest. The Sultan merely said that the treaties had been denounced, without any reference to the attitude of his allies. When the ceremony was concluded, Halil tore into the German chargé and accused him of a shameful breach of faith. By its reservation, the German government imputed to the Turks an inferiority and blood-thirstiness that took all heart out of the alliance. If the Turks were as bad as the Germans made them out, he continued, they would long ago have put all Catholics, Greeks, and Bulgars to the sword. Instead they had desisted, but would continue to do so only as long as Europeans in their country behaved in a way to justify the earlier clemency.[106]

Metternich was spared this tirade. He left Constantinople a few weeks before. The treaties question and the knotty diplomacy that accreted around it ended his career and brought him

[105] Chargé Radowitz to Foreign Ministry, Nov. 6, 1916, A.A. Türkei #204, Bd. 1, #A30094.
[106] Kühlmann to Bethmann, Nov. 14 and 21, 1916, *ibid.*, #A30876, #A31822.

back, a sacrifice to the army in Berlin. Falkenhayn again stepped boldly forward for the job, and Emperor William, who was described as "desperately" wanting a solution, concurred in his appointment.[107] However, the diplomatic service levelled a strong no-confidence vote against the new addition to its ranks, and Jagow was persuaded to head off the ambitious general. He was aided, perhaps unwittingly, by Erich Ludendorff and Paul von Hindenburg. These great heroes of the eastern fighting informed Falkenhayn that they expected him to meet all the Turkish demands for the sake of ultimate victory.[108] Falkenhayn did not take kindly to this advice, though he had pressed something similar on the unfortunate Metternich. In fact, he did not expect to perform the miracles that he had rigidly required of his predecessor and, the record shows, was loath to risk a failure. Jagow observed to him that the Turks might feel dragooned since yet another general was being sent to them and were likely to turn stiffer than ever. Moreover, as a member of the German government, he would be debarred from the role of covert opponent which he so enjoyed. In short, Falkenhayn would have to take orders, and that, in the end, he decided he could not do.[109]

Other names were then raised for the Pera embassy. The job was offered to Prince Hohenlohe-Langenburg, a former interim ambassador at the Sultan's court, but he turned it down for reasons of ill health. Arthur Zimmermann, Undersecretary at the Foreign Ministry, was also mentioned, though it was decided that the amount of business in Berlin would not allow his appointment at Constantinople. The government was then forced, with declared reluctance, to come back to the candidacy of Richard von Kühlmann, Ambassador to the Netherlands. The army was not enthusiastic about Kühlmann, though on the basis of his recent experience, it was difficult to say why.[110] Before being

[107] Bethmann to Foreign Ministry, Aug. 29, 1916, A.A. Deutschland #135, No. 1, Bd. 1, #A3068. The date shows that Falkenhayn had been pushing his candidacy for some time.

[108] Bethmann to Jagow, Sep. 12, 1916, *ibid.*, no number.

[109] Jagow to Bethmann, Aug. 30, 1916, *ibid.*, #A3065.

[110] Jagow to Bethmann, Sep. 12, 1916, *ibid.*, #A3237.

posted to the Hague, he had been a member of the embassies of Lichnowsky in London and of Wangenheim in Constantinople. In both cities, he served outwardly as a mere counselor; in reality, he was secretly charged to whip both his seniors into a more militant line.[111] His role in bringing about Turkish intervention in 1914 will be recalled.

Yet Kühlmann was a kind of split personality, whom fate had cast into roles contrary to his better nature. Left to himself, the man was as much a poet and artist as a workaday diplomat. In his sympathies and tastes, he was cosmopolitan and a good European, and these qualities made the army uneasy. He took little trouble to conceal his opposition to the war once he felt Germany could no longer win, and in The Hague embassy he was constantly alert to armistice projects and separate peace moves. He never favored unrestricted submarine warfare, and when, during the German occupation of Belgium, he was approached by a number of Flemish separatists, he told them that their hopes of annexation to the Reich were senseless and would never be approved by the Wilhelmstrasse. He worked always to make contact with Britain and rejected anything that would threaten her home ground or cool her toward negotiation.[112] To serve that latter end, and as a matter of personal pride, Kühlmann cultivated the friendship of well-travelled and widely known celebrities. One, the historian Friedrich Meinecke, was several times the Ambassador's guest during his Dutch service. To Meinecke he talked of his hopes for the future German empire, and according to the historian, these had nothing to do with Asia Minor, but were concentrated on central Africa.[113]

The army may have been aware of these speculations, because Hindenburg, who had lately succeeded Falkenhayn as chief of the General Staff, thought it necessary to admonish Kühlmann

---

[111] Friedrich Meinecke, *Strassburg, Freiburg, Berlin* (Stuttgart, 1949), p. 206.

[112] Kühlmann to Paul Weitz, May 30, 1915, A.A. Nachlass Paul Weitz, Bd. 6.

[113] Meinecke, *Strassburg, Freiburg, Berlin*, p. 208.

not to pursue an independent foreign policy.[114] Kühlmann gave assurances to that effect, but Hindenburg was not satisfied and continued to entertain the idea of replacing him with Zimmermann. An attempt was even made to send Kühlmann to Constantinople as only a chargé, but he insisted on and finally obtained the terms of a regular appointment.[115] In the end he was titled Ambassador Extraordinary, which made the Turks fear that he carried overwhelming power, though the people in Berlin knew it actually meant that he disposed of something far less. Pallavicini also interpreted his new colleague's appointment as provisional because of the army's dissatisfaction and deplored the fact that Germany, having changed her ambassador to Turkey three times in a year and a half, appeared to do it again. The Austrian observed that it was impossible for Berlin to get a clear picture of the situation under these circumstances, while at the same time he believed that it was easier for the Turks to exploit a man who was green and insecure in his job.[116] He might have added that the insecurity was aggravated by the German government itself.

The army, until it could evict the Ambassador, resolved to keep him isolated and infirm. As soon as Kühlmann arrived in Constantinople, the General Staff attempted to separate him from all the old Turkish hands. Ludendorff protested that Paul Weitz was allowed too free a run of the Pera embassy and too great access to papers that Wangenheim and Metternich should have classified strictly secret. The general carped that Weitz used embassy secretaries to type his reports to Frankfurt and then pocketed the money that should have been used to hire one on the outside.[117] Even if these charges were true, Ludendorff knew that Weitz's unique value should excuse a number of petty

[114] Pallavicini to Burian #88/p, Nov. 18, 1916, H.H.S.A. Türkei Karton 210.

[115] Bethmann to Jagow, Sep. 20, 1916, A.A. Deutschland #135, No. 1, Bd. 1, #A3346.

[116] Pallavicini to Burian #88/p, Nov. 18, 1916, H.H.S.A. Türkei Karton 210.

[117] Kühlmann to Bethmann, Dec. 11, 1916, A.A. Deutschland #135, No. 1, Bd. 1, #34220.

sins. The General was less concerned with upholding standards of professional integrity than with destroying a man who refused to be his dumb instrument.

With that other grey eminence of Turkish policy, Matthias Erzberger, the generals concerned themselves less. Erzberger's reputation as a diplomat collapsed with the second Egyptian campaign. After all his confident predictions, nothing more occurred than a few impotent raids on British posts in the Sinai Peninsula between April and August, 1916. The Turks lost over 50 per cent of the men detailed for this operation, and there were none of the revolutionary repercussions that Erzberger and his contacts had exuberantly expected. The only thing saving his reputation was the fact that the fighting did not come to a decisive end and, short of a general order for withdrawal, a Turkish comeback was not out of the question. Erzberger continued to hope and work for it, and in that manner compromised himself as much as the army could have wished. With money whose sources are obscure, he bribed the Khedive, Abbas Hilmi, as if the prospect of his restoration was still imminent and sure.

The Khedive cheerfully took the money and, as a diversion from the ordinary pleasures of his Swiss exile, did a little spying on Entente troop movements to prove his good faith. He maintained an agent in Paris, who had contacts with the French War Ministry, and Erzberger insisted that here was an excellent way of preventing the ingenious Abbas from making a separate accommodation with the British and French.[118] This kind of accommodation would naturally exclude the concessions, favors, and awards that Erzberger was trying to pry out of the Khedive with his money. But the French secret police found out the Egyptian plant and promptly registered a protest with the Swiss government. An investigation turned up several of Erzberger's letters among the belongings of the Khedive, who protested that his rights as a man and a sovereign were being infringed.[119] Nonetheless, his rage made no impression, Berlin was threatened

[118] Romberg to Bethmann, Nov. 7, 1916, A.A. Aegypten #3, Bd. 88, #A30395.
[119] Romberg to Bethmann, Nov. 10, 1916, *ibid.*, #A30610.

with the eviction of its embassy from Bern, and the Reichstag
deputy was mortified beyond recovery. The Turkish embassy in
Bern was said to have tipped off the French police. Erzberger
protested that he had merely used Abbas to transfer some charitable contributions to recipients in Italy, but the Wilhelmstrasse
knew better than to believe him, and the General Staff did not
want to.[120] He never advised the Pera embassy again.

For a man who, as it were, had lost both his hands, Kühlmann
at first did quite well. At the instance of Halil Bey, who wrote
Berlin about the matter, the government was persuaded to clear
away all ambiguities about his appointment and to confer some
sort of stable tenure. Then the Turks offered the Wilhelmstrasse
a separate convention that appeared to modify the recent nullification of the treaties and to exempt the Germans from the recurrent flurries of Committee chauvinism. Despite the recent conflict over the treaties, this document assured Germans in Turkey
special rights even above those of natives. They were to be permitted high places in business and the administration without
renouncing their citizenship, and with these inducements, it was
the express hope of the Sultan's ministers that the normal tide of
German emigration to America would be stemmed.[121] The
promises never got beyond paper, but his hosts had obviously
bidden the Ambassador to enjoy himself and work fruitfully at
his charge. However, Turkish encouragement ended here, and in
other areas positive obstacles appeared.

Count Czernin On Sharing the Spoils in Turkey and Rumania

These were offered Kühlmann not by the Turks, but by the
Austrians, whose government had recently come under a new
and younger hand. On November 21, 1916, Emperor Franz Joseph had passed away in the Hofburg and made place for his

---

[120] Erzberger to Foreign Ministry, Nov. 10, 1916, *ibid.*, #A30422;
Romberg to Bethmann, Nov. 20, 1916, Bd. 89, #A31692.

[121] War Office to Foreign Office, London #123/262213, Dec. 18, 1916,
P.R.O., F.O. 371/2783.

grandnephew Charles. Consequent on his accession, a general
shakeup of the Austrian bureaucracy removed Burian from the
Ballplatz and brought Ottokar Czernin, former Ambassador to
Rumania, as his successor. Charles had little liking for the Turkish alliance: it was not fit for a Catholic power. He had less for
the Germans, whom he considered overbearing, uncooperative,
and rude. About the time that Kühlmann was settling into his
new job, Charles was arguing the inopportuneness of unrestricted submarine warfare with the German navy. His opinions
were ignored, not too politely, and the admirals went ahead with
their plans. The experience only revived memories of earlier humiliating occasions when Charles had ineffectively tried to represent Austrian views of Italian policy to the German Emperor.[122]
Charles as sovereign therefore resolved to go his own way,
which quickly led him to the dark maneuvers of the Sixtus Affair. Czernin was an apt companion, though he disagreed with
his imperial master about details.

A keen competitor, Czernin was disposed to agree when Conrad von Hötzendorf referred to the Germans as "our secret enemies." He did not think that Austria could any longer tolerate
the war, but yet he hoped that she might somehow gain something from the struggle. At an earlier period, he pushed plans for
a Habsburg federation with Rumania and believed that it might
have been realized but for the unreasonable Magyar Stephen
Tisza, who insisted on persecuting the Rumanians of Transylvania. The war ended Czernin's plans for all time, but they help
explain why he repudiated the policies of his Magyar predecessor, Burian.

In the Ottoman Empire, the policy change was discernible by
a clear, sudden quickening of Austrian commercial activity. The
tempo alarmed not only the Wilhelmstrasse, but also the Navy
Department, which feared that measures might some day have
to be taken to contain Austria in the Adriatic Sea. The Foreign
Ministry was advised to put in a claim for Valona in Albania,

122 Arthur Polzer-Hoditz, *The Emperor Karl* (Boston, no date), pp. 193,
213.

though it would fall foul of Turkish and Italian, as well as Austrian ambitions.[123]

In the meantime, Charles and Czernin took up the protectorate of Ottoman Catholics, this time ignoring the claims of the German ally. Pallavicini discussed the question with Djemal Pasha, who was on leave in Constantinople from the Palestinian front. Djemal was more than a little taken with the idea because he was afraid of the imminent retribution of the Entente. Therefore, he had lately dispensed various kinds of relief and aid to the Syrian Catholics, urging them to recommend him kindly to the French. At the same time, he groped for Austrian mediation, indicating that in the field of religious protection, there was work enough for Paris and Vienna to share. Both he and Pallavicini agreed that Germany had no permanent place in Egypt.[124]

Implicit in all Djemal's remarks was the delusion that he would survive the war and even Turkey's defeat. He considered Talaat and Enver to be thoroughly discredited, for different reasons, in Ottoman and world opinion and Djavid, because of his Jewish background, disqualified from becoming their heir. He alone would be left, sufficiently well known to the people but, because of involvement with his Syrian command, safely above controversial and compromising political questions. Pallavicini believed this and banked on him to advance Austria's Near Eastern interests while securing his own.

Kühlmann, on the other hand, chronically backed Enver, who was known and everywhere reviled as the only pillar of the German alliance. That higher conscience that occasionally impelled

[123] Admiral Holtzendorff to Bethmann, Dec. 26, 1916, A.A. Nachlass von Hintze, no number.

[124] Pallavicini to Burian #96/p and #98/p, Dec. 16 and 23, 1916, H.H.S.A. Türkei Karton 210. In the course of the later negotiations, February, 1917, with Prince Sixtus of Bourbon-Parma, it became clear that Charles had much less definite ambitions in Turkey than his Foreign Minister. He would have declared in an agreement with Russia Austria's entire disinterest in the Ottoman Empire, but Czernin refused to allow any such precise renunciations to reach the French Foreign Ministry. Obviously, he wanted to keep the field open (Bayur, III/III, 515–516).

the German Ambassador brought him to protest to Enver the pil-
laging of the Greeks. Lossow was enlisted to keep up the pressure.
But though Turkey had secured the nullification of the Straits
treaties, to which she had cleverly attached the Greek issue,
Enver and Halil pled that they could not abate the persecutions
without sacrificing themselves to the Committee opposition.
With them, Kühlmann was reminded, would go the alliance.
They were already being accused of having sold the country to
the Germans and, like it or not, were forced to demonstrate their
patriotism in Greek suffering and blood.[125]

Halil did not exaggerate, though Kühlmann, who worried
more about Germany's standing in world opinion, kept up the
pressure. Ambassador Elkus told him that Washington was
watching the fate of the Greeks quite closely, and Kühlmann
was afraid that an unsatisfactory outcome might furnish one
more justification for America's joining the Entente.[126] His apprehensions of course did not forestall that event but his intimidation more immediately succeeded, quite inadvertently, in ex-
pelling both Halil Bey and the Grand Vizier, Said Halim, from
office. The Prince was too Egyptian and suspected of being too
ready to bargain with the British if they would deliver him his
estates intact. He was also regarded as too old-fashioned, even
obscurantist, in his opposition to the emancipation of Turkish
women. And lastly, he was taken in the Committee for a snob:
behind the backs of his colleagues, he had proposed to the Sultan that a new Ottoman peerage be recruited from the ranks of
the intellectuals, the bankers, and the scientists. The scheme
roused the equalitarian and baseborn Talaat to a fury, and he
was reported at the head of the movement that deprived the
Grand Vizier of his seals.[127] Yet the German Ambassador credited none of this, reproached himself for having moved clumsily,

125 Pallavicini to Czernin #4/p, Jan. 13, 1917, H.H.S.A. Türkei Karton
211.
126 Trauttmansdorff to Czernin #9/p, Jan. 30, 1917, *ibid.*
127 Trauttmansdorff to Czernin #11/p, Feb. 6, 1917, *ibid.*

and regretted the loss of the only "good European" in the ministry.[128]

Talaat took Said Halim's place, with Djavid at the Finance Ministry and Achmed Nessimi at the Ministry for Foreign Affairs. Enver remained at the War Ministry. He took particular delight in weathering this latest ministerial crisis and thought his survival proved his popularity among the people. His allies were less satisfied with the result: Kühlmann despaired of surmounting Enver's ego; and Pallavicini wanted him out of the way, together with Talaat, as a dangerous chauvinist. The Austrian embassy thought that this might yet happen, even though the two Committee leaders had survived their latest scrape with the party's dissenters, and reported that the army, as an institution distinct from its leaders, was now for the first time unpopular with the Turkish people. Food was short as always, but the parliamentary opposition leaders were now not scrupling to point out to the crowd that the shortages were the direct result of the army's rapacious needs. The Caucasian armies ate up everything that would ordinarily have been shipped out of Asia Minor to the capital, and though Enver was making efforts to tap the Bulgarian harvest, a railroad wreck on the frontier had choked off that source of supply.[129]

There was talk of sabotage and of willful extortion on the part of the Bulgarian government. The Turkish people had little liking for their ally in Sofia, and the current shortages uncovered a hostility never far below the surface since Bulgaria's entry into the war. That intervention had been consummated by an agreement published on September 22, 1915. By it the Turks recognized the left bank of the Maritza River as their frontier with Bulgaria, so that the railroad line up from Dedeagatch would run entirely within the territory of King Ferdinand. The city of Adrianople had to be surrendered in the transfer; the Committee accepted the loss grudgingly and tried to justify it as a necessity of war. A year and a half later, Austrian intelligence reports indi-

[128] Trauttmansdorff to Czernin Telegram #71, Feb. 5, 1917, *ibid.*
[129] Trauttmansdorff to Czernin #11/p (b), Feb. 6, 1917, *ibid.*

cated that the Turkish people were no longer disposed to believe this claim. There was a widespread popular feeling that the loss of Adrianople was only the first sacrifice to an unquenchable Bulgarian expansionism, and some Committee members were beginning to argue that the Union and Progress Party would fall if it could not recover the ancient Ottoman capital.[130]

Loudest was the Committee membership in Adrianople itself, who requested that the question be renegotiated with the Sofia government, but got no place with Enver and Talaat. According to Austrian reports, the Adrianople section was so outraged at this rebuff that it considered a revolution to force the government's hand. A number of Armenian assassins had been hired and, if the government did not come around, had secret orders to shoot down the Grand Vizier, the Ottoman War Minister, and King Ferdinand. The Austrian consul who reported this news to Pallavicini's embassy assumed that it would be relayed to the Porte at once, but the chargé, Charles von Trauttmansdorff, who was substituting while the Ambassador was on a brief leave in Vienna, decided to inform only the Bulgarian government. Trauttmansdorff justified his decision by declaring that any other would have been needlessly alarmist and provoked the Turks to an intensification of the Armenian persecutions.[131] While this was possibly true, the subsequent drift of Austrian diplomacy suggests that the chargé's decision was well in line with the thinking of Ottokar Czernin.

In the middle of March, the Austrian Foreign Minister held in Vienna a series of war councils with Bethmann and various members of the German and Austrian diplomatic services. He began by impressing on the Germans that the Dual Monarchy could not continue in the war for more than six months and cited hunger, typhus, floods, and the acute shortage of livestock, fertilizers, and industrial ores. Czernin therefore wanted to approach France and send the diplomat Count Albert Mensdorff to

[130] Trauttmansdorff to Czernin #12/p, Feb. 10, 1917, *ibid.*
[131] Trauttmansdorff to Czernin Telegram #58 and #12/p, Feb. 10 and 12, 1917, *ibid.*

Switzerland to put out feelers. Bethmann, on the other hand, was quite skeptical and doubted that France would talk unless she were promised the outright restoration of Alsace-Lorraine and of Belgium. The Chancellor did not feel that he could bring about such cessions in the face of a hostile German public opinion, not to speak of the General Staff, and urged his colleague to await a more conclusive outcome of the submarine warfare. Bethmann held that the Russian Revolution was directly attributable to its success. Nonetheless, Czernin dismissed any military victory as out of the question; the time had come, he said, to define the war aims of the Central Powers.[132]

He did not propose to acquaint Turkey and Bulgaria with these definitions until after they had been all but guaranteed by France. He had in mind a division of Rumania, recently conquered, to award part to Austria, part to Bulgaria, and part to Russia to turn her from revanchist intentions after the war. Aware of the state of opinion in Constantinople, Czernin must have known that the Bulgarian enlargements he contemplated would enrage the Turks. It was no wonder that he enjoined the strictest secrecy to cover the talks, because their content would make the Adrianople question seem trivial indeed.

Bethmann objected to the scheme; he wanted no quarrel with the Porte and saw no necessity for giving Russia anything at all. He further observed that anything offered St. Petersburg would only whet but hardly satisfy the appetite of the Slavs and make the incorporation of Constantinople seem more feasible. Czernin did not gainsay this and his pointed silence seemed to indicate that he was not closed to such a solution. Somewhat later, on March 26, he suggested that Germany under his dispensation might have the sovereignty of a restored Kingdom of Poland and of a newly created enclave embracing the mouth of the Danube. If Berlin would seal the bargain on this basis, Austria would reserve Wallachia for herself, the Dobrudja for Bulgaria, and Moldavia for the Russian provisional government.[133]

[132] Minutes of the Council, Mar. 16, 1917, A.A. Nachlass von Hintze, no number.

[133] Minutes of the Council, Mar. 16, 1917, and Mar. 26, 1917, *ibid.*

Instead of ending in agreement, the talks degenerated into a near argument. Bethmann refused to concur in the partition of Rumania and the aggrandizement of Bulgaria, declared such speculation premature, and practically called Czernin's statements about food shortages in the Dual Monarchy outright lies. The Chancellor insisted that the Austrian tales of woe did not tally with the reports of German travelers, but Czernin rejoined that he could produce documents to support his presentation in every detail. Hindenburg was sent a copy of the minutes of the Czernin conversations and for the army voiced his emphatic opposition to the Bulgarian proposals. In the General's view, a partition of Rumania was unnecessary, and the purposes of the Central Powers would be as well served by the accession of a Bulgarian prince to the Rumanian throne. The name of Prince Cyril was mentioned. He was German and could be expected to accord a long-term military alliance to Berlin and Vienna. Nothing more was needed, and the Rumanian frontier could substantially be left to stand.[134]

Hindenburg could not have been clearer nor Czernin more persistent. The point was never settled and kept the Central Powers on edge until the end of the war. The Ballplatz simply ignored Germany's wishes and pursued the incorporation of Rumania by every means open to it. By the summer of 1917, Czernin had drummed up much support for the partition among the Rumanian clergy and many of the intellectuals. Deputations of Rumanian prelates were received by the Archbishop of Vienna, feted by the Austrian Foreign Ministry, and allowed to wait upon Emperor Charles at the Hofburg.[135]

On the other hand, Czernin found it difficult to predict the reaction of the Magyars. They protested against any closer association with the Rumanians, because the latter were too antisemitic and would become a political liability in Budapest, where the

---

[134] Lersner to Foreign Ministry, Apr. 29, 1917, *ibid.* Part of Wallachia was possibly still to be ceded to Austria, but nothing more of the Rumanian kingdom to any other power.

[135] Wedel, German Ambassador in Vienna, to Chancellor Michaelis, Aug. 6, 1917, A.A. Rumänien #17, Bd. 4, #A26404.

Jews were so prominent. Tisza wanted the proposition tabled, and in his turn Czernin tried to withhold details of future negotiations from the Hungarian Prime Minister.[136] According to his memoirs, the bent of all his endeavors was purely economic and intended to secure for the Dual Monarchy nothing more than an abundant supply of Rumanian wheat.[137] Moreover, an arrangement with Rumania would help stave off a customs union with Germany, which Berlin had been urging on an unresponsive Vienna for over a year.[138] But when all was said and done, Czernin did want a clear-cut division of Rumania with Bulgaria, though for domestic and foreign reasons he was too embarrassed to say so publicly later.

Whatever was said was enough to alert the Turks, though they tended to blame Berlin and Sofia, rather than Vienna, for what was happening. Enver moved at once to checkmate the Bulgarians and to suggest to them how dangerous the consequences of their territorial rapacity might become. As an ally, he insisted on his right to review the Bulgarian lines. Permission, however, was denied him, because the Bulgarians were reported afraid of the incendiary effect he might have on their Moslem population. Barred from crossing the frontier, the Ottoman War Minister managed to get through to his agents, who spread all sorts of wild talk about an autonomous Macedonia and an Ottoman Albania. While Czernin and Bethmann conferred in Vienna, numerous Moslems deserted the Bulgarian ranks or ostentatiously put on Turkish uniforms mysteriously supplied to them. Under interrogation, the demonstrators admitted that they had been worked upon by Enver's people, and protests were immediately lodged with the Porte. The incidents, nevertheless, were not entirely suppressed, and the Bulgarians were reduced to menacing the Turks with one hand and decorating them with baubles with the

[136] Stolberg, German Ambassador in Vienna, to Foreign Ministry, Aug. 27, 1919, A.A. Rumänien #29, Bd. 1, #A23375. This is a retrospective analysis of the situation in 1917.

[137] Ottokar Czernin, *Im Weltkriege* (Berlin, 1919), p. 362.

[138] Stephen Count Burian, *Austria in Dissolution* (London, 1925), pp. 327–328.

other. Prince Cyril and a ranking Bulgarian army officer came to Constantinople to give the Sultan and Enver high awards, but they had difficulty getting permission for the trip, and then their reception was only lukewarm.[139] As a result of Enver's maneuvers, Bulgaria in the end did not become an active collaborator with Austria in her designs against Germany and the Turks. But at the same time, it cannot be said that the Committee chieftain succeeded in turning the Austrians from those designs or even in appreciably slowing them down.

To the contrary, what emerged in early 1917 was a complete and vigorous plan for Austrian economic penetration of the Ottoman Empire. Its premises were a negotiated end to the war and the cooperation and friendship of certain Young Turk leaders whom the Entente would allow to linger in office, such as Djavid Bey and Said Halim. The Austrian embassy maintained close contact with them even while it kept up more or less friendly contacts with the ill-omened Talaat and Enver. The ex-Grand Vizier was a fund of important information which never appeared in the German archives or only in the scantiest detail. It was from him that the Austrian Ambassador learned of a movement, begun by Djavid and nurtured by the parliamentary opposition, to reduce the annual appropriation for Enver's War Ministry from the customary nine to six million pounds. The intention, as Pallavicini could not doubt, was to force Enver's resignation or acquiescence in negotiations with France. Djavid's faction was furthermore reported as without any faith in the ultimate success of Germany's submarine campaign and convinced that the Germans, themselves aware of this, were getting ready to open talks at Turkey's expense.[140] It is odd that Djavid and Said Halim assumed that Austria was above such tricks, but the confiding tone they used to her ambassador and the warm encouragement they received from him indicate as much.

[139] Kühlmann to Foreign Ministry, Feb. 13, 1917, A.A. Bulgarien #17, Bd. 21, #A5140; Kühlmann to Bethmann, Apr. 22, 1917, *ibid.*, #A13672.

[140] Pallavicini to Czernin #20/p, Mar. 10, 1917, H.H.S.A. Türkei Karton 211.

Austria profited from the sympathy that, even in the Near East, was accorded the underdog. Moreover, her ambassador moved deftly and inoffensively while his colleague Kühlmann blundered and annoyed the Turks. The German Ambassador, like his predecessors, could not keep himself from the Armenians and possibly did not want to. The Committee confronted him with a demand that all male Armenians living in Germany, whom it numbered at three thousand, be extradited for service in the Sultan's army. Kühlmann and the Wilhelmstrasse refused the demand because they were certain the expulsion would mean certain death for the exiles. The Turks were instead assured that the Armenians would be required to serve the alliance in the Prussian army.

Then the Ambassador received an Armenian delegation which again requested that Germany exercise a protective guarantee over that distressed people, and for this episode no excuse to be made to the Porte could be found. Meanwhile, the incorrigible Professor Lepsius ground out brochures and pamphlets claiming that German banking and finance, the navy, the Chancellor, and even Hindenburg, all disgusted at the Armenian atrocities, favored peace and satisfaction of Britain's claims at Turkey's expense. The Foreign Ministry had to deny all this through Kühlmann, but it was impossible to shut up the professor because he had taken refuge in a Dutch coastal resort and there merrily spun out his fulminations and intrigue.[141]

Unlike the Wilhelmstrasse, the Ballplatz under Czernin was careful not to identify itself with any one people or geographical locality. There was no longer any talk of an Austrian Cilicia, as there had been in Berchtold's time, but only of mutual profit for Austrian and Turk and religious well-being for Christian and Moslem alike. The nearest Pallavicini came to anything like Germany's Armenian gambits was his interest in the Ottoman Jews during latter years of the war. He persuaded Czernin to allow

[141] German Evangelical Mission to War Ministry, Berlin, Jan. 18, 1917, A.A. Türkei #183, Bd. 46, no number; Romberg to Bethmann, Feb. 8, 1917, *ibid.*, #A4820.

him to transfer the contributions of Viennese Jews to their af-
flicted brethren in Jerusalem. About eight thousand people were
relieved of at least the direst misery of their poverty; the friendship of the Grand Rabbi, whom Pallavicini thought would be
serviceable with the British, was secured; and the House of
Rothschild made readier to capitalize Austrian Near Eastern enterprise after the war. According to Pallavicini, only investment
money and time were needed to get the edge of the Germans in
that market.[142] Meanwhile, he also advised that Austria move
quickly to the front to relieve Entente prisoners of war in Turkey. At the wish of Pope Benedict XV and on instructions from
the Ballplatz, a number of Austrian Capuchins were sent to the
internment camps. They all spoke English and French, were
very popular among the internees, and were assumed to have
added significantly to the fund of good will upon which their
government would draw at the conference table.[143]

Pallavicini's optimism was an almost giant stride beyond the
timorous claims he made for Austria in the earlier talks with
Matthias Erzberger. But in the year that had gone by, he had
seen German policy become more confused and directionless.
More important was the new blood Czernin brought to his job.
He did not consider himself a stopgap like Burian and always
put himself and his subordinates on the diplomatic offense. The
results of the new policy were immediate, effective, and to the
Germans, disturbing. The Austrians dispatched a number of experts knowledgeable in the work of the main Ottoman governmental bureaux. They stayed in the background and, upon inquiry, were described to the German embassy as prospective
faculty for a few commercial schools that the Austrians wanted
to establish in Constantinople. In reality, they were thought to
have been offered as alternatives to the Germans officially accredited to the Ottoman government. They gave advice, took no
fees, and aroused no hostility. Kühlmann warned that some of

[142] Pallavicini to Czernin Telegram #154, Mar. 8, 1917, H.H.S.A. Türkei
Karton 211.
[143] Pallavicini to Czernin #20/p(b), Mar. 10, 1917, *ibid.*

these men were intended to direct the electrification of Smyrna, while still others were reported to have laid out plans for new harbor works at Constantinople. Elaborate drawings of these had reached the desk of the prefect of the city without the Germans knowing anything about them, and it was feared that the negotiations had gone far enough so that the contract, reaching into millions of marks, would certainly be awarded. Moreover, Philipp Forchheimer, a professor from Graz, had been invited to lead the city's engineering school and, until he could train Turkish incumbents, would be empowered to hire his own compatriots to keep the public works in good repair and operating order.[144]

Kühlmann described the Ministry of Public Works as more important to Germany's postwar position than any other in the Ottoman bureaucracy. Its influence was unobtrusive but pervasive and permanent. He requested Bethmann practically to flood the Turks with German experts, lest Austria usurp more control and make her mischief irrevocable. Yet Bethmann could not rouse sufficient volunteers because of the low salaries offered and the conditions of service, which the Germans regarded as humiliating. The annual stipend was only two thousand Turkish pounds and the rank merely an undersecretary's. Furthermore, it was clearly specified that German undersecretaries would rank after Turks of the same order.[145]

The cost of living in wartime Turkey had risen so steeply and paper money was discounted at so severe a rate that the Germans were known to weep when they changed currency at the banks. The salaries offered by the Turks, inadequate to begin with, would dwindle by the day unless the commodity shortages abated. This was not likely. Kühlmann could therefore only attempt to bring the Turks to reason through argument, but this usually ended with the observation that another German loan would enable the Turkish government to pay a better wage.

[144] Kühlmann to Bethmann, Apr. 2, 1917, A.A. Türkei #139, Bd. 43, #A11241.

[145] Kühlmann to Bethmann, Apr. 11, 1917, *ibid.*

Moreover, it was difficult for the German Ambassador to carry his point because the Austrians at this very time offered to build the Turks a little railroad from Adabazar to Zonguldak in north-western Asia Minor. No conditions were attached to the work, and promises were given to complete it in the fantastically short space of two months. Material and wages would be supplied by Austria, and discussion about the liability of the Turks deferred until after the war. The German Ambassador thought that the proposals were not seriously intended and would founder if the Turks took them up.[146] But the very fact of such suggestions was in itself embarrassing to Berlin and encouraged assumptions by the Porte that the Central Powers would henceforth shoulder the expenses of the war alone. Kühlmann heard of someone in his circle who was insinuating that Germany did not expect to be fully paid for her engineering and materials on any Turkish railway enterprise but would be satisfied with the long-term profits. He was unable to establish this person's identity, but thought that he must have received comfort and advice from Pallavicini's staff.[147]

It soon became clear that the Adabazar-Zonguldak line was far from the limit of Austrian ambition. Vienna hoped to lace the entire northern coast of Asia Minor with railroads and in addition planned to prospect extensively for oil in Mesopotamia. The German embassy in Vienna learned that Czernin himself was encouraging the Wiener Bank-Verein and its associate banks to pool all available capital for Near Eastern undertakings. The Ballplatz was not even dismayed upon being informed that at some points the work contemplated would encroach upon concessions given earlier to German syndicates. Czernin at first professed ignorance but later simply declared that Austria, as a sovereign state, had a right to keep pace with Germany in the economic penetration of Anatolia. He grew very irritable about the matter, vowed to maintain his position, and advised that for

[146] Kühlmann to Foreign Ministry, Mar. 4, 1917, A.A. Türkei #152, Bd. 92, #A7396.
[147] Kühlmann to Foreign Ministry, Mar. 17, 1917, *ibid.*, Bd. 93, #A8971.

the sake of appearance, it would be better to adjust the question between the interested banks instead of wrangling over it in the foreign ministries.[148]

Beyond the polite warning issued from its Vienna mission, the German Foreign Ministry seemed reluctant to go. For a time it cherished the hope that the Turks would prefer to do business with the Germans, whom they knew from twenty-five years' experience. Yet the signs were multiplying that the problem could not be quietly adjusted between gentlemen and would require heavier diplomatic or military pressure. Professor Jaeckh, upon whom the Wilhelmstrasse depended to disseminate good will and German culture at Constantinople despite individual differences with him, was reported at his wit's end by the spring of 1917. He had hoped to revive faltering Turkish interest in German business through his Friendship House, a large building near the cistern of Justinian, conceived as a clubhouse and an exhibition hall. But on the day of its inauguration, the Turks of the capital and even the German merchant community boycotted the affair and went off to an Austrian fashion show being held nearby. Jaeckh and Kühlmann were furious and blamed one another, but the Turkish government was as much at fault and, despite its pledges, had donated barely enough ground to lay the cornerstone. His own countrymen ridiculed the splendid architect's drawing which Jaeckh carried in his pocket and behind his back petitioned members of the Reichstag to force him to release the contributions he had collected for the more vulgar enjoyments of the German denizens of Pera and Galata.[149]

Emperor William and the General Staff viewed all this with some alarm. They did not trust Czernin and were determined to make him renounce the rampant course of economic imperialism upon which he had embarked. In the process, the German Emperor and his generals were thrown closer together and united

[148] German Embassy, Vienna, to Bethmann, May 16, 1917, *ibid.*, Bd. 94, #A16142.

[149] Trauttmansdorff to Czernin #36/p, May 1, 1917, H.H.S.A. Türkei Karton 211.

against the Chancellor, Bethmann-Hollweg. The latter had diffi-
dently supported a negotiated peace and permitted the Foreign
Ministry to work toward it. Emperor William had not objected
or modified the course along which his Chancellor was drifting.
However, such a policy was no longer defensible against its critics, since the Austrians, who had once supported it, now seemed
to be selling it short. The result was that William became as outrageously expansionist as any of his generals and suggested conditions that the Entente could never accept.

This was the last thing Czernin wanted. Nevertheless, when
he came to Berlin in the middle of May, he found himself confronted by a set of German war aims that fully surpassed Austria's and probably would cancel out any advantages she might
have achieved behind his leadership. William demanded that
Malta, Cyprus, Egypt, Mesopotamia, Madeira, Cape Verde, and
the Azores be surrendered to Germany, with Gibraltar reverting
to Spain. In time, after the Italians had been expelled, the German navy also expected to build an elaborate station at Valona
in Albania.[150]

All these points were incorporated into a memorandum signed
by Czernin and Bethmann at Kreuznach on May 18, 1917. The
Austrian Foreign Minister could hardly withhold his approval
because it was pointed out to him how immense were the advantages accruing to Austria through the partition of Rumania, to
which Germany had apparently given her assent. But as soon as
he returned to Vienna, Czernin made it clear that he did not believe Germany bound to his proposals, or better, that given the
price, it was not worth Austria's while that she should be. In
reality, Czernin was trapped in the quandary of his ambitions, because the Germans were making it impossible for him both to
end the war and advance Austrian business in the Near East.
The suspicion was already in his mind that Emperor William
would not insist on his war aims if Austria were willing to sacrifice her program in Rumania. Czernin prepared the way for a

[150] Grünau to Foreign Ministry, May 13, 1917, A.A. Nachlass von
Hintze, no number.

dignified withdrawal by wondering aloud whether Austria would derive any solid advantages even if the Rumanian partition went through. He now held that Germany had so many contacts and so much money at her disposal that in the end Austria would have "only the shell while Germany has the kernel of Rumania." Czernin probably did not believe this, but could not at once out-maneuver the opposition of the German Emperor and his army. In the meantime, he warned against forcing his hand too far by refusing to help the Germans storm Valona.[151]

Had Czernin not postponed the partition of Rumania and the consequent enlargement of Bulgaria, the alliance of Turkey and the Central Powers would not likely have survived. Talaat's ministry would almost certainly have fallen and made place for men ready to open the Straits to the Entente. Even after the Bulgar-Rumanian crisis passed, the German generals remained alert against its revival. While William's bold talk had been intended to bluff Czernin into retreat, the military party began to press it as the valid aim of future negotiations. The Ministry of Marine commended the Emperor's foresight in regard to Valona and added that it would be even better if Germany staked out a liberal claim in the Albanian hinterland.[152]

With the Austrian Foreign Ministry checkmated, the German army labored to return vitality and confidence to the Turkish alliance. Ludendorff insisted that its value was basically unimpaired despite the fall of Baghdad in March. Moreover, whatever seeds of self-doubt and defeatism the Austrians had been able to sow were the result of German timidity and indecision and not of their own adroitness. The trouble, according to Ludendorff, was that Germany hitherto had been unwilling to challenge the Austrians on the spot. Because of sentiment, courtesy, and misplaced expedience by the Wilhelmstrasse, there had been too great an inclination to follow the suggestions of an ally whom Ludendorff thought better to order about.

[151] Wedel to Bethmann, May 23, 1917, *ibid.*

[152] Holtzendorff to Bethmann, May 29, 1917, *ibid.;* and Wedel to Foreign Ministry, July 16, 1917, *ibid.*

Consonant with this new and harder line, the General ordered the Foreign Ministry to facilitate the dispatch of businessmen to the Ottoman Empire in every possible way. He also wanted the banks to be officially encouraged to lend more money to industrialists so that they could set up branches in Constantinople and the provinces. Finally, he wanted the Foreign Minister to sit down with a Turkish representative and thrash out those points of German diplomacy that made the Turks ill at ease. He had in mind the Potsdam Convention of 1911, which was to be renounced along with all other forms of German involvement in Persia.[153]

Kühlmann flatly told Ludendorff that he was wrong. He had never favored the antics of Niedermayer and Wassmuss in Persia, but he did not think it wise to scrap the Potsdam Convention. While it gave some offense to the Turks by trespassing in an area the Sultan regarded as his sphere of influence, it testified to an era of Russo-German cooperation in the Middle East, a memory Kühlmann wanted recalled and revived. With that hope in mind, he warned the new Chancellor, Georg Michaelis, that German commerce in Turkey could not be expanded. The taxes and transportation facilities were detrimental and the shiftiness and moral laxity of the people incorrigible. They were always ready to hike a price or clip a profit, especially since the removal of the capitulations gave the foreign businessman no recourse.[154]

The day after this advice was given, Kühlmann received notice that he had been appointed Foreign Minister in the new Chancellor's cabinet. Pallavicini bade him an especially cordial farewell, because, as he informed Czernin, the news opened up "splendid" prospects of an early settlement of the war. Kühlmann knew the English milieu thoroughly and understood that the men in London regarded the Ottoman Empire as the keystone of their own designs for economic imperialism. In short, the new German

[153] Lersner to Foreign Ministry, May 21 and 22, 1917, A.A. Türkei #158, Bd. 17, #A16489, #A16634.
[154] Kühlmann to Michaelis, July 23, 1917, *ibid.*, #A21711.

Foreign Minister understood that Germany must vacate Alsace, Belgium, and Turkey before peace could be made.[155] Pallavicini was convinced that the new leadership would achieve all these things in short order, yet within a few months it was clear that Kühlmann and Michaelis would not move far beyond the policy of Jagow and Bethmann. For the best private intentions were withered by the army's ill will, and the new Ambassador in Constantinople had to adjust to it rather than to the consciousness, impending more and more in Berlin, that Germany and the Turkish ally might soon have to reckon with a gigantic collapse.

[155] Pallavicini to Czernin #60/p, July 24, 1917, H.H.S.A. Türkei Karton 211.

6

The Alliance Sundered

As on earlier occasions, the names of several army generals were bandied about for the Turkish embassy. Both Falkenhayn and the military plenipotentiary, Lossow, nearly got the job. But the appointment was finally conferred on Count Johann von Bernstorff, the former German Ambassador in Washington and a good friend of Colonel Edward M. House. Bernstorff was born in London and had as great a fondness for that city as for the American capital. He admired Lord Cromer and thought the British administration in Egypt a model colonial government. With the help of House and Wilson, to whom he fancied the line was still open, Bernstorff hoped that Germany might undertake something similar in Turkey.[1]

This did not suit Ludendorff. The General would not completely trust any ambassador not wearing military grey, and for him Bernstorff's ideas were too liberal. Disregarding Kühlmann's advice, he issued orders from General Headquarters that all officers serving with the military mission make private reports about the economic potential of the Turkish areas through which they traveled. The reports, subject to commentary by Liman von Sanders, were to be sent directly back to Germany and not shown to the staff of the Pera embassy.[2] Moreover, German professors at the University of Constantinople were to be enlisted in this work of analysis and survey, given army funds to supple-

[1] Count Bernstorff, *Memoirs* (New York, 1936), pp. 94, 188, 202.
[2] Lersner to Foreign Ministry, Aug. 15, 1917, A.A. Türkei #158, Bd. 18, number obscured.

ment their academic incomes, and assured of advancement in
the profession when they returned home.

For much of what Ludendorff wanted done, the Austrians had
already set the pace. They were setting up agricultural, biologi-
cal, and medical institutes throughout the Ottoman Empire, and
using Hungarian personnel, whose language had common features with Turkish. In light of all this, Ludendorff wanted no expense spared to bring Germany abreast in the race; but he did
not want any money given to the embassy or to the Turks themselves. For every economic concession taken from the Sultan's
government, Ludendorff would have given back, at some ratio to
be set by Germany, a hospital or a clinic, and he spoke of making serious beginnings in Constantinople, Smyrna, and Beirut.[3]

As an important premise for his plans, Ludendorff assumed
the imminent triumph of Enver Pasha over his Committee rivals.
Certain reservations about him notwithstanding, he was the only
Turkish leader whom the General Staff still trusted to turn the
country into a German satrapy. Ludendorff did not at all trust
in Talaat, who was suspected of being too much a nationalist
on the one hand and too ready to negotiate with the Entente on
the other. In the latter half of 1917, the General did much to
force the Grand Vizier into political eclipse while raising up the
War Minister, and the general political situation did the rest.

Ever since the first Petrograd revolution, the Turkish people
had been expecting the Grand Vizier to bring them peace. Russia was assumed to be now materially unable to prosecute the
war, and from some muddled pronouncements he had made, it
was even being stated that the provisional Foreign Minister,
Paul Miliukov, had no further appetite for Constantinople.
Rumor further spoke of a whole new party emerging in Russia
that would renounce the Straits for all time and settle instead for
a railroad access through Armenia to Alexandretta on the eastern
Mediterranean shore. The Russians were supposed ready to accept little more than a treaty guarantee for this line and to be
confident that it was more defensible against Turkish caprice

[3] "Recent Undertakings and Plans in Turkey," undated, *ibid.*, #A29285.

than the Marmora-Bosphorus complex.[4] But Miliukov never owned up to this "Alexandretta plan" and positively denied any renunciation of the Straits in London and Paris, where speculation was also rife.[5]

These denials did Talaat considerable harm, as did the failure of Henry Morgenthau's mission in June, 1917. The former American Ambassador was convinced that Talaat, promised an easy peace, was ready to open the Straits to Entente submarines, which would sink the *Goeben* and *Breslau*. In the ensuing confusion, Enver was to have been shot. But Morgenthau, who discussed these plans with the British at Gibraltar, was held at arm's length by them and by Chaim Weizmann, the Zionist leader who inspired much of London's Near Eastern policy at the time. The Zionists did not want the Turks given any guarantee of territorial integrity that would deprive the Jews of a homeland, and the British were persuaded that Morgenthau exceeded his instructions or that he was a German agent attempting to extricate the Reich from impending military collapse.[6]

The feelers of which Morgenthau had made so much were thrown out by members of the Turkish parliamentary opposition, to some extent with the Grand Vizier's approval. In their disappointment, these people now decided that nothing more could be expected from Talaat. They worked for his fall and used the course of German politics to advance their ends. Pallavicini reported that the entire city was alarmed by the retirement of Bethmann-Hollweg and afraid that the new men were summoned to make peace behind Turkey's back. The return of the

---

[4] Cresson, Consul at Tiflis, to Ambassador Francis in Petrograd, Apr. 15, 1917, D.S., #867.00/797. It will be recalled that the Germans had intelligence of this project in May, 1916 (Chapter 5, note 76).

[5] E. Adamow, ed., *Die europaischen Mächte und die Türkei während des Weltkrieges: Konstantinopel und die Meerengen* (Dresden, 1930), II, #326, 328, 332.

[6] Cecil Spring Rice to Foreign Office #1591/114918, #1635/117007, #1660/117850, June 9, 11, 12, 1917, P.R.O., F.O. 371/3057. For an account of this affair, see also Cyrus Adler and Aaron Margalith, *With Firmness in the Right: American Diplomatic Action Affecting Jews, 1840–1945* (New York, 1946), pp. 74–76.

Prussian Crown Prince to Berlin was blown up to portend Emperor William's abdication. Furthermore, the Turks followed every speech of Matthias Erzberger with increasing disapproval and alarm. He was described as the coming man, who would follow a strictly Catholic policy and betray the children of the Prophet. And if he did not do it, then the German socialists eventually would. The socialists were suspected of being ready to sell out all Germany's interests and friends overseas in return for cash, basic foodstuffs, and raw materials that the Reich would badly need at the end of the war.[7]

Talaat walked in fear of his life, and not all the watchfulness

---

[7] Pallavicini to Czernin #61/p(b), July 28, 1917, H.H.S.A. Türkei Karton 211. These suspicions were undoubtedly occasioned by socialist opposition to the ratification of a new set of consular and extradition treaties brought to the Reichstag in May, 1917. Both the Majority and Independent Social Democrats criticized the extradition treaty because of its loose definition of the term "anarchist." The socialists argued that Germany would be compelled to surrender anyone who had fallen afoul of the Young Turk government, in addition to genuine anarchists; and that on this basis the persecuted Armenians could not legally find asylum in the Reich. The socialists also added that the Reichstag should have been consulted before the Turkish alliance was contracted in the first place! See *Stenographische Berichte über die Verhandlungen des Reichstags, 1914–1920.* Bd. 310, 105 Sitzung, pp. 3198–3209.

The principle behind these treaties was that of perfect legal reciprocity; they embodied Germany's practical recognition that the old capitulations were null and void. It will be recalled that Germany was always reluctant to depart from any system like the capitulations, in which all the powers had had a hand. Witness the case of the treaties of 1856, 1871, and 1878. This would explain why agreement about the capitulations came so late in the war. If Bayur may be believed, on November 27, 1917, Bernstorff forced Talaat to sign a revision of the consular series that the Reichstag had debated the previous May. According to this revision, the series would stand after the end of the war only if the other powers also agreed to renounce their capitulatory rights. Since at that time, even Austria had not yet recognized the abolition of the capitulations and in fact disapproved of the concessions Berlin had already made, the Turks rightly suspected Berlin of trying to break its earlier promises. But then the Austrians themselves signed a series of consular, residence, property, and legal aid treaties on March 13, 1918, so that Berlin lost whatever recourse it was seeking. Among the Turks, however, bad feeling remained (Bayur, III/III, 496–498).

of the Committee spies sufficed to put his mind at ease. The clergy were hostile to him and allowed placards to go up in the mosques calling for his immediate resignation. At the end of July, hundreds of bottles containing more denunciations of the Grand Vizier were floated on the waves of the Bosphorus. These were thought to have been released by a Russian submarine and did assure the Turks that the Petrograd government had renounced the Straits. But the frantic Talaat told his associates that he thought the whole thing a deadly ruse perpetrated against him by his enemies, who had printed the broadsides in the city and then set them afloat. Among these enemies, Pallavicini numbered the ex-Grand Vizier, Said Halim, with whom he had frequent and cordial intercourse at their adjoining summer residences in Therapia.[8]

By his own wits and with German assistance, Talaat hoped yet to bail himself out. Already crushed by an overwhelming press of business, he now assumed the personal direction of food relief for the whole empire. Most foreign observers felt that his decision was a serious mistake and would only compound his problems. The relief agency was infested with notorious profiteers, many of them Talaat's reliable party hacks in the legislature whom he could not afford to dismiss. They would probably have defeated his efforts, had he attempted to purge them, but the Grand Vizier instead sought an accommodation that made him an accomplice in their crimes. He permitted his cronies to ply the black market and set prices at will, but on the understanding that the profits would be split with him to build schools, hospitals, and asylums. He hoped still to save his unpopular leadership, but in the end suffered only disillusionment and failed to bind his friends to their bargain.[9] At any rate, the Turkish people could never be made to understand the scheme, and even if the Germans had given the additional grain allocations for which Talaat begged, its breakdown could not have been long

8 Pallavicini to Czernin #61/p(c), July 28, 1917, H.H.S.A. Türkei Karton 211.

9 Pallavicini to Czernin #65/p, Aug. 11, 1917, *ibid.*

delayed. Ludendorff, however, denied him the foodstuffs he wanted, or rather sent them to Enver Pasha, whose stature and prestige were enormously inflated.[10]

Said Halim remarked to Pallavicini that it would take only a high concentration of troops in the capital, aggravating the food shortage, to topple the Grand Vizier. The Prince foresaw in this his own restoration to office, while the Austrian contemplated a settlement over Turkey with the Entente.[11] Most of the Sultan's units were then being sped to the southern fronts to participate in Falkenhayn's celebrated Yilderim offensive to recapture Baghdad, and the conditions for riot and rebellion therefore seemed unlikely to arise. Yet the Austrian embassy labored to bring them about and only minimally supported the plans the Germans had drawn up for Mesopotamia. Pallavicini even persuaded Liman von Sanders, his frequent and unguarded communicant, to sympathize with his designs. Liman held that Falkenhayn would fail at Baghdad and that his forces could be better employed in Greece against the army of the French general Maurice Sarrail.[12]

Falkenhayn was already unpopular with the Turkish field commanders and compromised both by his actions and words. When informed that paper money was accepted reluctantly in Constantinople and not at all in the provinces, he simply ordered foodstuffs for the Baghdad buildup seized. He also advertised that he intended to emulate Cromer in Egypt and rule Turkey with vice-regal high-handedness when he was appointed ambassador at the completion of a successful campaign.[13] All this boded ill for Yilderim.

At the same time, Sarrail in the Balkans had done no decisive fighting against Bulgaria, though his presence contributed to the

[10] Waldburg to Foreign Ministry, Aug. 4, 1917, A.A. Türkei #134, Bd. 38, #A26001.

[11] Pallavicini to Czernin #63/p, Aug. 4, 1917, H.H.S.A. Türkei Karton 211.

[12] Pallavicini to Czernin #55/p, July 7, 1917, *ibid.*

[13] Pallavicini to Czernin #59/p, July 21, 1917, *ibid.*

abdication of the Germanophile King Constantine of Greece and the restoration of Premier Venizelos, the man of the Entente. However, Sarrail subsequently fell out with the Greek leader and was accused of lobbying for French businessmen and for permanent French political jurisdiction in the Salonika area. A quick, hard attack by the Central Powers might have dislodged him, with not even the Greeks to mourn his end.[14] While Liman might have taken these things into account, they did not weigh heavily with Pallavicini.

Czernin also supported an attack on Sarrail and instructed all Austrian representatives in the Ottoman Empire to work for it. Pallavicini reinforced his arguments with the depositions of Captain Thomas Nomikos, former head of the Greek Merchant Marine Association. Nomikos testified that the Greek army was still loyal to Constantine, while the partisans of Venizelos were daily deserting in larger numbers. He believed that if a large Turco-German force were taken by submarines from Bulgaria to Greece and landed behind Sarrail's lines, it would be possible to liquidate that front and capture the whole Entente contingent. Furthermore, Nomikos asserted that royalist Greeks would cooperate, and in the end so convinced the German embassy that he was given a subsidy by Bernstorff.[15]

Nevertheless, the High Command did not favor this strategy. Falkenhayn feared it would reduce the manpower available for Mesopotamia and Palestine, and Talaat was worried that the troops passing through the capital to the Salonika lines would instead turn on his administration. Using these arguments, the German military leadership was able to dismiss the wishes of the Austrians as unsound. Actually, no one in Vienna needed to be convinced of this, because the motives of Czernin and Pallavicini had all along been political and, aside from the hope of raising a

[14] Alan Palmer, *The Gardeners of Salonika* (New York, 1965), pp 94–95.
[15] Pallavicini to Czernin #68/p, Aug. 21, 1917, H.H.S.A. Türkei Karton 211.

revolt in the Turkish army, were conceived only to embarrass the Germans in still another question. For the German Emperor and his generals were again interested in Rumania.

In August, William made a personal tour of the country and was so impressed with its economic and industrial potential that he declared it should become an appendage for one of his sons. His War Ministry heartily confirmed that opinion, and the navy, its sights set on abundant bases and fuel oil after the war, could not have been more delighted.[16] But all this clashed with Austria's Black Sea ambitions and was flagrantly irreconcilable with Germany's earlier contention that Rumania should not be partitioned nor revert in any manner to foreign control.

William quickly realized that his sally into Rumania had been an act of bad faith and was at pains to reassure Pallavicini about it when he saw him in Constantinople during October.[17] The German Emperor apparently also reconsidered his government's attitude toward Enver Pasha, because the Ottoman War Minister had taken advantage of his ally's preoccupation with Salonika and Rumania to get out of line. Unlike Talaat, who hoped to gain a peace from the Petrograd revolution, Enver wanted to use the chaos in Russia to extend the Ottoman frontier and incorporate the Caucasus, where so many kinsmen of the Turks lived. In 1917 this idea was only embryonic, but already distasteful enough to alarm William and bring him to Constantinople on a state visit.

It was unlike his two earlier trips, being briefer and less showy. The Emperor even shortened the banquet menus in consideration of the prevailing lack of food. But he still exuded confidence and assured everyone that he would drub his British cousins into surrender. For his entry into Pera, the Turks lined the streets with crowds of unveiled schoolgirls and women, and

[16] Grünau to Michaelis, Aug. 12, 1917; Grünau to Michaelis, Aug. 13, 1917; and Michaelis to Grünau, Aug. 14, 1917, A.A. Nachlass von Hintze, no numbers.

[17] Pallavicini to Czernin Telegram #582, Oct. 17, 1917. H.H.S.A. Türkei Karton 211.

for this the Emperor pointedly congratulated Talaat and encouraged him to further progress and reform. However, Pallavicini privately reported to Czernin that the appearance of reform was a hoax, and William was obliged against his preference to deal with the War Minister, rather than with the Sultan or the Grand Vizier.[18] What transpired between them could not be fully determined. The Austrian embassy believed that the real purpose of the trip was to negotiate an extension of the Turco-German alliance, due to expire in July, 1920.[19] But according to a later British intelligence summary, the Emperor had been made to promise to do everything to augment the Sultan's authority as caliph, to guarantee his prewar territories, and to restore to him Arabia and Armenia.[20]

The coming months were to show how elastically Enver defined Armenia and the claims of the caliphate. For the present, he made it clear that he thought a railroad line to Diarbekr the best way to implement those claims, even though it could only be built at the cost of stopping all work on the main Baghdad line. Two weeks after the Emperor returned to Berlin, the directors of the Baghdad Railway and the Deutsche Bank protested that Enver's demand was outrageous and inconceivable. The company's chief engineer went to see Bernstorff at the embassy and told him that even the present commitments involved the risk of bankruptcy and that the loss for 1916 had reached ten million marks. Passenger and freight business along the main route had fallen much below expectation and around Diarbekr would be even less. Far from undertaking new projects, the company needed an immediate eight-million-mark credit to cover the cost of old ones.[21]

In Berlin, the Treasury Secretary declared that he would never

[18] Pallavicini to Czernin Telegram #584 and #84/p, Oct. 19 and 20, 1917, *ibid.*

[19] Pallavicini to Czernin Telegram #573, Oct. 11, 1917, *ibid.*

[20] Memorandum of British Embassy, Washington, Jan. 21, 1918, D.S., #762.67/6.

[21] Bernstorff to Foreign Ministry, Nov. 6, 1917, A.A. Türkei #152, Bd. 98, #A36938; Bernstorff to Michaelis, Nov. 7, 1917, *ibid.*, #A36943.

allocate money for the Diarbekr line, but Enver tried to change
his mind with blackmail and intimidation. All food supplies were
cut off from the work gangs at the Taurus and Amanus tunnels,
and the banks of Constantinople were ordered to change German marks at a very severe rate of discount. Then Djavid Bey,
the Ottoman Minister of Finance, entered the controversy and
offered to take up half of the loss for 1916, though Enver made
the construction of the Diarbekr line a condition for even this
concession. The Baghdad Company was so desperate, and the
German War Ministry so concerned to preserve the alliance, that
both were ready to concur in Djavid's proposition. But the Wilhelmstrasse on Bernstorff's advice warned against it and insisted
that the wily Djavid was out to create a dangerous precedent. If
the Germans accepted only half of their losses, they stood a risk
of never getting more should similar circumstances recur in the
future. Furthermore, by agreeing to the Turkish proposals, the
company would be collaborating in the violation of its own
contract.[22]

Bernstorff's argument was technically correct but in essence
far removed from that of Ludendorff, which emphasized that all
further Egyptian and Palestinian campaigning depended on
completion of the Baghdad line. This work, the General repeatedly insisted, had to be done at any cost and on any terms, unless Germany were prepared to lose the Fertile Crescent to Turkey's enemies and her own.[23] Yet it is apparent that the German
Ambassador and the Foreign Ministry were preparing for just
such a loss, while hoping still to turn it into a partial advantage.

This crisis reached a nebulous and for the Germans thoroughly unsatisfactory end on January 8, 1918, when Djavid
signed with the Foreign Ministry an agreement that the Baghdad Company would be compensated "in a satisfactory manner"
for its losses. The 50 per cent Turkish guarantee was not mentioned because the Treasury and Foreign Ministries considered it

[22] Bernstorff to Foreign Ministry, Nov. 13, 1917, A.A. Türkei #152,
Bd. 98, #A38025; Gwinner to Bernstorff, Dec. 15, 1917, ibid., Bd. 99,
#A11967; Bernstorff to Foreign Ministry, Dec. 20, 1917, ibid., #A12768.
[23] War Ministry to Foreign Ministry, Jan. 9, 1918, ibid., #A1265.

unwise to be bound to it. The Deutsche Bank was not placated at all and continued to advance arguments showing that the Sultan's government could pay up immediately and in full,[24] but the War Ministry forbade these to be pressed. The Turks would not have paid much attention whatever was done by Berlin. Enver in the meantime continued to plot an intensive Caucasus campaign to the detriment of defensive operations in Palestine and Mesopotamia, and when his German Chief-of-Staff, Bronsart, would not agree with him, relieved him of his command. General Hans von Seeckt was then named to take Bronsart's place. He was instructed to make every accommodation to the Ottoman War Minister, and incidentally to keep close watch on Bernstorff and Pallavicini.[25]

Seeckt subsequently achieved great distinction in Germany's service, but his work in Turkey during 1918 gave no hint of the later, more masterful man. Privately he made sound rather than particularly shrewd analyses of the Turkish war effort, but in public he carried out Ludendorff's policy of capitulating to Enver wherever possible and of restraining Bernstorff, who was disposed to take a harder line. Enver and the General hit it off well and maintained a kind of friendship even after the end of the war.[26] But Enver never left any doubt that he considered his the position of strength, and Seeckt had to swallow without protest almost daily newspaper notices that Turkey should assume control of all the railroads as soon as peace was made. In the opinion of one of his associates, Seeckt's ability to bargain was severely limited when the *Breslau* was sunk and the *Goeben* badly damaged on January 21 during an attack on Chios and Mytilene.[27] The disabling of the ships removed one more German lien on the Young Turk leadership.

Pallavicini likened it to Canossa, and Bernstorff insisted that

[24] Lersner to Foreign Ministry, Jan. 8, 1918, *ibid.*, #A1111; Gwinner to Foreign Ministry, Jan. 25, 1918, *ibid.*, #A4225.

[25] Seeckt to Foreign Ministry, Feb. 27, 1918, *ibid.*, Bd. 100, #A10155; Seeckt to his wife, Dec. 20, 1917, Seeckt Papers.

[26] Seeckt to his wife, Jan. 28, 1918, *ibid.*

[27] A Memoir of Seeckt in Turkey by Major General Rohdewald, written Sep. 3, 1938, *ibid.*

the only way out was to make an end of the war and the Turkish alliance.[28] The Ambassador reasoned that half the provinces of the Ottoman Empire were now lost to the enemy and what remained promised little for German capitalism. Moreover, the exhaustion of the Reich might be such as to require all the resources of capital and industry for rehabilitation at home rather than for enterprises abroad. Bernstorff urged that further agreements with the Turks be deferred and that pressure from them be repelled outright.[29] But Ludendorff feared that the Committee might set about making a separate peace with the Entente, endangering the current negotiations with the Russians at Brest-Litovsk. If the solid front of the Central Powers were now to crack, Lenin might break off the talks and hurl his forces back into the war. Therefore the Turks and their torments had still to be suffered, or at best to be contained by the resources of diplomacy.

Such resources were increasingly difficult to apply. The Foreign Ministry brought no will or conviction to the job, and the Turks insisted that the claims of equity and nationalism alike made their aims in the Caucasus irrefutable. While Djavid was bargaining in Berlin about the Baghdad Railway contract, Woodrow Wilson published his Fourteen Points. Enver cleverly seized upon them to argue that the peoples of the Caucasus, if given a free vote, would choose the government of the Sultan over rule by the Bolsheviks,[30] and Djavid went so far as to suggest that the United States would provide Turkey with a full and generous alternative if the finances of the Reich proved too difficult to tap in the future. Djavid suddenly absolved Robert College, an American institution, of five thousand pounds of Turkish taxes, and on express orders from Talaat several telephones, torn out when the Porte had broken relations with the United States, were conspicuously reinstalled in the college buildings.

[28] Pallavicini to Czernin #11/p, Feb. 5, 1918, H.H.S.A. Türkei Karton 212.

[29] This argument is recapitulated by Kühlmann (Kühlmann to War Ministry, June 1, 1918, A.A. Türkei #152, Bd. 101, #A22953).

[30] Pallavicini to Czernin Telegram #29, Jan. 14, 1918, H.H.S.A. Türkei Karton 212.

The purpose of all these gestures, as Committee spokesmen were frank to admit, was to secure from Washington massive aid for railroad building after the war.[31] No such assurances were of course ever given by the Wilson administration, but in the meantime State Department personnel graciously entertained emissaries of the Committee in Switzerland. These men were ostensibly instructed to purchase foodstuffs, but the Germans knew that they had come to neutral ground first and foremost to talk peace. Djavid declared almost jokingly that he would be satisfied if his Swiss intrigues were repaid by an appointment as Ambassador to Paris after the war. The French, he claimed, liked him, and the Americans would add their support in return for all his little kindnesses.[32]

The clearinghouse for all these negotiations, in which every prominent Turkish leader except Enver was supposed to be involved, was the Ottoman League for Peace and Liberty, formed in Bern by the grandson of the celebrated reformer Midhat Pasha. Its program was to compel the Porte to make peace, to reconcile the races alienated by the Young Turkish leadership, and finally to modernize the Ottoman Empire and establish real freedom of religion and race. To a certain extent, the league was patronized by the British, and its members had already been invited to talk up their program among Turkish prisoners of war.[33] But what really alarmed Berlin was that Austrian and Hungarian nationals were rumored working with its ranks. Informants of the German embassy in Bern saw some Austrians at the league's meetings and believed that they had not come in a private capacity but instead to facilitate diplomatic introductions and to open up sources of cash in Vienna and Budapest.[34] How

[31] Louis Heck, Near Eastern Secretary at Bern, to Secretary of State, Feb. 7, 1918, D.S., #867.00/813; Memorandum by Paul Weitz, Mar. 1, 1918, A.A. Türkei #190, Bd. 3, #A11707.

[32] Rumbold to Foreign Office #456/57400, Mar. 30, 1918, P.R.O., F.O. 371/3050.

[33] Chargé Hugh Wilson at Bern to Secretary of State, Jan. 11, 1918, D.S., #867.00/812.

[34] Consul Rossenfelder in Zürich to Hertling, Mar. 22, 1918, A.A. Türkei #169, Bd. 8, #A13404.

abundant these might become, the Germans could only guess, but they did know that salesmen of the Skoda Works were discussing terms for a future railroad network in northern Anatolia, and these discussions were thought to be part of a more comprehensive plan to allow Austria to reorganize the Imperial Ottoman Bank and fill its most important executive positions.[35]

Ludendorff was not concerned to sift rumor from fact, but only to move quickly to render both innocuous. He and the War Ministry cooperated in sounding out a number of smaller German banks that might be expected to scrape up capital to meet the American and Austrian competitors in Turkey and to maintain the German interests should the harassed and exhausted Deutsche Bank, formerly the leader in the Near East, ever decide to opt out. Seeckt also wrote personally to the influential magnate Walther Rathenau and attempted to interest him and his friends in new investment houses dealing with the Ottoman Empire.[36] But the soldiers were met more by polite curiosity than hard cash and, without abandoning interference completely, gradually returned the initiative in Turkish affairs to the Wilhelmstrasse for the remainder of the war.

The record of this diplomacy is not a long one. The maneuvers were few, rather obvious, and eventually unsuccessful. In the first place, efforts were made to play off the extreme Egyptian nationalists against the Committee regime in Constantinople. Germany had formerly kept these men at arm's length or put on the payroll only those who would exchange Turkey's political for Germany's economic suzerainty in their country. Now, however, the German Ambassador in Bern began to pay small doles to the indigent Egyptian politicians and students who languished in the cheap hotels of Switzerland. The British military administration at Cairo had forbidden any money to be sent to these peo-

[35] Bernstorff to Foreign Ministry, Oct. 30, 1917, A.A. Türkei #155, Bd. 5, #A36110; Vice Consul Edelman, Geneva, to Secretary of State, July 16, 1918, D.S., #867.00/820.

[36] Dr. Erich Alexander, Director of the Deutsche Orientbank, to the Ministry of Economics, Mar. 13, 1918, A.A. Türkei #152, Bd. 101, #A20133; Seeckt to his wife, Mar. 22, 1918, Seeckt Papers.

ple from home, and in many cases their suffering was acute. But through it all they insisted upon the full independence of their country, with no halfway compromises allowing the exploitation of foreign powers. For Germany, as for Turkey, there should be nothing save to meet with Egypt as a full equal after the war. The Foreign Ministry did succeed in persuading one of the exiled nationalist leaders, Mohammed Ferid, to agree in principle to the internationalization of the Suez Canal, but beyond that the Egyptian was unwilling to go, and the Germans still gave him and his colleagues their money. They were reconciled to doing the Committee some present damage, while renouncing any future profit at the expense of its vassal. Meanwhile, the Turkish Ambassador in Switzerland announced that he would give every Egyptian exile a monthly subsidy of three hundred francs. That this was not done for any humanitarian motive but rather to combat the German propaganda became clear when Hakki Pasha, the Turkish Ambassador in Berlin, protested the whole affair at the Wilhelmstrasse. When he got no satisfaction, he left the German capital temporarily as a gesture of protest.[37]

While Germans and Turks fought with francs in Switzerland, the Wilhelmstrasse opened up a new diplomatic offensive against the Porte in Palestine and Armenia. In the preceding September, the Yilderim campaign to recapture Baghdad had

[37] Bernstorff to Foreign Ministry, Feb. 13, 1918, A.A. Aegypten #3, Bd. 90, #A5360; Romberg to Hertling, April 22, 1918, *ibid.*, Bd. 91, #A7627; Montgelas to Hertling, May 29, 1918, *ibid.*, #A23168. Evidently Mohammed Ferid had long distrusted the Germans. In *Frankfurter Zeitung*, September 28, 1917, he criticized the Wilhelmstrasse for the vagueness of its Egyptian policy and urged the press to bring pressure to bear on the government for a clear-cut statement. The Turkish Ambassador in Switzerland, Fuad Selim Bey, was particularly obnoxious to the Germans. He was fond of insisting that they must hold out for the integrity of the whole Ottoman Empire. He asserted that the defeat of tsardom was not only the work of Hindenburg, but also the result of the defense and closure of the Dardanelles (*Frankfurter Zeitung*, January 13, 1918). It may also be remarked that to some extent, Mohammed Ferid seems not to have been his own man, but rather the agent of Djavid Bey, for whom he frequently mediated with the French. In short, he was the last person upon whom the Germans should have relied (Bayur, III/II, 165–166).

been abandoned and most of the manpower transferred to Palestine to stop a British advance up the Syrian coast. Nevertheless, the Turkish army was badly beaten at Gaza in November, 1917, and a month later forced to surrender Jerusalem to the enemy. Since that time, Enver had been insisting to Berlin that the restoration of the Holy City must become a German war aim. But as the Pasha's plans for Greater Turkey in the Caucasus called for the Committee to negotiate but not fight for Jerusalem, the German Foreign Ministry was less than ever inclined to give a commitment and speculated about a solution for the Holy Places that would diminish the prestige of the Porte and at the same time, it was hoped, recover world opinion and Christian good will for the Reich.

It was to be intimated to the Turks that Germany would not demand the restoration to them of Jerusalem and Bethlehem, unless she were offered very good reasons for doing so. Short of these, the Wilhelmstrasse would make increasingly clear, the best solution might be to internationalize the Holy Places and put them under a "college of custodians" seating representatives named by the Pope, the Ecumenical Patriarch, and a conference of the Protestant churches. The plan also might pacify the government's religious critics at home and persuade groups like the Catholic Center to vote the necessary credits to bring the war to an honorable conclusion.

Bernstorff favored this plan and solicited the opinions of the German consuls in the Levantine towns still held by the Turkish forces. Many of these suggested that a German prince be enthroned and territory in addition to Jerusalem and Bethlehem brought under his scepter. But in his final draft on the question, the Ambassador opted for the college of custodians, significantly adding to it two representatives for the Arabs and the Jews. What contribution they would offer the administration of the Holy Places, Bernstorff did not say. But they could make an incalculable amount of trouble for the Turks, as well as for each other, and that recommended the idea to the Foreign Ministry.[38]

[38] Kühlmann to Bernstorff, Feb. 28, 1918, A.A. Türkei #175, Bd. 2, #A993; Bernstorff to Hertling, Mar. 30, 1918, *ibid.*, #A1698. It may be

Talaat himself had once spoken of conceding the Jews a greater share in the government of Palestine, while stopping short of promising to make it their national homeland. But the Young Turks were no more ready to confer genuine autonomy on the local people there than they were in Armenia. Therefore Bernstorff recommended that Armenia be diplomatically tilled, even as the long-buried but deep-rooted hostilities between Zionism and Pan-Arabism were to be ploughed up into the light. The Armenians were at this time part of the Republic of Transcaucasia, born as the result of the Russian Revolution but barely able to draw breath because of racial friction among its three peoples: Armenians, Azerbaijani (Turco-Tartars), and Georgians. Almost the sole bond of these confederates was their suspicion, even hatred, of the Turks, to whose rule the Treaty of Brest-Litovsk had returned them. The Brest treaty gave the Sultan Kars, Ardahan, and Batum, and the Russo-Turkish frontier of 1877. The signatories of the pact hoped that Turkey would permit some kind of free plebiscite to secure legal and popular support for her rule over the Caucasian peoples. The Porte, however, did not trouble with such technicalities—it was not entirely certain of a favorable outcome—and Enver, as has been shown, massed his forces in increasing strength close to the frontiers of the in-

---

that the custodial scheme was in part intended to satisfy Jewish opinion within Germany. In May, 1917, the Bethmann ministry had been severely criticized in the Reichstag for allowing the plunder and deportation of the Jews in Gaza and Joppa. The government admitted that some Jews had been evicted from these areas, but alleged that the Turks had left their houses and farms intact and under the care of a kind of Jewish police force, whose jurisdiction the Ottoman government recognized. In other words, any analogy to Armenia was denied. See *Stenographische Berichte über die Verhandlungen des Reichstags 1914–1920*, Bd. 321, Aktenstücke #851, #990.

Talaat tried to give the impression that the Jews were not regarded as a particular problem by the Committee. In reference to the Balfour Declaration, he stated that the Ottoman government would welcome their immigration, especially since, with the capitulations removed, they would have no choice but to become loyal subjects of the Sultan, instead of Russian agents as hitherto. But the reporter of the *Frankfurter Zeitung*, March 2, 1918, indicates that his paper required some time to bring Talaat to make a statement on the Jewish question.

cipient republic. Because of this external pressure and the ethnic quarrels within, the Transcaucasian hybrid fell apart on May 26, 1918, with each of the three peoples striking out on its own. However, the Armenians did not believe themselves able to travel far without German support. Bernstorff called for "immediate action," an official Reich protectorate over the new Armenian Republic of Erivan, and the use of German combat troops to intercept the Turkish columns encroaching on the Armenian lands.[39]

Germany invited, but was refused, the cooperation of her Austrian ally. Burian, again in charge of the Foreign Ministry, thought it would be enough to stop the Turkish advance with a formal recognition for the Erivan republicans. He was afraid that anything more would be taken by the Bolsheviks as a menace to their security and bring them back into the war. In reality, however, he feared that the Germans would not be content to use the protectorate as a pressure device to force the Turks out of Anatolia and toward the Palestine front, but would instead turn it into a going and permanent concern.[40]

Above all else, the Austrian government was determined to prevent this. It had long regarded the loss of Syria and Palestine with relative indifference, but by 1918 the importance of excluding Germany from the Black Sea littoral had turned into a matter of imperial life or death. The Brest treaty gave Germany Russia's Baltic provinces, and Austria did not trust herself to wrest the Adriatic from Italian control. Only by the turbid flow of the Danube into the Black Sea was escape still possible from the closing ring of German economic encirclement, and should it be shut off, Austria would end in bondage to a middle-European tariff union controlled from Berlin.[41]

[39] Bernstorff to Foreign Ministry, May 23 and July 18, 1918, A.A. Türkei #183, Bd. 51, 52, #A21877, #A30714.

[40] Burian to Austrian Embassy, Berlin, Aug. 9, 1918, *ibid.*, Bd. 53, #A33900; Memorandum by Under Secretary of State Bussche, Aug. 11, 1918, *ibid.*, #A33610.

[41] Pallavicini to Czernin #30/p, Mar. 30, 1918, H.H.S.A. Türkei Karton 212. The Middle-European tariff union was raised by Berlin several

For this reason, Austria labored to pin Transcaucasia on the horns of the Turkish crescent lest it pass under the smothering wing of the Hohenzollern eagle. The Ballplatz raised the Bulgar-Rumanian question again and managed to force on it an evolution that made any Turkish withdrawal from the Caucasus less than ever possible. In May, 1918, the Central Powers imposed on Rumania the Peace of Bucharest. It provided that the controversial Dobrudja should be administered by a condominium of the four victor states. But none of these regarded the matter as definitely closed, because Ludendorff was secretly angling to achieve permanent German economic control in the area, and the Bulgarians were saying even as they signed the treaty that they viewed the condominium as only a transient formality. In short, Bulgaria insisted that the Germans, Austrians, and Turks waive all their claims and relinquish the entire Rumanian Dobrudja to King Ferdinand.[42]

The German Foreign Ministry at first attempted to stand fast for the condominium and then worked for a compromise that would have allowed Bulgaria to keep the Dobrudja, while obliging her to surrender the Maritza district and Adrianople as compensation to Turkey. In terms of area alone, the exchange was not a fair one, and the Porte rejected it at once. But aside from the obvious inequity, the Bulgarian government would have nothing to do with the retrocession of Adrianople and pleaded that its army would likely revolt if any steps were taken to consummate it.[43]

For Enver Pasha, the stakes were roughly the same. During an

---

times during the war, always against the stubborn opposition of Vienna. Yet the Germans always liked to maintain that there was a difference on this point between Austrian official and popular opinion. The Austrian people, the German papers argued, wanted such a union. See a long discussion of the problem in *Frankfurter Zeitung*, December 19, 1915.

[42] Lersner to Foreign Ministry, May 16, 1918, A.A. Bulgarien #17, Bd. 22, #A20797; Oberndorff to Foreign Ministry, May 15, 1918, *ibid.*, #A20846.

[43] Chargé Richthofen at Sofia to Hertling, July 24, 1918, *ibid.*, Bd. 23, #A31680.

interview with Seeckt at his country house, he told the General
that every one of his officers considered the fortifications of Constantinople useless as long as Adrianople remained in foreign
hands. At the same time, the war had wearied and worn the
Pasha, and he was readier than in the old days for compromise.
His demands tended still to be sharp and peremptory, but Seeckt
noticed that physically he was not in control of himself and became unusually irritable with his children and his old father. In
this less than resolute frame of mind, he admitted that the Committee would settle for the return of some Aegean islands held
by Greece and of the Dodecanese and Rhodes, currently under
Italian occupation. The last of course had not the significance of
Adrianople, but their recovery would at least efface the shame of
the Tripolitanian if not of the Balkan Wars.

Seeckt forwarded this proposition to Berlin, where Ludendorff
gave it his approval. The General even held that the return of
the islands to Turkey would be in Germany's maritime interest.
However, the Austrians vetoed the plan and pointed out that if
Italian expansionism were not satisifed in the Mediterranean, it
might turn dangerously active in the Tyrol. Austria's solution
was simply to leave nothing except Kars, Ardahan, and Batum
for Turkey's satisfaction and not to worry if the Turks moved
farther east of those places. Indeed, Austria would begin to
worry if they did not.[44]

Under pressure from the Ballplatz, Foreign Minister
Kühlmann came to believe that if Bulgaria did not soon get the
entire Dobrudja, she would leave the war and take Austria with
her. Bernstorff was of the same opinion and extracted from the
Porte a promise that all claims in the Dobrudja and in the Maritza Valley would be waived if Germany supported the Ottoman
advance in Transcaucasia. The Ambassador commented that
Germany would lose little, since Georgia was hopelessly poor
and Armenia would forever suspect the Germans of collaborating in the massacre of its people. Azerbaijan, he thought, was

[44] Legation Secretary Berckheim to Foreign Ministry, May 24, 1918,
ibid., Bd. 22, #A21948; Memorandum of the Austrian Embassy at Berlin,
Aug. 21, 1918, *ibid.*, Bd. 23, #A35403.

rich enough in natural resources, but its inhabitants were more hopelessly oriental than the Turks and unlikely ever to evince a taste for European commodities. His final justification was that Austria wished the Turk upheld in the Caucasus so that Bulgaria might be secure in the Dobrudja. The idea was Czernin's, its proponent was Burian, and by an irony of fate its executant was to be the German Empire.[45]

During the summer of 1918, the Turks with one hand signed treaties of peace and friendship with the Caucasian republics, while with the other they exterminated their citizens with a will. Enver detailed some of his best troops for these operations, promising them rapid promotion and higher pay. The consequent drain on the Palestinian units became enormous, for only the sick and mortally exhausted could resist the lure of money and fame. A sweltering heat of 131° made an end of many in the weakened army, and Allenby's Australians accounted for the rest. Liman, who held the Palestinian command, Lossow, and Ludendorff all protested to the Ottoman War Minister, but he ignored them. His excuse was the refractory attitude of his allies in the Dobrudja or, when that failed, the wild Pan-Turanian ambitions that had taken possession of his febrile and unreasoning brain.

The Turkish people probably supported these schemes more than some of the Pasha's previous aims, because they knew more about them and saw them discussed almost daily in the newspapers. Earlier in the summer, old Mohammed V died, and his successor, the younger Vahideddin, lifted the press censorship. The new ruler hated both the Committee and the Germans, but he exulted in the prospect of numbering the annexation of the Caucasus among the glorious deeds of his reign. As a coronation gift, he amnestied all persons court-martialed from the active service and invited all army deserters to reveal themselves to authorities.[46] The German embassy took these proclamations as an

[45] Bernstorff to Foreign Ministry, July 30, 1918, *ibid.*, #A32288; Oberndorff to Hertling, Aug. 7, 1918, *ibid.*, #A33660.

[46] Vice Consul Edelman, Geneva, to Secretary of State, Aug. 13, 1918, D.S., #867.00/822.

insult, because the military mission was often responsible for the application of the disciplinary code. Nevertheless, Bernstorff's protests were ignored by the palace, and the Ambassador had no means of redress except to privately advise the German technical experts to return home at their earliest convenience.[47]

This Bernstorff dispatch would not seem to support the argument that the Germans desperately tried to hold on to their Turkish interests up to the last minute. The best evidence for such a contention is of course the Treaty of Poti, signed on May 28 and regulating the relations between the Berlin government and the successor republic of Georgia. The Georgians, as has been pointed out, feared occupation by the advancing Turks and to avoid its worst consequences accepted a German military guarantee of their sovereignty. Among the most important provisions of the pact were those permitting the Germans to guard and use the railroad lines for the transportation of men and supplies and to set up a mining monopoly to deliver large quantities of raw ore, particularly manganese, to the Reich.

Quite naturally, the Poti treaty was quickly accepted by Lossow, who represented Germany at the negotiations, and by Ludendorff, who approvingly read over its clauses in Berlin. Ludendorff later wrote in his memoirs that he considered it essential for Germany to take tons of rawstuffs and barrels of oil from the area in order to win the war. However, it should be recalled that the initiative for the Poti treaty came mostly from the Georgians themselves. Furthermore, the Wilhelmstrasse received the treaty coldly, immediately sought to assure the Bolsheviks in Petrograd that it was not directed against their interests, and finally made nothing whatever of a scheme, mutually concocted by Emperor William and Ludendorff, to enthrone a German prince as ruler of a Georgian kingdom.[48]

It is not unlikely that Lossow negotiated at Poti without a

[47] Bernstorff to Foreign Ministry, July 17, 1918, A.A. Türkei #139, Bd. 47, #A30475.

[48] Firuz Kazemzadeh, *The Struggle for Transcaucasia 1917–1921* (New York, 1951), pp. 115, 122–127, 147, 148–151.

complete set of instructions from Berlin or that such instructions, having been given, were drastically reconsidered after some time for reflection had elapsed.[49] This was clearly the impression given to a Georgian delegation, headed by the Foreign Minister, Akakii Chkhenkeli, when it arrived in Berlin in June, 1918. The delegates were brilliantly feted, but politely informed that it might become necessary for Germany to disavow the claim of Georgian sovereignty if Soviet Russia were later to object. Despite Chkhenkeli's protests, the Germans refused to consider themselves already bound by the Poti agreement whatever the Russian reaction. In support of their arguments, it could be pointed out to the Georgian Foreign Minister that his own colleagues had signed with the Ottoman Empire the peace treaty of Batum on June 4, 1918.[50] This document made over to the Turks substantially the same railroad privileges that Poti had given to the Germans a few days earlier. Berlin anticipated some bitter exchanges with the Porte over this matter and blamed the Georgians for its embarrassment.

Yet even without this excuse, the documents do not indicate that German diplomacy was prepared to hold Georgia at all cost or exploit it to the uttermost. Months before, Bernstorff urged the Wilhelmstrasse to work for the recall of Lossow before he brought off some compromising maneuver.[51] Now that the General had done just that, the Ambassador, as has been already shown, attempted to reduce the number of his compatriots in the Ottoman Empire to a point where they could not materially assist the purposes of the military.

[49] Kress von Kressenstein to Chancellor Hertling, July 13, 1918, A.A. Türkei #158, Bd. 20, #A31679. Kress, who commanded German troops in the Caucasus, warns the Chancellor against getting deeply involved in any Caucasian ventures.

[50] Kazemzadeh, *The Struggle for Transcaucasia,* p. 149. Lenin's government later agreed to Germany's treaty arrangements with Georgia, and the Wilhelmstrasse went on to write a more comprehensive engagement covering consular representation, religious freedom, economic affairs, etc. All this was nullified by the end of the war.

[51] Bernstorff to Bussche, private, Mar. 2, 1918, A.A. Türkei #139, Bd. 46, #A1103.

Before the war ended, the Turks and the Germans quarreled bitterly about their priorities on the Georgian railroad system. Ludendorff sent a battalion to Georgia that in the end found itself pointing its guns at the Turkish ally. Accompanying these soldiers came representatives of Krupp, Deutsche Luxemburgische Aktiengesellschaft, Gewerkschaft Deutscher Kaiser, and other prominent German firms. All of them professed to find the prospects for exploitation very favorable, especially with the backing of the army's guns. But in the meanwhile, Bulgaria surrendered to the Entente on September 29, and with the defenses of Constantinople exposed, the cabinet of Talaat Pasha was unable to continue beyond October 7. After some difficulty in finding a new Grand Vizier, the Sultan finally conferred the post on Izzet Pasha, the renowned general and Albanian intriguer of some years before. Izzet assured the German embassy that Turkey would make no separate peace, but both Bernstorff and General von Seeckt thought that intention ought to be reinforced by immediately recalling all available German units to the defense of the Turkish capital.[52] To meet the Entente threat, the Turkish forces also left the Caucasus.

Even this final crisis did not weld together the Central Powers and their Ottoman ally. Izzet was no sooner in office than he had an argument with Pallavicini, recently returned from a summer's leave in Austria. He reproached him for his secret hostility and scored the whole policy of the Ballplatz, which aimed at excluding Turkey from her rightful share of Albania.[53] Izzet had a long memory. As to the Germans, while they thought Izzet's integrity fairly sound, they did not entirely trust it to withstand the popular bitterness threatening to overwhelm the Germans. The newspapers were speaking of "burying" the German alliance, British prisoners of war were ambling comfortably about the streets, and in the hospitals, others among the Turks' erst-

[52] Bernstorff to Foreign Ministry, Oct. 8, 1918, A.A. Türkei #158, Bd. 21, #A42167; Grünau to Foreign Ministry, Oct. 12, 1918, *ibid.*, #A42748.
[53] Pallavicini to Burian #623, Oct. 16, 1918, H.H.S.A. Türkei Karton 212.

while captives were delighting street crowds with their imitation of the German goose step. Under these circumstances, Bernstorff opened his embassy to store the gold reserves of the city's German banks. The Turks had recently asked for an audit of such holdings, and there was no telling to what use they would put such information.[54]

The army for once completely approved the Ambassador's action. Seeckt and Bernstorff worked together to persuade Izzet to classify as "nonessential" as many German military as possible. These were to be returned home immediately so that an armistice would not catch too many of them in the grip of the Entente. Apparently, Ludendorff wanted to take even further precautions against the arrival of the British and French, because he raised the possibility of destroying "most railroad and telegraph lines in Asia Minor . . . if the war takes its present course."[55] Such action seemingly would have included the Baghdad Railway itself. However, because of a strenuous protest from the new Foreign Minister, Paul von Hintze, who feared "a permanent negative effect" on Turkish and world opinion, no such action was ever carried out.[56]

Nevertheless, this exchange between the Wilhelmstrasse and Supreme Headquarters is still important as suggesting the collapse of Ludendorff's Near Eastern war aims. The Georgian maneuvers, previously discussed, are no exception to this conclusion, because if Ludendorff would have sacrificed the Baghdad line, for twenty-five years the most celebrated and talked about achievement of German imperialism, then he would have given even shorter shrift to the enterprises his office sketched out

[54] *Frankfurter Zeitung*, November 1, 1918, contains a good synopsis of Turkish newspaper opinion during the armistice crisis. For the antics of British prisoners, see Francis Yeats-Brown, *Bloody Years, a Decade of Plot and Counter-Plot by the Golden Horn* (New York, 1932), pp. 198, 212. On Bernstorff and the German banks, see Bernstorff to Foreign Ministry, October 7, 1918, A.A. Türkei #158, Bd. 21, #A42148.

[55] Lersner to Foreign Ministry, Oct. 27, 1918, *ibid.*, #A45461.

[56] Hintze to Lersner at General Headquarters, Oct. 28, 1918, *ibid.*, #A45461.

in the Caucasus. For the most part, these represented only the dreams of a few months, and not, like the Baghdad line, the investment and labor of many years.

On October 17, 1918, Izzet sent General Charles Townshend, who since Kut-el-Amara had been enjoying a comfortable captivity in Constantinople, to negotiate an armistice off Mudros with the commander of the British Mediterranean fleet, Admiral Somerset Gough-Calthorpe. These talks did not issue in a formal curtailment of hostilities until October 30. Between these dates, Izzet had in effect arrived at the separate peace he had numerous times forsworn to the Germans. Given the military situation, no one was disposed to contest the Grand Vizier's decision, because, as has been shown, steps were taken to anticipate it long before October 18, when General von Seeckt was informed by the Porte that the armistice talks were in progress.

Curiously enough, however, the Austrians were busy building up their position just as the Germans were speedily liquidating their own. For at least two months before the armistice, the Ballplatz worked vigorously to assure its interests in the Ottoman Empire whatever the outcome of the war. It entrusted the work not to Pallavicini, who was recalled for a temporary "rest" during that summer, but to Baron J. von Szilassy, the former Austrian minister in Athens and a man once praised by Berchtold as "the first to inaugurate Austrian colonial policy." [57]

This referred to an incident in 1913 when Berchtold developed an interest in staking out the Ottoman province of Adalia for eventual annexation by the Dual Monarchy. At the time Pallavicini was against any such schemes and returned to the Ballplatz to argue his case. But Berchtold was encouraged to strike for Adalia by the ambitious Magyar Szilassy, Pallavicini's junior by many years. In behalf of the Austrian Foreign Minister, Szilassy went to Berlin and obtained the German Foreign Ministry's consent not to the eventual cession of all Adalia, but at least to a city within that area, Alaya. The Deutsche Bank had some prior in-

---

[57] Baron J. von Szilassy, *Der Untergang der Donau-Monarchie, Diplomatische Erinnerungen* (Berlin, 1921), p. 257.

terest in Alaya, which it now renounced, so Szilassy, and apparently Berchtold, thought they had turned quite a triumph. Indeed nothing more ever came of it, but his work was deemed sufficient to qualify Szilassy as Pallavicini's interim replacement in the summer of 1918.[58]

The Baron now called for an intensive Austrian sales campaign in northern Anatolia and along the Black Sea shore. He described both areas as "the natural economic extension of the Danube valley." Because of the friction between the Turks and Berlin over Enver's Caucasus campaign, he believed the Committee would welcome Austro-Hungarian settlers into Anatolia and recommended in the meantime that certain kinds of political malcontents, Serbs, Czechs, and especially Magyars, should be indoctrinated for eventual resettlement in the Ottoman Empire. According to Szilassy, the last of the peoples mentioned had advantages that would eventually overcome any German competition. The Magyars were tactful, half-oriental, and considered first cousins by the Turks.

There is no documentary evidence that Szilassy ever brought up the resettlement scheme at the Porte. It is not likely that the Committee would have agreed to it even as a weapon against the Germans, because the Ottoman Empire had enough potential and actual rebels of its own. However, before terminating his mission, Szilassy did bring the Turks to accept a kind of Latin patriarch in Constantinople for the Roman Catholic rite. He was to have been archbishop of the capital, with a suffragan at Smyrna, and to have been chosen from the prominent Hungarian clergy. The Turks did not even insist that the archbishop-patriarch, who would hold ministerial rank, accept Ottoman citizenship, and Szilassy regarded this fact as one more assurance that he would serve the interests of Vienna as much as those of Rome.[59]

[58] Szilassy, *Der Untergang der Donau-Monarchie*, pp. 255–256, 278.

[59] Szilassy to Burian #66/p and #77/p, July 27 and September 7, 1918, H.H.S.A. Türkei Karton 212. The Turks suspected that Germany had attempted to win the Constantinople patriarchate for one of her own

But the armistice of Mudros put an end to all such plans, as did the Austrian and Hungarian revolutions for which the prevision of the old-school diplomats had made little place.

The Mudros armistice ordered all German and Austrian personnel out of the Ottoman Empire within a month. Very few chose to wait that long, and Bernstorff was packed and ready to go three days before the document was signed. He suddenly turned very afraid of Entente revenge. On October 27, he boarded a torpedo boat for the Rumanian coast and subsequently travelled overland to Berlin. To excuse any undue haste about his departure, he notified the Wilhelmstrasse that in this time of crisis Germany "needed all her good workers." He fancied himself one such, and Pallavicini thought he was putting in an early bid to lead the Foreign Ministry itself. If this was Bernstorff's aim, Germany's new Social Democratic masters quickly disappointed him, though he later took an honorable part in his country's activities at the League of Nations.

For the moment, however, it was felt that Bernstorff had made inadequate provision for the Pera embassy. All German diplomatic business was entrusted to the Swedish Ambassador, but he handled it carelessly and hardly exerted himself to evacuate the frantic German merchants. Meanwhile, his wife appropriated the German embassy limousine, was driven all around Constantinople, and forwarded numerous bills for fuel and maintenance to the mortified and outraged gentlemen of Berlin. Had it not been for the staunch and timely intervention of the Dutch Ambassa-

---

nationals and that for a time she had the favorable interests of the Papal Secretariat of State. For this end, it was rumored that Falkenhayn deliberately reduced the food supply in Jerusalem to make impossible the defense of the city against Allenby's advance in December, 1917. The Germans were afraid that in any protracted defense, the Holy Places would be destroyed and Catholic support thus forfeited. If there is any truth in this story, the tactics were obviously not adequate to defeat the later efforts of Szilassy. See Bayur, III/III, 393–394.

dor, the Germans would have found their passage homeward even more rigorous.[60]

It was the intention of the Sultan to try the Committee leaders for treason and secure their execution as a sop to the Entente. Enver Pasha never doubted that condign justice would be meted out to him, and he told Seeckt that Britain's direct control or hostile influence would bar him from any area where he might want to seek asylum. Seeckt then offered him and Talaat a place on a German ship. It was accepted, and in that manner the two men left the country together with many lesser Young Turkish lights. The grand Vizier Izzet was either double-crossed by the German general or deliberately winked at the escape. His negligence, if it was that, cost him his post. His cabinet fell on November 9, and the venerable, conservative Tewfik Pasha led a new ministry which could do little more than take dictation from the western allies.

At any rate, fate spared the lives of the Ottoman triumvirs for only a few more years. Talaat arrived in Berlin, where he lived in a modest pension almost completely ignored by the republican government. From time to time, he gave interviews or wrote articles for the press, most of them protesting his innocence of the Armenian massacres or detailing attempts to dissolve the German alliance.[61] He at least convinced his countrymen that he had tried to serve the nation's best interests, and during the Second World War, they accorded him the honor of reburial in the city where he had once held sway. But he did not convince the Armenians that he was clean of their blood, and in 1921 an assassin of their race brought him down in a Berlin street.

In 1922, Djemal was killed by an Armenian in Tiflis, and later in the year, Enver met a soldier's death in southern Russia. Before this, he shuttled back and forth between Berlin and Mos-

[60] Bernstorff to Foreign Ministry, Oct. 27, 1918, A.A. Deutschland #135, No. 1, Bd. 6, #A45701; Pallavicini to Burian #675, Oct. 27, 1918, H.H.S.A. Türkei Karton 212.

[61] Aubrey Herbert, *Ben Kendim, A Record of Eastern Travel* (London, 1923), pp. 309, 314.

cow, attempting to be serviceable to both the German and Soviet governments and in the process ingratiate himself with Mustafa Kemal too. He kept in contact with Seeckt, if not personally (this is impossible to check) then clearly by correspondence. There are several letters from the Pasha to the General in the Seeckt papers. In these Enver urged the German government to close an alliance with the Soviet Union. Specifically he urged Seeckt to facilitate the delivery of weapons and industrial parts to the Soviets, together with any secret intelligence information he might have about the Polish army, which both powers hated and feared. From the papers, it also appears that Enver tried to interest the German government in a Soviet move against Afghanistan. Some of the arms sought from Berlin were probably to be used to redraw the Soviet frontier at that little country's expense.[62] However, this project never advanced beyond its beginnings, and these, from the available evidence, must have been quite rudimentary. For whatever reason, Enver fell out of Soviet grace and was shot down fighting Red troops in Uzbekistan.

Almost the last to leave was old Pallavicini. He stayed in Constantinople until November 30, well after the Entente ships had passed through the Straits and discharged hundreds of soldiers on the conquered city. Such persons as remained at the German embassy did not know what to make of his behavior. It seemed an act of muddled courage to some, but other observers thought the veteran Austrian might be up to secret negotiations, now that the Germans were no longer around to eavesdrop. Tewfik's new Foreign Minister, Mustafa Pasha, had served some years as Ambassador in Vienna and knew Pallavicini very well. It was thought that the Turk would listen closely to his advice, disavow under Austrian direction any resistance to the Entente, and in this way win for Vienna some custodial supervision of what remained of Central Power interests in the Near East.

In the end, the peace treaties, dealing harshly with both Austria and Germany, showed that, if in fact it had anything to remember kindly of Pallavicini, the Entente had a short memory.

[62] Enver to Seeckt, Aug. 25 and 26, 1920, Seeckt Papers.

But the Ambassador did set a seal of bitterness and gall on this closing phase of Austro-German activity in Turkey. During the month he remained after Bernstorff's departure, the German refugees repeatedly begged him to find the means for their escape. He finally put them off with a promise that he had wired for an Austrian ship to carry them to Genoa. The ship finally arrived, but it had space for only a few passengers.[63] Most of the Germans could not board. They cursed Pallavicini, but he had already left them far behind.

Liman was the only prominent figure detained by the Entente. Seeckt advised him to prepare his retreat, but against all reason he stayed at his Palestinian command. The Turks no longer took his orders, but he still would not turn over these troops to a Turkish officer. His peculiar antics increased as the position in the field became more hopeless. Before he was at last forced to depart, he awarded his two daughters Turkish military decorations on the grounds that they had been under fire during the British siege of Haifa. The Turks protested the action as an offense both to their military and social ethics and indicated that they were well rid of him when he made his way north.

Liman sailed from Constantinople about the middle of February, 1919. He got as far as Malta, where the British ordered his ship into port and arrested him. Until the following August he was kept a prisoner on rather vague charges. The nearest the British came to an indictment was to accuse him of having plotted the murder of the Armenians. It took numerous pleas of the German Foreign Ministry, an appeal for Swiss intervention, and even some consideration at the Paris Peace Conference to win his release. By that time, the General claimed the Maltese climate had broken his health and made him almost totally deaf.[64]

[63] Wedel to Foreign Ministry, Dec. 29, 1918, A.A. Deutschland #135, No. 1, Bd. 6, #54583.

[64] Lersner to Foreign Ministry, Mar. 30, 1919, A.A. Türkei #139, Bd. 48, #A10010; Hammerstein to Haking, May 31, 1919, *ibid.*, no number.

Conclusion

A summary of the reasons for the failure of the Central Powers in the Ottoman Empire can well begin with the remarks General Hans von Seeckt prepared on his way back to Germany in late 1918. He held that the war shattered the alliance, which otherwise might have been profitably continued. However, probing a bit more deeply, Seeckt asserted that the mere presence of the Germans—and of any foreigners—in the Ottoman Empire sapped the Turks' will to fight. Excessive contact with the West deprived the race of its national consciousness and ability to exist as a separate political entity. Even if the Entente had not won the war and the Central Powers preserved their Near Eastern position intact, no long-range improvement for this malaise could be expected. For the axioms of the European state system forced Germany to be associated in most things with Austria, and the influence of the Austrians upon the Turks was, if anything, even more pernicious than that of Britain and France. The Austrians were not a race but a political jumble. Given their historical circumstances, they could not understand patriotism, but only improvise ways to live without it and dodge its effects on other peoples. This characteristic of the Dual Monarchy, Seeckt thought, would at first make it very much at home in a Turkey that cosmopolitanism was rendering decadent and corrupt. It would also appeal to rootless peoples like the Armenians and Phanariot Greeks. For this reason, had the war not intervened, Germany would have found Austrian competition keen in any areas where these two peoples were resident. But in the end, this mixture of mock civilization and overripe culture would bring them all down.[1]

In reading over these remarks, more than due allowance must be made for Seeckt's outrageous racial snobbery. A narrow-minded militarism also colored his judgment, though he was quite right when he charged that the German Foreign Ministry frequently attempted to oppose and upset the wishes of the High Command. Yet when all is said and done, the essence of Seeckt's argument is sound, and he hints at many issues upon which documents not available in his time have since thrown light. As far back as the embassy of Marschall von Bieberstein, the Germans began to feel that there was little of value to be salvaged from the Ottoman Empire. Despite all their activity and investment and the brilliant representation of Marschall, Germany had simply not achieved sufficient security and guarantees against the future. Marschall was not inclined to admit this flatly, but even he attempted to introduce German settlers into the Ottoman Empire to oversee and develop German projects on the spot. In other words, neither the Germans nor the Turks trusted each other, and for this attitude there was blame on both sides. In the meantime, Marschall was reduced to all kinds of humiliating and undignified tactics to curry favor at the Sublime Porte, but the evidence indicates that even his patience was at last exhausted. To a greater or less extent, his successors were subjected to the same trials, and in most of the negotiations immediately before and during the war, the Turks appear to have held the upper hand.

In part, German diplomacy worked with this disadvantage because the popular press and public opinion at home gave little encouragement or support. The evidence suggests that the German people at large regarded the Turks as interesting, exotic, perverse, or amusing, but never as vital to the welfare of the Reich. The alliance remained too narrowly the concern of the

[1] This paragraph and the following one are a summary and interpretation of Seeckt's memorandum "Reasons for Turkey's Collapse," Nov. 4, 1918 (Seeckt Papers).

diplomats, the generals, the businessmen, and the academicians. The average German, as he showed when he dealt directly with the Turk, did not understand it. At heart he probably disapproved of it, especially when the Turks began to massacre the Armenians. The religious difference between the German and Ottoman peoples was not a crucial factor in the working of the alliance, but both sides remained aware of it and this awareness was not always a salutary or constructive force. Where the Austrian Foreign Ministry was concerned, at least some of the reckonings about diplomatic and military policy were made with a Christian bias. The last Austrian Emperor was susceptible to such influence, as were Pallavicini and probably Czernin.

In some ways William II was the best example of a Christian ruler being unable to work with a Moslem state on a basis of complete parity. In 1889 he himself inaugurated the era of good feeling. It was he who proclaimed himself the protector of the Moslems of the world. Yet, though this pronouncement drew down upon his head the denunciations of the Entente press and deepened the enmity of London and Paris, the German Emperor rarely followed up with his actions what he said in his speeches. His own honeymoon with the Ottoman Empire ended with the Balkan Wars. The smashing defeats inflicted on the Ottoman Empire were understood in Europe as an indictment of the training given the Turks by the German military mission. The German General Staff evidently concurred in this opinion and rather unchivalrously pushed the blame on General von der Goltz. But no matter who was to blame for the outcome of the Balkan battles, the confidence of Berlin in Constantinople had been shaken, and Emperor William began to assert that Turkey must save herself as best she could, expect no special favors from Germany in the future, and if necessary even bow before the triumph of Serbian or Bulgarian arms in the Balkan Peninsula.

The Emperor, however, did not deal as severely with the Turks as he had threatened. When the World War began, William spoke the decisive word leading to the signing of the alliance of August, 1914, but his earlier remarks were not entirely cleared away by any stroke of the pen, and they lingered to sow suspicion and intrigue in the counsels of those who were publicly allies. The Austrian Foreign Ministry was bewildered and appalled by Germany's apparent indifference to the prospect of an expanding Serbia, the more so since the German Emperor rudely rebuffed Berchtold when the latter protested the vagaries of the Wilhelmstrasse. Furthermore, the Austrians could not approve any rapprochement between Germany and Russia over the disposition of Turkish Anatolia and Armenia. Such a rapprochement appears to have been sought by the German Foreign Minister, Jagow, and his Ambassador in Constantinople, Hans von Wangenheim.

It was not only to her threatened isolation that Austria objected nor to a violation of the old bonds between Vienna and Berlin tied by Bismarck. Rather, the Austrians were frightened by a special aspect of the Armenian schemes of Jagow and Wangenheim. This was, briefly put, that Turkey in return for yielding to a Russo-German political or economic condominium in Anatolia-Armenia was to be assured compensation in the Balkans. Neither the German nor the Russian Foreign Ministries were opposed to an Ottoman restoration in Albania. It could be argued that the Sultan once held sway there and that his government had been less chaotic than the regime of the Christian prince, William of Wied. The great powers imposed Wied on the Albanians in 1913 but thereafter did little to uphold him. His religion was an offense to the Moslem dignitaries of the country; Serbia and Greece conspired to get portions of Albania for themselves; and Germany and Russia came to prefer an Ottoman prince. But Austria, though she shared the doubts about the stability of the Wied administration, did not want to substitute Turkish control for it. She preferred the Balkan *status quo,* because any tampering with it seemed to her likely to raise a storm of Serbian and Greek counterclaims and irredentist intrigues. If hostilities broke out again in the Balkan Peninsula, Austria had no assurance that they could be confined to Albania. The exchanges between Pallavicini and Berchtold show that any Balkan fighting was expected to spill over Austria's southern frontier.

Pallavicini recommended to Berchtold that Turkey be offered a formal alliance with the Central Powers to reduce her capacity for Balkan troublemaking and to bind her with a debt of honor. The military benefits of an alliance with the Ottoman Empire seem to have weighed very lightly with the Austrians in the World War. They attempted to persuade the Turks to mount an offensive north from the Black Sea so as to remove Russian pressure from their own front, but when they were rebuffed by Enver Pasha, the Austrians lost all but a diplomatic interest in the Turkish alliance. The Germans, on the other hand, were satisfied to use the Turks as a military makeweight, tying down Entente troops that otherwise could have been used in European fighting. Beyond that modest point the Germans were reluctant to plan, though for diplomatic reasons, apart from purely military considerations, the Germans allowed themselves to become involved in the first Egyptian campaign of 1915. This campaign proved an overextension of Ottoman resources.

Because they approached the Ottoman alliance from different motives, Germany and Austria soon disagreed as to how it should be implemented at specific points. The Egyptian campaign of 1915 was an early instance of this disagreement. The German General Staff favored the capture of the Suez Canal to cut off Britain's troop reinforcements from India and, just as importantly, to use Egypt as a pawn to compel the British to negotiations. The latter motive was endorsed by the German Foreign Ministry. However, the Austrians would have preferred the Turco-German forces to keep out of Egypt. If they advanced against that country, Vienna feared that Italy would consider her own interests jeopardized in Tripolitania. These interests were none too secure, since Italy had only wrenched Tripolitania from the Turks in 1912. The Austrians contended that if the Turks and Germans now gave any challenge to the Italians in this former Ottoman province, Italy would bolt the Triple Alliance and make common cause with the Entente. Eventually Italy did just this, partly because the Germans ignored the Austrian arguments and continued the buildup for the Egyptian campaign. In Vienna it was suspected that Germany planned to carve out an Egyptian satrapy for exploitation after the war.

There were later occasions of discord. A few may be recapitulated here. Throughout the Egyptian and Dardanelles campaigning, the problem of supplying the Ottoman Empire from central Europe became acute. Germany made strenuous diplomatic efforts to open up passage through Rumania and Bulgaria, the latter neutral until late 1915. However, the Austrian War Ministry permitted Austrian businessmen to use transportational facilities that should have serviced the Turkish front to bring nonessential Austrian manufactures into the Balkan market. Though the fate of the Turks was in the balance at the Dardanelles, responsible Austrian officials allowed business to be plied as usual, using the exceptional conditions of wartime to outsell German competitors in Eastern Europe.

In the matter of the Baghdad Railway, that other major line of supply, the Austrians were less of a hindrance but certainly no help. Germany was unable to persuade the Ottoman government to share significantly in the cost of completing the Baghdad Railway. The Turks insisted that the railway was a German enterprise, primarily for German profit, though they fanned rumors that they intended to nationalize the whole network after the war. The Germans protested any such step, but their arguments were weakened when the Austrians intimated to the Sublime Porte that they would undertake various contracts for public improvements in Turkey at terms more advantageous than those offered by Berlin.

By 1917, Berlin and Vienna were at loggerheads about almost every question of the Turkish alliance. Matters were not helped when Ottokar Czernin was appointed to lead the Ballplatz. Considered by some a defeatist, by others merely a realist, the Austro-Hungarian Foreign Minister wanted a negotiated end to the war. To achieve this he urged that Rumania, recently conquered by the Central Powers, be partitioned among the Austrians, the

Bulgarians, and the Russians as a means of inducing them to
leave the war. Czernin evolved this whole scheme in close secrecy with the German Chancellor, Bethmann, telling the Turks
nothing about it at all. But what the Sublime Porte inferred
alarmed it considerably, and had the partition been carried
through without her agreement, Turkey would probably have
broken her alliance with the Central Powers and forced them to
negotiate a general peace. Czernin knew all this, because the
Turks had long made it clear that they would not tolerate an enlargement of Bulgaria without compensating advantages for
themselves. And so did the Germans, who were barely able to
thwart Czernin's designs with countermaneuvers of their own.

Thus, the alliance of Turkey and the Central Powers became a
self-defeating proposition. In light of the various problems reviewed in this book, it may be questioned whether Germany
would have been able to uphold a strong position in the Near
East even if she had won the war. Austria would not have accepted it, and the chauvinistic Young Turks would have fought
it. Aside from the militancy of the Young Turks, there was the
problem of the various regional nationalisms that were beginning to flourish. In their fumbling negotiations with the Egyptian nationalists and in their gross underestimate of the significance and strength of Arab nationalism, the Germans seemed
unable to reckon with the forces of the future. These forces had
certain liberal and equalitarian overtones which ran counter to
Germany's own reactionary constitution and feudal culture. Consequently the Germans were obliged to a makeshift accommodation with a few slippery politicians on the Committee of Union
and Progress. Yet when the World War opened, the methods of
the Committee were already as outmoded as those of Abdul
Hamid. Essentially Germany had placed her bets with the past,
but she could no more arrest the march of History than the
triumph of Entente arms.

Bibliography

Unpublished Materials

For the most part, this book is based upon unpublished records of the German and Austrian Foreign Ministries. These have been supplemented by documents drawn from the Public Record Office, London, and the archives of the Department of State, Washington, D.C. Much of the German material is on microfilm reels held by The National Archives, Washington, D.C.; the University of California, Berkeley; and the University of Michigan, Ann Arbor. Specific locations are found in *A Catalogue of Files and Microfilms of the German Foreign Ministry Archives, 1867–1920*, published by the American Historical Association for the Study of War Documents, 1959. A list of the original file numbers is given below. Appropriate file numbers are also given for the Austrian and British materials. The American papers are individually numbered rather than filed in volumes, and therefore it will be necessary for the reader to refer to the notes for fuller citation.

German Foreign Ministry Files
Aegypten 3
Albanien 1
Bulgarien 6; 17
Deutschland 127, No. 6; 128, No. 2; 128, No. 5; 135, No. 1; 167, No. 1
Orientalia Generalia 2; 5; 9, No. 2
Rumanien 17; 29
Türkei 110, No. 2; 110, No. 5; 134; 139; 142; 144; 152; 153; 154; 155; 158; 159, No. 1; 159, No. 2; 161; 165; 168; 169; 171; 175; 179; 183; 189; 190; 204

Verträge No. 94; 95; 98; 103
Weltkrieg 11u; 16
Nachlass Paul von Hintze; Hans von Miquel; Paul Weitz
Austrian Foreign Ministry Files
Allgemeines Karton 941–948
Türkei Karton 207–212; 466
Bavarian State Archives, Munich
File MA95027
British Foreign Office Papers (Public Record Office, London)
   371–2140; 371–2479; 371–2481; 371–2487; 371–2489; 371–2492;
   371–2767; 371–2783; 371–3050; 371–3057
Papers of Ernst Jaeckh at Yale University Library
Papers of Hans von Seeckt, on microfilm at Houghton Library, Harvard University, Reels 19, 24, and 26 were used.

Official Documentary Collections

Austria. *Österreich-Ungarns Aussenpolitik.* Edited by Ludwig Bittner and Hans Uebersberger. Vols. VI, VII, VIII. Vienna, 1930.

France. Ministère des Affaires Etrangères. *Documents Diplomatiques Français 1871–1914.* 3d Series (1911–1914), Vols. IX, X, XI. Paris, 1936.

Germany. *Die deutschen Dokumente zum Kriegsausbruch. Vollständige Sammlung der von Karl Kautsky Zusammengestellten amtlichen Aktenstücke.* 4 vols. Berlin, 1919.

——. *Neue Gefahrenzonen im Orient, 1913–1914.* Vol. XXXVIII *of Die grosse Politik der europaischen Kabinette, 1871–1914.* Edited by Johannes Lepsius, Albrecht Mendelssohn Bartholdy, and Friedrich Thimme. Berlin, 1927.

——. *Stenographische Berichte über die Verhandlungen des Reichstags, 1914–1920.* 20 vols. Berlin, 1917–1920.

Great Britain. *British Documents on the Origins of the War, 1898–1914.* Edited by G. P. Gooch and Harold Temperley, Vol. X, Parts 1 and 2. London, 1936, 1938.

——. *Correspondence Respecting Events Leading to the Rupture of Relations with Turkey.* Parliamentary Papers, Vol. LXXXIV, No. 13. London, 1914.

Italy. *I Documenti Diplomatici Italiani.* Series 5, Vol. I. Edited by Augusto Torre. Rome, 1954.

Russia. *Das Zaristische Russland im Weltkriege. Neue Dokumente aus den russischen Staatsarchiven.* Edited by M. Pokrovski. Berlin, 1927.

——. *Die europaischen Mächte und die Türkei während des Welt-*

krieges: Konstantinopel und die Meerengen. Nach den Geheim dokumenten des ehem. Ministeriums für Auswärtige Angelegenheiten. Edited by E. A. Adamov. 4 vols. Dresden, 1930–1932.

——. *Die Internationalen Beziehungen im Zeitalter des Imperialismus. Dokumente aus den Archiven der Zarischen und der Provisorischen Regierung.* Edited by M. Pokrovski. Ser. 1 and 2. 11 vols. Berlin, 1931–1936.

——. *Iswolski im Weltkriege. Der Diplomatische Schriftwechsel Iswolskis aus den Jahren 1914–1917.* Edited by Friedrich Stieve. Berlin, 1925.

United States. *Papers Relating to the Foreign Relations of the United States. Supplements 1915–1918, The World War.* Washington, 1928–1933.

Secondary Sources

Aaronsohn, Alexander. *With the Turks in Palestine.* Boston, 1916.

Adler, Cyrus, and Margalith, Aaron. *With Firmness in the Right.* New York, 1946.

Aflalo, F. G. *Regilding the Crescent.* London, 1911.

The Aga Khan. *The Memoirs of Age Khan, World Enough and Time.* New York, 1954.

Albertini, Luigi. *The Origins of the War of 1914.* 3 vols. London, 1952–1957.

Allen, W. E. D., and Muratoff, P. *Caucasian Battlefields. A History of the Wars on the Turco-Caucasian Border 1828–1921.* Cambridge, 1953.

Anderson, M. S. *The Eastern Question 1774–1923.* London, 1966.

Austria. *Oesterreich-Ungarns letzter Krieg 1914–1918.* Edited by E. Glaise-Horstenau. 8 vols. Vienna, 1931–1938.

Baumgart, Winfried. *Deutsche Ostpolitik 1918. Von Brest-Litowsk biz zum Ende des Ersten Weltkrieges.* Vienna, 1966.

Bayur, Yusuf Hikmet. *Türk Inkilâbi Tarihi.* Vols. II/II, II/III, III/I, III/II, III/III. Ankara, 1951–1957.

Benson, E. F. *Crescent and Iron Cross.* New York, 1918.

Bernstorff, Johann von. *Memoirs.* Translated by Eric Sutton. New York, 1936.

Bethmann-Hollweg, Theobald von. *Betrachtungen zum Weltkriege.* Berlin, 1921.

Blaisdell, Donald C. *European Financial Control in the Ottoman Empire.* New York, 1966.

Burian, Stephen. *Austria in Dissolution.* London, 1925.

Chapman, Maybelle Kennedy. *Great Britain and the Bagdad Railway,
1888–1914.* Northampton, Mass., 1948.

Conrad von Hötzendorf, Franz. *Aus meiner Dienstzeit 1906–18.* Vols.
IV–V. Vienna, 1923–1925.

Czernin, Ottokar. *Im Weltkriege.* Berlin, 1919.

Dallin, Alexander. *Russian Diplomacy and Eastern Europe, 1914–
1917.* New York, 1963.

Daniel, Robert L. "The Armenian Question and American-Turkish
Relations, 1914–1927." *Mississippi Valley Historical Review,* XLVI
(1959–1960), 252–275.

Davison, R. H. "The Armenian Crisis, 1912–1914." *American Historical Review,* LIII (1948), 481–505.

Demirhan, Pertev. *General-Feldmarschall Colmar von der Goltz.*
Göttingen, 1960.

De Novo, John A. *American Interests and Policies in the Middle East
1900–1939.* Minneapolis, 1963.

Djemal Pasha. *Memoirs of a Turkish Statesman, 1913–1919.* New
York, 1922.

Earle, Edward Meade. "The Secret Anglo-German Convention of
1914 Regarding Asiatic Turkey." *Political Science Quarterly,*
XXXVIII (1923), 24–44.

————. *Turkey, The Great Powers, and The Bagdad Railway.* New
York, 1924.

Einstein, Lewis. *Inside Constantinople.* London, 1917.

Emin, Ahmed. *Turkey in the World War.* New Haven, 1930.

Epstein, Klaus. *Matthias Erzberger and the Dilemma of German
Democracy.* Princeton, 1959.

Erzberger, M. *Erlebnisse im Weltkrieg.* Berlin, 1920.

Evans, Laurence. *United States Policy and The Partition of Turkey,
1914–1924.* Baltimore, 1965.

Falkenhayn, Erich von. *General Headquarters, 1914–1916, and its
Critical Decisions.* London, 1919.

Feis, Herbert. *Europe, the World's Banker, 1870–1914.* New Haven,
1930.

Fischer, Fritz. *Griff nach der Weltmacht.* Düsseldorf, 1961.

————. "Deutsche Kriegsziele, Revolutionierung und Separatfrieden im
Osten 1914–1918." *Historische Zeitschrift,* CLXXXVIII (1959),
249–310.

Fisher, Sidney N. *The Middle East.* New York, 1959.

Frankfurter Zeitung. 1914–1918.

Gehrke, Ulrich. *Persien in der deutschen Orientpolitik während des
Ersten Weltkrieges.* Stuttgart, n.d.

Germany. Marine-Archiv und Kriegswissenschaftliche Abteilung der Marine. *Der Krieg zur See 1914–1918: Der Krieg in den türkischen Gewässern.* Edited by Hermann Lorey. 2 vols. Berlin, 1928–1938.

Germany. Reichsarchiv und Kriegsgeschichtliche Forschungsanstalt des Heeres. *Der Weltkrieg.* 14 vols. Berlin, 1925–1944.

Giesl, Wladimir. *Zwei Jahrzehnte im nahen Orient.* Berlin, 1927.

Gleich, Gerold von. *Vom Balkan nach Bagdad.* Berlin, 1921.

Goltz, Colmar von der. *Denkwürdigkeiten.* Edited by Friedrich von der Goltz. Berlin, 1929.

Gordon, Leland James. *American Relations with Turkey, 1830–1930.* Philadelphia, 1932.

Gottlieb, W. W. *Studies in Secret Diplomacy during the First World War.* London, 1957.

Great Britain. *Campaigns in Mesopotamia, 1914–1918.* Edited by F. J. Moberly. 4 vols. London, 1923–1927.

Great Britain. *History of the Great War: Military Operations Egypt and Palestine.* Edited by George MacMunn and Cyril Falls. 3 vols. London, 1928–1930.

Great Britain. *Military Operations, Gallipoli.* Edited by C. F. Aspinall-Oglander. 2 vols. London, 1929–1932.

Guse, Felix. *Die Kaukasusfront im Weltkrieg bis zum Frieden von Brest.* Leipzig, 1940.

Hallgarten, George W. F. *Imperialismus vor 1914.* Vol. II. Munich, 1951.

Hamilton, Ian. *Gallipoli Diary.* Vol. II. London, 1920.

Helfferich, Karl. *Der Weltkrieg.* Karlsruhe, 1925.

Hentig, Werner-Otto von. *Ins verschlossene Land.* Potsdam, 1928.

Herbert, Aubrey. *Ben Kendim, A Record of Eastern Travel.* London, 1923.

Herzfeld, Hans. "Die Liman-Krise und die Politik der Grossmächte in der Jahreswende 1913/14." *Berliner Monatshefte,* II (1933), 837–858, 973–993.

Holborn, Hajo. "Deutschland und die Türkei 1878/1890." *Archiv für Politik und Geschichte,* V (1925), 111–159.

Howard, Harry. *The Partition of Turkey, 1913–1923.* Norman, Okla., 1931.

Inal, Ibnulemin Mahmud Kemal. *Osmanli devrinde son sadriazamlar* [Last Grand Viziers of the Ottoman Period]. 14 vols. Istanbul, 1940–1953.

Izzet Pascha. *Denkwürdigkeiten.* Edited by Karl Klinghardt. Leipzig, 1927.

Jabotinsky, Vladimir. *Turkey and the War.* London, 1917.

Jaeckh, Ernst. *Der Goldene Pflug, Lebensernte eines Weltbürgers.* Stuttgart, 1954.

——. *The Rising Crescent.* New York, 1944.

James, Robert Rhodes. *Gallipoli.* New York, 1965.

Janssen, Karl-Heinz. *Der Kanzler und der General. Die Führungskrise um Bethmann Hollweg und Falkenhayn 1914–1916.* Göttingen, 1967.

Jäschke, Gotthard. "Der Turanismus der Jungtürken. Zur osmanischen Aussenpolitik im Weltkriege." *Welt des Islams,* XXIII (1941), 1–54.

——. "Zum Eintritt der Türkei in den Ersten Weltkrieg." *Welt des Islams,* new series, IV (1955).

Kann, Robert A. *Die Sixtusaffäre und die geheimen Friedensverhandlungen Oesterreich-Ungarns im ersten Weltkrieg.* Munich, 1966.

Kannengiesser, Hans. *The Campaign in Gallipoli.* London, 1928.

Kazemzadeh, Firuz. *The Struggle for Transcaucasia, 1917–1921.* New York, 1951.

Kedourie, Elie. *England and the Middle East, The Destruction of the Ottoman Empire, 1914–1921.* London, 1956.

Kerner, Robert J. "Austrian Plans for a Balkan Settlement, 1915–1916." *The New Europe,* XVI, No. 207 (1920), 280–284.

——. "Russia, The Straits, and Constantinople, 1914–1915." *Journal of Modern History,* I, No. 2 (June, 1929), 400–415.

——. "The Mission of Liman von Sanders." *Slavonic Review,* VI (1927–1928), 12–27, 344–363, 543–560; VII (1928), 90–112.

Kiesling, Hans von. *Mit Feldmarschall von der Goltz Pascha im Mesopotamien und Persien.* Leipzig, 1922.

Kinross, Patrick Balfour. *Ataturk.* New York, 1965.

Klein, Fritz. "Die Rivalität zwischen Deutschland und Oesterreich-Ungarn in der Türkei am Vorabend des ersten Weltkrieges." *Politik im Krieg 1914–1918.* Edited by Fritz Klein. Berlin, 1964.

Kress von Kressenstein, Friedrich. *Mit den Türken zum Suezkanal.* Berlin, 1938.

Kühlmann, Richard von. *Erinnerungen.* Heidelberg, 1948.

Landes, David S. *Bankers and Pashas: International Finance and Economic Imperialism in Egypt.* Cambridge, Mass., 1958.

Larcher, M. *La Guerre Turque dans la Guerre Mondiale.* Paris, 1926.

Lepsius, Johannes. *Deutschland und Armenien 1914–1918.* Potsdam, 1919.

Lewis, Bernard. *The Emergence of Modern Turkey.* London, 1961.

Fürst Lichnowsky. *Auf dem Wege zum Abgrund.* 2 vols. Dresden, 1927.

Liman von Sanders, Otto. *Five Years in Turkey*. Translated by Carl Reichmann. Annapolis, 1927.

Lindow, Erich. *Freiherr Marschall von Bieberstein als Botschafter in Konstantinopel 1897–1912*. Danzig, 1934.

Lloyd, George Ambrose. *Egypt Since Cromer*. Vol. I. London, 1933.

Ludendorff Erich von. *Ludendorff's Own Story*. Vol I. New York, 1919.

Lührs, Hans. *Gegenspieler des Obersten Lawrence*. Berlin, 1936.

Mandelstam, André. *Le Sort de l'Empire Ottoman*. Paris, 1917.

Marczali, Henrik. "Papers of Count Tisza, 1914–1918." *American Historical Review*, XXIX, No. 2 (January, 1924), 301–315.

Martin, Bradford G. *German-Persian Diplomatic Relations, 1873–1912*. 'S-Gravenhage, 1959.

Mazard, Jean A. *Le Régime des Capitulations en Turquie pendant la Guerre de 1914*. Alger, 1923.

Mehlan, Arno. "Das deutsch-bulgarische Weltkriegsbündnis." *Historische Vierteljahresschrift*, XXX (1935), 771–805.

Meinecke, Friedrich. *Strassburg, Freiburg, Berlin*. Stuttgart, 1949.

Meyer, Henry Cord. *Mitteleuropa in German Thought and Action, 1815–1945*. The Hague, 1955.

Mikusch, Dagobert von. *Wassmuss der deutsche Lawrence*. Leipzig, 1937.

Moorehead, Alan. *Gallipoli*. New York, 1956.

Morgenthau, Henry. *All in a Life-Time*. New York, 1922.

——. *Ambassador Morgenthau's Story*. New York, 1918.

Mühlmann, Carl. *Das Deutsch-Türkische Waffenbündnis im Weltkriege*. Leipzig, 1940.

——. *Der Kampf um die Dardanellen*. Oldenburg, 1927.

——. *Deutschland und die Türkei 1913–1914*. Berlin, 1929.

——. *Oberste Heeresleitung und Balkan im Weltkrieg 1914/1918*. Berlin, 1942.

Mutius, Gerhard von. "Die Türkei 1911–1914." *Preussische Jahrbücher*, CCXXXVI (1934), 212–220.

Nadolny, Rudolf. *Mein Beitrag*. Wiesbaden, 1955.

Napier, H. D. *The Experiences of a Military Attaché in the Balkans*. London, 1924.

Nekludoff, A. *Diplomatic Reminiscences, 1911–1917*. New York, 1920.

Nicolai, W. *The German Secret Service*. London, 1924.

Nicolson, Harold. *Sir Arthur Nicolson, First Lord Carnock*. London, 1930.

Niedermayer, Oskar von. *Unter der Glutsonne Irans*. Munich, 1925.

Nogales, Rafael de. *Four Years Beneath the Crescent*. New York, 1926.

——. *Memoirs of a Soldier of Fortune*. New York, 1932.

O'Connor, Frederick. *On the Frontier and Beyond, A Record of Thirty Years' Service*. London, 1931.

Ostrorog, Leon. *The Turkish Problem*. London, 1919.

Palmer, Alan. *The Gardeners of Salonika*. New York, 1965.

Patrick, Mary Mills. *A Bosporus Adventure, Constantinople Woman's College*. Stanford University, 1934.

——. *Under Five Sultans*. New York, 1929.

Poincaré, Raymond. *Au service de la France*. Vol. VI. Paris, 1930.

Polzer-Hoditz, Arthur. *The Emperor Karl*. Boston, n.d.

Pomiankowski, Joseph. *Der Zusammenbruch des Ottomanischen Reiches*. Vienna, 1928.

Potts, James M. "The Loss of Bulgaria." *Russian Diplomacy and Eastern Europe, 1914–1917*. New York, 1963.

Ragey, Louis. *La Question du Chemin de Fer de Bagdad, 1893–1914*. Paris, 1936.

Ramsaur, Ernest E., Jr., *The Young Turks: Prelude to the Revolution of 1908*. Princeton, 1957.

Rathmann, Lothar. *Berlin-Bagdad. Die imperialistische Nahostpolitik des kaiserlichen Deutschland*. Berlin, 1962.

——. *Stossrichtung Nahost 1914–1918. Zur Expansionspolitik des deutschen Imperialismus im ersten Weltkrieg*. Berlin, 1963.

Renouvin, Pierre. *The Immediate Origins of the War*. New Haven, 1928.

Rivière, Louis. *Un Centre de Guerre Secrète, Madrid, 1914–1918*. Paris, 1936.

Rohrbach, Paul. *Um des Teufels Handschrift*. Hamburg, 1953.

Rosen, Friedrich. *Aus einen diplomatischen Wanderleben*. Berlin, 1931.

Ryan, Andrew. *The Last of the Dragomans*. London, 1951.

Sâbis, Ali Ihsan. *Harb Hatiralarim* [War Memoirs]. 3 vols. Istanbul and Ankara, 1943–1952. Vol. II. Ankara, 1951.

Savinsky, A. *Recollections of a Russian Diplomat*. London, n.d.

Sazonov, Serge. *Fateful Years 1909–1916*. New York, 1928.

Schacht, Hjalmar. *76 Jahre meines Lebens*. Bad Wörishofen, 1953.

Schweder, Paul. *Im türkischen Hauptquartier*. Leipzig, 1916.

Scipio, Lynn A. *My Thirty Years in Turkey*. Rindge, New Hampshire, 1955.

Seeckt, Hans von. *Aus seinem Leben, 1918–1936*. Edited by Friedrich von Rabenau. Leipzig, 1940.

Seton-Watson, R. W. "Unprinted Documents. Austro-German Plans for the Future of Serbia (1915)." *Slavonic and East European Review,* VII, No. 21 (March, 1929), 705–724.

——. "William II's Balkan Policy." *The Slavonic Review,* VII, No. 19, 1–29.

Silberstein, Gerard E. "The Central Powers and the Second Turkish Alliance 1915." *Slavic Review,* XXIV (1965), 77–89.

Skendi, Stavro. *The Albanian National Awakening 1878–1912.* Princeton, 1967.

Smith, C. Jay, Jr. "Great Britain and the 1914–1915 Straits Agreement with Russia." *American Historical Review,* LXX (1965), 1015–1034.

Snouck-Hurgronje, C. *The Holy War "Made in Germany."* New York, 1915.

Sousa, Nasim. *The Capitulatory Regime of Turkey.* Baltimore, 1933.

Steglich, Wolfgang. *Bündnissicherung oder Verstandigungsfrieden.* Göttingen, 1958.

Steuber, Werner. *Jilderim. Deutsche Streiter auf heiligem Boden.* Oldenburg, 1922.

Stuermer, Harry. *Two War Years in Constantinople.* London, 1917.

Swire, J. *Albania, The Rise of a Kingdom.* New York, 1930.

Sykes, Christopher. *Wassmuss, "the German Lawrence."* London, 1936.

Szilassy, J. von. *Der Untergang der Donau-Monarchie, Diplomatische Erinnerungen.* Berlin, 1921.

Talaat Pasha. "Posthumous Memoirs of Talaat Pasha." *Current History,* XV (1921), 287–295.

Thomas, Lewis V., and Frye, Richard N. *The United States and Turkey and Iran.* Cambridge, Mass., 1952.

Trumpener, Ulrich. "German Military Aid to Turkey in 1914." *Journal of Modern History,* XXXII (1960), 145–149.

——. "Liman von Sanders and the German-Ottoman Alliance." *Journal of Contemporary History,* IV (1966), 179–192.

——. *Germany and the Ottoman Empire, 1914–1918.* Princeton, 1968.

Ussher, Clarence D. *An American Physician in Turkey.* Boston, 1917.

Vernier, Bernard. *La Politique Islamique de l'Allemagne.* Paris, 1939.

Vopicka, Charles J. *Secrets of the Balkans.* Chicago, 1921.

Weltman, Saadia. "Germany, Turkey, and the Zionist Movement, 1914–1918." *Review of Politics,* XXIII (1961), 246–269.

Wolf, John B. *The Diplomatic History of the Bagdad Railroad.* Columbia, Mo., 1936.

Yalman, Ahmed Emin. *Turkey in My Time.* Norman, Okla., 1956.

Yeats-Brown, Francis. *Bloody Years, A Decade of Plot and Counter-Plot by the Golden Horn.* New York, 1932.

Zeine, Zeine N. *Arab-Turkish Relations and the Emergence of Arab Nationalism.* Beirut, 1958.

Zeman, Z. A. B., and Scharlau, W. B. *The Merchant of Revolution, The Life of Alexander Israel Helphand.* London, 1965.

Ziemke, Kurt. *Die neue Türkei.* Berlin, 1930.

Index

EAGLES ON THE CRESCENT

*Germany, Austria, and the Diplomacy
of the Turkish Alliance, 1914–1918*

Designed by R. E. Rosenbaum.
Composed by Vail-Ballou Press, Inc.,
in 10 point linotype Caledonia, 3 points leaded,
with display lines in monotype Perpetua.
Printed from type by Vail-Ballou Press, Inc.,
on Warren's No. 66 Text, 60 pound basis,
with the Cornell University Press watermark.
Bound by Vail-Ballou Press, Inc.,
in Interlaken ALP book cloth
and stamped in All Purpose red foil.